THE CLEAN PACKAGE

A PIONEER ASSEMBLAGE

JOSHUA DEWAIN FOSTER

Copyright © 2023 Joshua Dewain Foster

Published by Foster Literary

First Printing February 2023

Hardcover: 979-8-9860973-1-2
Paperback: 979-8-9860973-4-3
eBook: 979-8-9860973-3-6

Cover Art by Spencer Erickson, Son of Erik Design

All rights reserved.

To request information or permissions, contact the publishers at www.FosterLit.com

PUBLISHER'S NOTE:

This is a work of fiction and nonfiction. Names, characters, places, and incidents either are the product of the author's imagination or are used fictitiously, and any resemblance to actual persons, living or dead, events, or locales is entirely coincidental—except when they are not.

for my father,

Boyd S Foster,

who insists I keep my rows straight

&

for my mother,

Laurie Manwaring Foster,

who compels me to be creative not crass

FOREWARD

Georgia Pearle Foster

The first time I saw Joshua Dewain Foster, he was giving a public reading of "Bring on the Spins" which is also printed here for the first time since its initial publication in *Tin House*. I had just come off a decade in which I'd entirely refused to read any writer who was white, straight, and male, thinking I'd had enough of them taking priority in all those years of my early education, and I had been to so many literary readings that I had begun to finally get bored of literary readings. All of which is to say that, when the man first stepped to the microphone in front of the great windows in the University of Houston's library, I was possibly the least receptive audience member he could have found. I wasn't interested in him as a man, much less as a man who wrote. Then he opened his mouth and spilled out a prose paced and turned unlike any I'd ever heard, on a subject in which interest had never occurred to me, and I sat back and thought, huh. Maybe I should give this one a chance. What I found when I finally convinced him to throw some pages my way: a voice that's generous and unpresumptuous, rare in infectious enthusiasm, funny without being cruel, surprising, and surprisingly tender. I have never regretted opening a page that Foster has passed to me since.

Sure, by now we share a name, a home, several beasts, human children, and the literary company that's bringing you this book, but I assure you the romance came much later. The work has always come first. First there were the pages between us, and respect, and a shared desire to bring books to a willing audience.

In terms of pleasing an audience, Foster has a seemingly impossible task ahead of him, but I think if anyone can manage it, he can. He comes from a solid stock of Latter-day Saints in the Intermountain West, the country of television inventor Philo T. Farnsworth and novelist Vardis Fisher, and while he's historically been up for a row with his birthright faith and his culture on several finer points, he is not interested in turning his people into a caricature, nor into easy politicized fodder for the wider reading public. Readers unfamiliar with Foster's world may find themselves in disbelief at characters like Rose and Mike or Kimberly and Harry, much like the New York poet whom Vardis Fisher describes reacting to one of his novels: "If Mr. Fisher thinks life is like that, I'm here to tell him it isn't!" Having spent these last years as an outsider in the Idaho mountain valleys, I have to agree with Fisher's rebuttal to that New York poet's charge when he wrote simply, "But it was." Fisher expounded, less simply, " It was the kind of life that destroyed the weak and added the meaning of their death to the strong." There, too, Fisher isn't wrong.

On the other hand, readers who hail from the rolling sagebrush valleys in this mountainous corridor, particularly those who grew up, like Foster did, in The Church of Jesus Christ of Latter-day Saints, have good reason to be nervous about any creative project that threatens to show them to a wider readership. How many times have we seen members of the faith twisted into an easy laughingstock, on Broadway, in pop culture, in documentary exposé? Those who are active members of the faith will have to extend a little grace for (as they say in hushed tones) language, and they may find some sinning between the covers. If they can muster the generosity to push on anyway, they may be pleased to find their daily world here on earth rendered skillfully and earnestly, with a pleasure in the language itself unlike any writer they've found before.

This collection carries pieces of fiction and nonfiction drafted across a stretch of fifteen years, beginning in early 2020, before we knew a pandemic would settle into our days, and reaching back to 2005, a decade before we met. The telescope through time chronicles enormous growth in the writer's experience of the world, and an expansion of the interior voice that he throws across the characters, all those ever-shifting first person "I's" which are not Foster, but also not wholly not Foster.

If you're interested in which stories are essays, which is to say, apparently true, and which stories are true short stories, which is to say, definitely fiction, you can find the list in the appendix at the end of the book, but I'd hazard a caution here: there's fact in Foster's fiction, and there's fiction in his fact. Sure, the cover illustration for this first edition of *The Crown Package* is ostensibly him, but, distorted and elaborated as it is, the man on the cover shouldn't be construed to be him. Lately, when asked about it, he's taken to showing a sly smile as he shrugs and says, "It's all fake news—truthful as a selfie."

CONTENTS

THE CLEAN PACKAGE

OH, I'D MADE SOME MISTAKES—WHAT NUMBER WAS THIS ... I SAID A PRAYER IN MY HEART AND BELTED UP AND GOT US OUT ON THE WINTER ROADS ... I WANTED TO MAKE NOTHING EASY, NO DEAD GIVEAWAYS ... THESE DETAILS I HAVE NEVER FORGOTTEN ... SHOULD I GO ON WITH MY SOB STORY, MY ACHING CRACK, MY BROKEN PARTS ... I AM NOT A PERSON WHO LIKES TO DISAPPOINT ... IF I DIE, I MIGHT RESURRECT, I FIGURE, I HOPE, I DOUBT ... I AM NOT THE SAVIOR; I AM HIS COUSIN ... I COULD HARDLY TALK FROM LOSS OF BREATH ... I'D DONE A GOOD THING, PROUD OF MY ANIMAL HUSBANDRY ... I AM NOT A WRITER, BECAUSE ... I AM WELL-PLEASED WITH YOUR SERVICE TO THIS COMPANY ... I AM HERE TO RECALL, TO INVESTIGATE, TO REPORT, TO EXPERIENCE THIS MIDWAY PURGATORY ... I AIN'T SPENDING MY LIFE FEELING LIKE ... I OWN THEM ALL ... I MAKE FRIENDS WITH A POLICEMAN ... I HAVE, I HAVE BLOOD ... I'M JUST DOING AS I'M TOLD ... I SHOT A CAT ... ABOUT THE SCARIEST SHOT I EVER SHOT ... I THOUGHT ABOUT PULLING RANK ... I OPENED MY MOUTH ... I ACHIEVED LEVITATION ... THAT'S A FAULT OF MINE — TAKING THINGS TOO FAR ... I'M A BIT OVER-THE-TOP ... I FALL TO MY KNEES ... I BOX UP MY WORK CLOTHES AND BURY THEM IN THE CLOSET AND QUIT, THIS TIME FOR GOOD

SAILING: A DUET

2020

PEARLE

It was around this season last year that we first toured the property where we now live. Love built this place, the original owner had told us with her hands full of sterling rings, none of them a wedding band. A swoon to her voice as she said, This place was built to house love. Sing that to the same cadence as Fantasy, it gets the best of me. The Loft: six acres of parking lot and gardens edged in evergreens and lilacs, and two log cabin buildings—one that started as a restaurant, and a second that sprouted as a space to hold wedding receptions and parties anywhere other than a local Church hall. It was the first of its kind in Eastern Idaho.

In sailing terms, the sail loft is the room where sails get drafted, cut, and made into something that can catch the next wind. So it makes sense, this place being called The Loft. My job here, to help people cut the ceremonial sails that will carry them into new versions of their lives, forging new families. Or that's how I see it on a good day. On a bad day, I think Foster and I are camping in the basement of other people's hope, and those sails look like fantasies someone else crafted and stuck me to tend, a purgatory for our many prior matrimonial failures. We live with four divorces between us, at least seven diplomas on our shared walls, six of them verifiable, two dogs, a spoiled tuxedo cat, two garbage cats that came with the place, and my two teenagers at the dinner table each night.

The first month we were at The Loft, Foster found a baby bib in the garden and bestowed it to me. I threw it out. It keeps reappearing: last night, on my pillow. Before that, on the bathroom counter, in the bottom bathroom drawer. This morning I saw it draped on our headboard, which he claims was my doing. I don't remember that.

Sailing Cutie, the bib proclaims in an insufferable white cursive. The bib is the soft but somehow bitter pink of the Wal-Mart baby section, a cheap pink, like a Pepto bottle left too long to the elements. Machine embroidered on the bib, a sail boat with a dark pink bow stitched to the mast, dark pink stitching around one white sail, cerulean stitching around the other blue sail. The same blue for the anchor, and navy for the hull, and I think to myself, of course the supposedly masculine colors get to be the parts of the boat that are functional. Water-tight hull, anchor and sail, all blues. Meanwhile the pinks are merely decorative. Then I think, the bitterness of the pink is probably my own damn bitterness at being pink in spite of all my reaching toward anything else, queerness and solo-ness especially, at having gone through the whole supposedly fulfilling stretch of young motherhood mostly broke and alone, my children now in their teens and readying their wings, condescending to me over the homemade chicken soup I've made them when I have a literal PhD in the topic they're teaching me about. But myword, my children were beautiful. Bright blonde, sharp and so quippy that I kept regular notes on the gorgeous things they'd say. They're still beautiful, in the way that teenagers are beautiful, constantly morphing and bursting, passing through the uncomfortable but necessary transom from postlarva youngling to grown human being. And of course I'm also proud of them, and comfortable in my assurance that they'll go on being brilliant and beautiful and do something necessary for the world, that is if they can manage to keep their teeth and fingernails clean without my nagging. It's just that the marathon of keeping them alive and focused in a direction for nearly a whole generation now has got me about worn out.

The bib has a brown stain along one full side of its pink, faded because I keep washing it. I keep throwing it in with the dish towels, in our laundry room full of wedding linens for the event center we both run, where we also live (in the basement). In my head, the stain has been there all along, mud from languishing in the rain after being dropped from the hand of some distracted auntie at one of the twenty-three weddings we hosted last summer. That's probably not right, though. Foster is too attentive to misplaced objects and to the lawn care to have left it there in the mud for that long. I'm sure he picked it clean off the grass and brought it in to our shared bathroom counter, where it stayed, mocking me. The bib's presence was there both times I drew my own blood for the at-home fertility test. Just to see where we are, what the options are or aren't, because I am aging and Foster hasn't yet had children, not that he knows he wants them. And oh holy hell, could I do it again? The first test failed. I over-bled on the blotter paper. I was sure I wasn't giving enough with those little plastic lancets they'd sent, and so in my typical manner of overdoing everything, I took a straight razor to my fingertips. The company sent another kit. That time everything came out normal, fine enough for someone whose womb is geriatric.

Each time I throw the bib in the Speed Queen and waste another cycle on it, I ask myself why. I've thrown it away at least thrice. Every time, Foster pulls it out and finds another place where it can haunt me. I never would have put a bib like this on my child. A bib is just another thing to wash. Between diaper blowouts, spitups, and teething drool, infants have to be changed so often that it never seemed practical to me to Velcro yet another piece of fabric across their chests. Plenty of days, I gave up on fabric entirely and toted my babies around the house in only their diapers. As far as I'm concerned, this particular bib is no more or less useful than any bib. It's a gesture, a symbol, with little real application. All summer, I told myself the same thing about all the weddings we hosted. The tradition, the fanfare, the same array of awful and awfully sentimental songs on repeat. Cut as many sails as you like. They're nothing without the right wind.

But then, I ask myself, if it's only some symbol, why did I find time to sob in our basement stairwell after every ceremony? Honestly. I'm poet enough that there've been plenty of times I've loved the symbol and the image more than the real, daily thing they were supposed to mean. I'm not supposed to love diamonds, those useless upcharged things with their industry's ethical atrocities, but I loved my wedding jewelry all the way to the moment I pawned it off to pay the electric bill, both times, as marriage seemed important enough for me to try at least twice. And as I watched those princess cuts on my finger twist in the light, set in platinum, I loved, too, what they symbolized—the visage I carried, both times, of the fresh-faced young man who loved me enough to put two full months of work into something that served nothing more important than this reminder of his devotion. The fresh-faced young man who had fathered my child, and spent days lingering with me in the sand, beachside back in our coastal home county. It's not far to never-neverland, sings Christopher Cross. Fantasy, it gets the best of me.

Those diamond rings had meant hope, and in my twenties I sold my hope for pennies on the dollar. How else was a girl supposed to keep her lights on after love had died? I pawned those rings and went back to my books with my children on my back.

After we'd taken our first tour of The Loft and its accompanying basement dwelling, Foster and I scheduled a trip to my home county in Alabama to talk to my lawyer, and the one of my two ex-husbands who still had visitation with the kids. It was March 2019. We'd be graduating in May, two newly minted Doctors of the Literary, having pushed through the last few years together. What a way to spend our final Spring Break, dragging this love to tour all my failed sails.

The first day of our trip also happened to be my sister's baby shower. Of course I only had an inappropriately black dress to wear, which looked strange against the pastel petit fours piped with icing pacifiers. I bought her a multipack of matching socks, hats, and yes, bibs, in an array of white and gray, and imagined them scattered and lost to the furniture in the blur of her firstborn's first months. It was a warmer thought than it sounds. Some part of me truly misses those years I spent smelling like curdled milk, afraid to wear black because it would show so many smears, afraid to wear cotton because of how it'd reveal those letdown leaks. And maybe this is the point of sentimentality, at least when it comes to babies. Spend the time describing your days with an infant to anyone, and it's mostly bodily fluids, laundry, blistered nipples, and the ever-banal-but-too-real-not-to-mention exhaustion. But there's that other intangible: the moment when the child sighs, sleeping on your chest, and you see that you've broken off a piece of yourself and grown it into the future, a future you can only hope will expand into worlds you won't live to see. And smacked on the back of that comes the hubris they'll have when they do grow into people who know they're rising to replace you, too foolish yet to realize how much they, too, will fail to perfect the world behind you, just as you know your own parents failed.

At the end of the baby shower, as I was sweeping the room for the last of the paper plates with their remnants of chips-and-dip and pastel buttermints, I got a text message from Foster: *I'm bleeding. Anldso pretty jacked up.* Nothing else in the message save a location pin. I showed it to my sister-in-law, she showed me her phone with its own garbled text flares from my step-twin, and we agreed it was time to go pick the boys up.

By the time we got to the far end of the suburban golf course where Foster and my brother were throwing discs over exposed sewer pipes and into the dense swamp woods, they had entirely forgotten they'd texted us. Pearle! It's a miracle! How'd you find us?! Foster grinned and pointed to his calves, filthy and wet and vined with blood. I knew these woods well enough to know he'd got caught in a mess of brambles. I turned to my brother, HolyHell. How many hours I leave him with you, and this happens?

And of course my step-twin, lover of costume and revelry, participant in no less than one and no more than three Mardi Gras organizations, had already concocted another scheme. He had somehow collected a batch of sailor hats, and he wanted all of us together, in sailor hats, at the neighborhood yacht club for karaoke night, where we would sing together in those sailor hats.

It's at least part my step-twin's fault that I'm such a curmudgeon. He's the sort of jokester who'll get you nearly beat up any time you go anyplace together. Once, when we were twelve, I left for the bathroom at a homecoming game in Brewton, Alabama and came back to him telling a throng of cornfed Southern Baptist boys that I was known for my witchcraft skills. As soon as I'd heard the plan, I resolved I wouldn't be singing. I probably wouldn't be wearing those dumb hats, either.

I listen to a song like Sailing, and how can I not be irritated at the gauzy ease that seems to mark so much music from my parents' generation? And this brother of mine, he loves it unquestioningly. I envy that about him, his ability to jump on whatever ship his joy has built and go with it. Meanwhile I can't seem to trust most ships not to thrust me overboard or make me sick. When I was small, my father had his captain's license, and would sometimes run charter boats for deep sea fishing trips. Once, before my step-twin's father married my mother, I was out on one of those charter boats with my parents and their gaggle of friends, all in flipflops, tiny shorts or string bikinis on their slender-as-a-line-of-cocaine frames. I imagine it was about four years post-Sailing. There was the salt air, and the dolphins chattering boatside, their skin flecked with light as they sprang. I was young enough to imagine mermaids down there in the deep. And then I got sick enough to sully the hair of at least two or three mermaids, and someone carried me down to the cabin to moan to myself, alone, for the rest of the trip.

Christopher Cross makes an unsettling promise: that there's a way to be taken away without danger. That peace really exists somewhere, that compromise won't come on the back of the someone who's already the most disadvantaged. You say boat shoes, I think sweat and blisters. What a damn inheritance.

FOSTER

This trip to Mobile Bay was the fourth time I'd visited Pearle country, and it'd never been this frazzled. I, for one, was scared crapless, understanding the synchronicity and alignment of all this. In January, Pearle and I had entered our last semester at the University of Houston, both with quality manuscripts and peak hope in a bleak job market situation. My agent, or, ex-agent, was shopping my novel then. I didn't feel great about it, blamed the fake news. That same month, Pearle and I video-conferenced in on a line with all thirty-two of my parents' progeny. My parents had news to share. They opened the LDS official email once we were all ready: they had been called to serve, as Mission President and Companion to Mission President in some remote Pacific Islands—the Marshalls, Kiribati, Narau—for three years. Little coral mushrooms growing out of the deep dark blue. My mother slid her glasses down her nose and chuckled and couldn't get a word out, so surprised and shocked. She was really clucking. And my father, he sat back, stared off into the abyss. The story I'd always heard was that they had signed up for a six-month mission to Southern

Canada, where they could take their dog and pickup and food storage. I watched him running his commitments and career as a farmer and rancher through the ticker of his mind. He stared off, yawned big, opened his eyes. They had a June departure.

After the news, I didn't sleep well for a few nights. Things had not been great between me and my parents. They were sick of me abandoning them and the family farm and our morals and standards in the sweaty pursuit of high art. I was critical of the Church, this governing organization and spiritual politick to which we all adhered, to varying degrees. I had lodged my complaints and withdrawn, stood my ground, ran my mouth, and because of this, hardly anyone could stand me anymore. The last time I'd seen my parents face-to-face had not been pretty. There was a yelling match with my mother in the parking lot of an orange gas station; I leveled truth upon my father in his big cowboy F-350 while we were eating tortas from the taco truck. I was so mad I only ate half, and I hardly ever waste food.

And yet, I still felt inclined to call my father. He'd looked sucker-punched by the call. I knew how much responsibility there was to care for back in Idaho, because when I hadn't been in sweaty pursuit of high art, I had worked every job on the family farm, from pulling weeds at the granaries to counting potatoes with the bankers. I deeply respected my parents, had worked in the dirt with my father since I could see over a dashboard, graduated into the office to be trained by my mother in the books and legalities. I had built their spreadsheets and organized and backed-up their data and synced their phones and connected them. They loved me through my first divorce, completely shocked and scared, but my second wife and I left after a barley crop disaster, thinking I could never manage risk and crop failure like farmers had to, and that really fractured things. By my mid-thirties, I wanted that dependable, full-benefits, shared-moldy-office-institutional future. So I told my parents, before I left for the PHD, trailering my then-wife's musical instruments and my books with my farm pickup, I told them I wouldn't be coming back. The farm life was not for me. They were the leaders, caretakers, toilers. I was an artist, for crap sakes. We'd tried it enough times to know better.

I left, knowing there was more sweet-bitter to come. My life changed a few more times in adult and complicated ways—that all-American story of eros and aftermath—and now here I was, fiercely with Pearle and her kids and our cats and her dog, our books in the same hallway. A new kind of family, at least for me, and one I wanted to continue post-doc, so I was staying up at night thinking about the obligation I had to my parents and this labor of love, and my history of missions, and their history too, and how easy it is to lose everything, and the delay and heartache of rebuild and the hard-knock ticks of the mortal clock, and the truth of crashing dreams, of best ideas— creative and personal—capsizing, and my plodding and sunburned and volcanic genealogy, and all that my people had bled into their eons and stars and hills and hay and dust, and the lack of prof jobs or book deals, and thinking became dreaming, and maybe that became prayer, asking for direction on how this little crew of Pearle's could ever fit into it, if they wanted to.

Then I talked to Pearle about everything that was weighing on me, and she heard me out, and she said, That sounds like something you and your father need to talk about.

So I called him. He almost always answers me, in part because I know when to call him, when he's happy and clear-headed and undivided, which is usually sitting in his pickup on Bluetooth. In Houston, I sat out in my own car, in front of the flat I shared with Pearle and the kids, with sunglasses and a beanie on, cold then for Texas.

This call was short. I told my father the truth: we were different because we had to be, and there was no use in allowing this wedge to settle and split us. I was sorry, and as he knew, loyal as a cow dog, and dependable, and indebted. And if there was a need for me in Idaho, and a way to include Pearle and the kids, then maybe there was a reason I'd finished the degree a year early—just in time to move back home.

My father was chewing something beefy, and focused on that, quiet in thought. He said he didn't know; he'd reach out if anything came to mind. I thought that was fair. We hung up. I told Pearle that was that, and we kept our gigs and dissertation schedules.

But then something strange and big happened—my mother had this old family cheese-and-kitsch store, a log cabin building they'd bought from the original owner a few years back, and now the neighbor wanted to sell the adjoining reception hall. My father called me, giddy but cool. He'd always wanted the whole corner property to eventually sell to the church for the first temple in Rigby. The purchase as-is would include the log cabin events center and its business operations, an industrial kitchen, nigh on three decades of rustic-romantic wedding decor, and the living quarters beneath the building, a three-bedroom, two-bath basement house with a west-facing set of concrete bunker stairs.

Pearle and the kids and I, we all hashed it out. In February, we flew to Idaho for a few days to talk more with my parents and meet with the neighbor and maybe pop into School District 251, my alma mater, and also attend the funeral of the untimely death of one our best family friends, a young man who was a hunting guide and fishing guru, son of my father's best friend and hunting partner. Death abounded here; it felt heavy to be home, but necessary. And, in that way, the ideas and energy all started to pile up. Pearle and I stayed up talking to my parents. The former owner invited us to tour the premises and living quarters, and had a tray of fresh-baked chocolate chip cookies waiting. The basement house felt Nineties Nostalgic. I'd always been made to sleep in the cellar, and to have a whole downstairs, well, to me it felt like a comfortable beaver dam. What a dream. The kids were stoked to have separate bedrooms with functioning doors, and that the showerhead had neon settings. Pearle and I eyed up a two-person jetted tub in the master bathroom.

We started to imagine ourselves in new ways, Pearle and me. Could we? Should we? Even though it was a big boat, it was a small cabin, and lonely living. And but what about the kids! The kids? Idk, idk. We didn't say yes; we said we'd need to really look into some things. We were writers, after all, in our bones, not party planners. We all returned to Houston. By March, my father was joyfully negotiating with the neighbor, and Pearle and I were sweating pre-anxiously, and playing coy, not committing. Rejections came in on my novel, doors continued to close. The agent removed herself from the book, took a job internally. I thanked her, was sad, told her I was sorry that I could never make her any money.

Suffice it to say, when Pearle and I arrived in Mobile, we were feeling an urgent anxiety about locking something down. We got into Mobile and dropped the kids off with one of her ex-husbands, the one who's still around, and went and crashed at her step-brother's mom's house. It all felt very familiar, and no one really knew what we were in town for. Baby shower gossip talk. I was very much looking forward to it all. I was going disc golfing with Pearle's step-brother Daniel. A very family move. Knowing Daniel had a finely weird sense of humor and plenty of pop culture wisdom and great taste in snacks. He admitted to not being the most active Disc Golfer, but had gone enough to know his subdivision had a course in the heart of it. I had two bags of discs, and enough stress to chuck all day.

The next morning, before the baby shower started, Daniel picked me up, and we wound around this massive wooded hilly runneled maze of houses and cul-de-sacs. LAKE FOREST. It may have well been its own township, or kingdom, confusing in name but effectively descriptive. Daniel told me facts and fodder that sounded regionally accurate and fascinating. Daniel and his wife and their three cats and dog all just bought a house in Lake Forest, just around the wormy road from where he'd lived with Pearle as a kid, the one in which they stuffed a toilet in the basement full of potatoes just to see how many he could fit in there. Cost the family a lot of money with that prank, not to mention the loss of the spuds. He says one of his high school friends owns that house now, has a homemade arcade in it. No kids though.

It took a while to drive through Lake Forest. Daniel was tan and swarthy and smiley, and had on sunglasses. Very boaty looking. I was wearing shorts in public, a rare look, for the sport of it, cankle out, and running shoes and a bandana. The windows were down, and the spring air was hot, and the trees misty and the Spanish moss green and wet, and the sun was out, and we could have been going to the pier where apparently the subdivision had a yacht club, which I couldn't really visualize how close we were to Mobile Bay, just another hill over to the water. And, that like any bay, there would be piers and accesses and businesses. It smelled coastal, and felt that way, when we parked and got out of the car in the lot smack dab in the middle of the course, and up and down which snaked Daphne Alabama City Parks Septic Crew, pumping sewage above-ground through huge flexible piping. The exposed sewer and weekend-parked dozers and tractors and flatbed trucks left by the department made for interesting obstacles.

I gave Daniel a bag of discs; he got out a cooler and surprised me with an ice-cold tall boy can of the latest Red Bull, pomegranate, and we started at box one, heading west, up and downhill, toward the water, drinking and throwing, getting our heart rates up.

There's always some comradery and chatter in the first nine holes. Daniel, who I could see now, really had a dock vibe in his new digs. He explained H.O.A.s to me. We mostly talked and didn't keep real score and felt good about throwing all these bogies. Daniel put on some music from his phone, a Google XL, just like I had, and streamed some of his new favorite music since moving to Lake Forest: Yacht Rock.

So far, I had liked everything fine about the day but the soundtrack was really slowing me down. This softy salty meander. Was it all powdered drug metaphor? I could never tell. I tuned it out, drank, threw. Went through a few before the music got better. Kiwi-flavored, I remember, then Pinapple. The taurine kicked in and so did the aggressive disc habitat. My throws wobbled, then veered, then shanked. I didn't care. I was sea-side vibing, shaking with energy, this music made perfect sense.

At some point, Daniel told me more about the yacht club, which sounded to me like a country club for ball golfers, just add sails and safe harbor. That was where Stacey and Daniel had been hanging out on various weekends, particularly, karaoke night.

And I must have been really revved, because I said I'd sing some karaoke with Daniel, you bet, anytime. I'd be there for him.

The tenth got sparkly, transcendent. I had sweat through every piece of clothing on my slick wet body. We'd walked up and down and back a hill, to the car, replenished the cooler, and tee-ed off down into a swamp full of sewage tractors, and I was probably rattling off how much I loved Pearle and her poems and politics and murmured all about it through my drive. Launched my driver through a bramble wall into someone's Lake Forest backyard. I sprinted straight off into the trees, barely pausing to pick my way through and dart in and grab the neon plastic, and by the time I came out and caught up with Daniel, my shirt was torn and I was bleeding down both shins. Felt great though, wasn't thinking about anything but my salvage shot. A trio of bros with super cool backpacks came up on us playing really fast and I wanted to challenge and race them, but Daniel convinced me to sit so we found a bench and opened another one, this a zero-sugar Monster Raspberry Lemonade, and let them play through. Daniel turned up the music. I stood up and did the The Running Man. The guys made sure to avoid us. Then suddenly I was out of the window, too elevated, and again, yacht rock sucked, that was undeniable.

We were beyond the point of productive conversation. Daniel scrolled his phone, searching Miami Vice tunes, and I was squinting at those pros who jumped us. Each one threw three-hundred feet, and around trees and trucks and shiz too. I was amazed at how good people could be at things, and ashamed I wasn't better in every way. I bet if I practiced and had real faith I could launch this disc all the way up the hill, over the trees and alligators, to the sandy beach. I stood up to try but I wasn't feeling great about anything, belched chemicals that burnt my nose. Why wasn't I more careful? Classier? In less credit card debt? Even if this all worked out in Mobile, how would the kids really do in Idaho? How would Pearle? How would I? I grieved ex-family members from my past lives, the book, my own literary dreams. I was aggravated and alone and bleeding in a foreign and hostile region.

I was about to puke, when Daniel was like, Will you look up there? His phone sang: The canvas can do miracles, believe me.

Down the hill strolled Stacey and Pearle in fanciful Sunday gowns. I learned this, when they got up close. I was stupefied, grateful, amazed.

How had Pearle come to find me, lost as I was, bloody in the water, torn up, paddleless, out of my latitude and longitude? Castaway miracles, only. And more so, I was so glad she was here finally, but did she have a solution to my deep and abiding consumption of caffeinated beverages? And would she let me pick her up and sprint her to the car?

PEARLE

Before dawn on the day of our appointment with the lawyer, I couldn't quit thinking of the wide Western sky. The summer before, Foster and I had driven all the way from Texas to Idaho to stay in an empty cinder-block ranch-style surrounded by fields and potato cellars, and on the way through Wyoming he started waxing on about the desert. I'd never seen so much open ground, marveled at the juniper and sagebrush. Imagine all this, thousands of years ago, all an ocean floor. I blinked into the dark and tried not to feel seasick. At one point in my life I'd over-identified with jellyfish, wanting what I thought must be an existence of clear calm in the dark. But all this talk I'd heard from Foster of water rights in the West had me nervous. What happens to a liquid creature in the desert dust? In a place where water's scarce enough to draw and fight contracts over it? What if I dried up? And the kids? It's not like either of us was particularly adept at making love stay. We had a pile of try between us and an even bigger pile of debt, much of it accrued in past lives, past attempts at making family. Finally, I reached across the bed in the dark and convinced Foster to get up with me and go to Waffle House. We sat in what had once been the smoking section, back when I was sixteen and dropped out of school and drawing a paycheck there, and talked through the conversation we'd be having with my lawyer later that day: how at risk would my custody of my youngest child be, given that we were living in sin and planning to move cross-country? And should I have my first husband's paternity rights revoked, given that we hadn't seen him or any sign of his care in how many years? What sort of contracts would I need?

After our plates were cleared, we set to walking the gator trail to burn off the nerves together. Except for when we fail, we do this most mornings. Walking. In Houston, we'd walk four or five miles around Buffalo Bayou, or the track at the downtown Y when it rained. In Idaho, we hiked. Lately, we go upstairs and pace circles around the dance floor before dawn, our rowdy collie puppy swiping our calves.

So we didn't think much of setting out down the boardwalk trail along the interstate that runs across Mobile Bay, at least not until we'd got going. The early morning mist was out over the water, and maybe there was an alligator or two in the reeds, but mostly there was that unsettling echo of cars across the overpass overhead, thathunk thathunk. And I'd been saying it all week, but there's no place I hate more on this earth than Daphne, Alabama. The place is mostly an interstate fast food strip and a sewer treatment plant that overspills into the bay and gums up the air. Daphne, where I'd been pulled over and searched by the cops what felt like at least once a month when I was a teenager, targeted for my manic panicked home haircuts, the piercings, my penchant for combat boots with ripped up dresses or old man slacks cut below the knee. They never did find a thing when they tossed my car. I've always been pretty square.

Another reason I hate Daphne: I could probably play Are You My Baby's Father? on any given day in that miserable city. They're both still there, in apartments a few miles apart. When I still lived local, years ago, sometimes they'd pick the kids up in the same damn truck, grinning together like some snaggle-toothed faux-wrestling tag team. For a while, I'd called them My Two Dads.

As we rounded the sidewalk coming off the boardwalk, I'd said to Foster, I'm sure this sounds ridiculous, but I can feel my firstborn's father. Stumbling down the sidewalk in frayed wide-legged denim, grizzled, tie-dyed, something about the man's energy made Foster put a hand on my lower back and shuffle closer. I walked faster, craned and squinted, trying to get a good look at the man's eyebrows. Was it? Could it be? Nope. Not him.

And then the next one was him. Barely nine a.m. on a weekday, and my first ex-husband was walking from the Circle K in a pair of kitchen shoes and chef's pants, black striped and ballooned, and a stained white undershirt. Seventeen years since the wedding photos. He'd lost a fair chunk of his teeth and not bothered to replace them. He had a rollie cigarette in his left hand, and a glass bottle in a brown paper bag in his right. Hey how y'all doin this morning, he said with a chin flick, no recognition until I tossed an, Alright, how 'bout you, over my shoulder. I wasn't about to stop and try to reminisce, about what, all the birthdays and bank holidays he'd missed? Or the night he broke out my backdoor window to "use the phone," or the time he'd cleared out my bank account to pay a dealer debt and left me and the baby with no power in December? That was H's dad, I muttered to Foster, who did the double-take, incredulous, and then pivoted on his heel to walk backwards in this sort of ridiculous, sort of beautiful, puffed-up-and-protective stance.

Later, after sitting with Foster in my lawyer's office, we'll have dinner in a Thai restaurant with the other of My Two Dads. The plan was to let him know what was coming in the mail: the relocation letter, which my lawyer had perused already, which would inform him that we intended to abscond to the Idaho wilds with the kids after we'd finished in Houston, and include all the state mandated details of prospective visitation schedules, et cetera. And as we're sitting there— Foster by my side and another version of my family, kids included, across the table—all of us pulling spring rolls from the same plate, for a moment things feel normal. Thanks to Foster's easy charm, my ex seems to have forgotten to think all Mormons are kin to Warren Jeffs, and I somehow forget my litany of complaints against him, which are justified and many, and it all feels, for a moment, like family. I feel generous enough to pick up the check.

FOSTER

On the last big day of the trip, Pearle and I had a scheduled call with the seller, and then a follow-up call on that call with my father, whom we had recently learned sold his valley house and offered the neighbor all the cash proceeds for the reception center, the sale would happen on the guarantee that Pearle and I were on board to manage. The seller wanted to say yes, but needed reassured we were for real and not some truck stop, like was going around town.

On the first call, we assured her we were ready to leave our classrooms for the cult of small-business management as soon as we could. We all had a good scary relaxing laugh in my car on the Bluetooth, then closed the deal. We were all all in. The neighbor was ecstatic, was going to hang up and call my dad.

A few minutes later, the call came to us from my father: "So are you two managers even ready for this? Do you have a pen and paper? Let's make a list ..."

Awkward, neither of us really spoke up. Pearle took notes, I asked clarifying questions. The new reality: there was a spot somewhere for us. Apple trees and space for kids and dogs. And work, work, endless work, tending to the investments and best bad ideas of others, taking the rickety helm while they set off on more hero narratives.

After a minute, my father's voice fell drastically. Had something changed on our end? Were we totally both-feet-in, locked down, sure? And we were, made sure he knew it fully. In that case, he'd deliver a check of earnest money before the banks closed, and we'd work out the rest as it came at us, now that we were in business together, back in cahoots with the family. The laughs and praise of my father: rare, genuine. I was really coming home, this time with Pearle, and her crew. He could barely believe it, and really, neither could I, but we both were pretty darn happy about it. Pearle was just as stunned, smiling to herself in the co-pilot seat. She had confided to me how much she loved the mountains, the cows, the sagebrush, and who knew what kind of poems she could make in the deep wells.

It started raining again, getting cold and cloudy, dark. We belted up, hummed through the slow wet city of Mobile and onto the causeway, the sun setting in an orange line to our backs. We had a half-hour to kill before meeting for dinner, and suddenly I was feeling frigid and tired, Alabama was cold for the first time that week. I felt stoked that I had money coming in the future that was not student-loan, so I drove to the Daphne Dollar General, parked and left Pearle in the car, ran in and found a red flannel shirt made from the same fleece material as a lumberjack Snuggie. Never a piece of apparel that looked less Southern. Three dollars. Hell, I had that, cash. I bit off the tags and handed those to the cashier, told him to keep my pennies too. I put it on, buttoned it up, warmed me like a Large but thinned me because it was a Medium. That's what happens when things go your way. You start to feel like you had something to do with it, get a little high-headed, puffed up, you look better than you should.

I strutted out to the car and Pearle took one look and started laughing. In that kind of mood, Pearle shaking her head at my faux bravado, we drove the speed limit down the main drag and then on a dark slender road to the parking lot of the Lake Forest Yacht Club, where most of Pearle's Bama Family, minus her ex-men and children, for the last night, were waiting for us to eat dinner, and take in the local talent. In the white wooded archway of the entry, which looked suspiciously closed, stood Daniel and Stacey, and Pearle's pregnant sister Katie with her husband Chris, and Pearle's step-mom and long-term man, who was also the father to her daughter's husband. This was the kind of family that made sense to me, a tangled and complicated but funny one, and once Pearle and I got up close, Daniel handed us two white captain's hats. Everyone else already had theirs. I put mine on, lofty, spacious, tall, the brim, tiny, but visible. Pearle held onto hers, rolled her eyes, said Absolutely not.

Daniel led us up to steps to a dark outer ballroom and then through some closed doors that opened onto seventy, eighty seated and standing People of the Gulf, mesh-back fishing shirts and cargo shorts and Roll Tide baseball caps, watching us saunter in with our captain's hats, having never seen any of us before, all singing along to Steely Dan? Both sides were startled, and we all diverted our eyes, and our party hustled to a big undressed round-top table on the far side, facing the karaoke DJ but as far away as we could get.

Daniel stood up and took some menus from a rack on the wall, which was great, because we were all starved, and a customer, a woman a lot like us, just there for dinner and drinks and some entertainment, came over to our table and gathered up the menus and told us what there was: fried fish and shrimp, fries, po-boys, cheap beer. I think she was mad because her whole table looked viciously hangry and waiting on a food order. I didn't like the treatment. All these good southern mannered folks had taken off their captain's hats now that we were inside and seated, but I kept mine on, seeing that it bothered the other table. They forgot us when a silver-haired shorty took on Simon and Garfunkel, both parts.

In casual conversation, something came up that I'd heard before: both Daniel and Stacey and Katie and Chris had tied the knot that this very yacht club. But when I heard it this time, I heard it differently, since Pearle and I were new partners in the love business, co-managers of beauty, innocence, freedom. We talked about their wedding and wedding decorations for a half-hour.

Pearle and I went to the bar and got two fresh Diet Cokes, then out to the pier deck and got in some deep breaths. Daniel came from the bar with the last six good IPAs and a Sugar Free Red Bulls for me. I heard more about their weddings, the in-fights, the highs and lows, the dancing at the end, always dancing, and remembered the pictures Pearle showed me on her Instagram more than once, in new context, and isn't that all worth it, the sweetest part of love? The selfies?

We looked out to the black water of the gulf when the talking is done. And just like any aluminum can, I love the first one, and reconsider my choices from the second on. I was a family man now, soon to be back in Mormon Country, I couldn't be smoking coffin nails. I finally had something to live for again, and celebrate.

We all finished what we were drinking and went inside. Some new favorite was singing another bad song from an era that wasn't mine. Who cared? I stood there and watched and saw that literally everyone else in the building did. A big boy sidled up to me then—he'd been sitting with the menu-woman, I recognized—and I looked up into his soft nostrils.

Hey, he said. What's up with you and your friends?

I scanned him up and down.

They're my new family, I said. I'm not from here.

He looked over to his mother, and back to me, sort of.

He asked me: What's up with the hat?

The nerve. Didn't he know who I was? A soon-to-be Doctor of the

High Arts, a cowboy captain, a man on a mission from God once again?

It holds down my hair, I said, flat-out.

That clearly shut him up because he shut up. So I went and sat down, and told Pearle to put on her hat, which she did, for a couple selfie, and then told everyone at the table what happened. They laughed. We watched three pretty okay performances. Then those that smoked went out for a smoke, and we went out and smelled the whiffs of tobacco. We always had a habit of being bad for each other. Wedding memories ensued, and so did my deepest fears and regrets. Oh, I'd made some mistakes—what number was this? On the docks, in a cold light yellow rain, we finished our last drops, all of us, and entered again the gallery to cross the room and go out to the cars. I was ready to get on the road, reality a heavy lift.

So we entered again the gallery, and immediately Daniel had his claws on me, walking me up the aisle to the DJ station, where the man in the sparkling jacket held up two wireless mics. Terror set in. We walked past the angry mother and son. I realized, that of course, Daniel had never forgotten what I had so hyperly promised. I don't know when he signed us up for a slot, but he had.

Now, I am not a singer, and the stage has never called my name, and I was dressed in confusing and anachronistic fashion and definately needed more caffeine. My heart beat pounding beneath my ears, I felt the beady eyes of the many mother-son couples in the room. Daniel, who had his back to me, was giggling. That knuckle-head; what a guy. Pearle had her phone out, recording. I'd been duped. I felt very queasy, and knock-kneed.

Not the first time, not the last time, I thought. This was a hang-on and ride-it-out situation. So I took the mic and turned my back to the crowd and tried to calm myself. I leaned over to Daniel and asked him what the buck were we singing.

Sailing, Daniel said, by Christopher Cross.

I stared at it, hard. I had no idea.

The title came onto the lyric screen.

Then the music started. The wavy instrumental strings. And I thought, briefly, incorrectly: Oh, I know this. I've heard this. Right???

But then the strings faded, the pleasantness of the orchestra too, and some synthesized rhythms marked the true beginning, and baseline anxiety, of the song: reality escape by schooner. The further we got from the shore of the stringed instruments, and into the deep of beach-coke-80s America, I had serious doubts about turning around to face the crowd, and wanted to stop-drop-and-roll behind the DJ station, leave Daniel alone in his own mess.

But I didn't. I grimaced, rotated, showed myself, put one hand in my pocket, struck the mildest pose. The words were appearing, ready to be sung. I shook my head no to Daniel, let him go first. As he mildly waded in, I tried to grasp any familiarity with this song, which everyone in the room immediately grooved to, as if Soft Nostrils had appeared behind us in a flowing buttoned fish shirt and neon sunglasses and a saxophone. Which, these first lines, they still give me shivers, make my blood run cold, for their softness, their nonsensical praise:

> *Well, it's not far down to paradise, at least it's not for me*
> *And if the wind is right you can sail away and find tranquility*
> *Oh, the canvas can do miracles, just you wait and see.*
> *Believe me.*

That made zero sense, and I had no idea what logically came next. So I would anticipate, and try, and fail. That happened for four minutes. Honestly, I don't know how I made it through the entire set, other than the strange recess intervals found throughout in which I could close my eyes and pull my hat brim down and shuffle in place. Even when I did attempt to sing, mic down and six inches from my mouth, my eyes affixed to a swordfish on the back wall, my captain's hat itching and weighing heavy, a-rhythmically moving my hips to a foreign flamingo sound, I put my arm around Daniel, that rat fink, and sang incorrectly:

> *Sailing—it takes me away!*

That was my best line, and it got a claps. Totally undeserved.

I knew then that "Sailing" by Christopher Cross was a bad song that made gullible people do irrational things. How many ship-heists because of this? And how many subsequent ship-wrecks? Clapping?

Me, I held on for dear life, with Daniel, in our karaoke life-raft until it was finally over. When I gave my mic back to the DJ, I looked him right in the chestnut moustache and said: Thank you, and I am sorry. Never had this shirt, or singing in public, been a dumber, cozier idea. I walked straight out of the building then, planning to never return. Pearle was desperate to find something to eat and then go to Daniels and finally get to play VR-Ocean Floor. I agreed too, if there was some water to drink.

We met Daniel and Stacey at the nearest Publix, and grouped up to get a cart. We had plans to buy fruits and crackers and maybe electrolytes. Outside that stuffy yacht club, the night suddenly felt full of hope and options and fresh. We all put on our captain's hats, my idea. I guess I'd never taken mine off, still refused. On the entrance security camera we saw ourselves. I took a picture of the picture with my phone, which was really just a super selfie, a pic of me, of us, on a screen, back then, but also still.

We took a little cart and wheeled into the mostly-empty store. There was an employee replenishing the citrus display. An old white man, not rattled by our rude hats. He stopped culling the grapefruits and straightened and watched us walk by. And he crossed his arms and sort of congratulated me and said: Hey, hey, hey look who's ship came in.

I buttoned my fake flannel collar button, smoothed down my shirt, adjusted my hat, replied: Captain, you got it backwards.

We're just fixing to set sail.

Both my step-siblings got married at that yacht club, thanks to my step-mom's deep HOA discount, inclusive packaging, and the allure of the bayfront view. At the first wedding, I wore this strapless mid-thigh satin purple thing that I was convinced made me look like a suffocated tulip, my sister and my new sister-in-law's sisters all in a bouquet to match. I'd burnt my forehead the week before trying to figure out how to operate a curling iron, and left the rehearsal dinner early to sob on my steering wheel the whole way home. I had just kicked out my second husband a second and final time, on the same day my temporary employment contract had ended, and me and the kids were headed back to the food stamp office. But the photos! Those lilac dresses against the fuschias and corals in that sunset over the bay, my siblings radiant together, my children young and bright in the golden hour. The canvas can do miracles, just you wait and see.

I hate that yacht club nearly as much as I hate Daphne, but I love my step-twin's unflappable effervescence, his enviable humor in the face of a disapproving crowd. The night we showed up with Foster, I was having none of the sailor hats, the warm Cokes, or the deep-fried plates of deep fried. But when Foster got onstage in that dollar store plaid, mic in hand and arm around my step-twin, all nerves and try in the face of sockless, khaki'd hostility? It occurred to me how many other hostile bodies he'd braved alongside me, usually with far more humor and grace than I mustered myself. If I distrust Christopher Cross's diaphanous, synthetic promises of being taken away, of dreams, innocence, of being free, someone pulsing "believe me" in my ear, what I know I can trust is the earnest and daily attempt to show up and look something like family. Foster asked me to put on the damn sailor's cap, and I put on the cap to try this togetherness again. I'd rather be landlocked in our valley bowl of long-dried ocean, the aquifer far beneath me, trimming the lilacs and deadheading the petunias. We know by now how to stand against the wind. Whoever needed a mast, anyway.

WHAT HAPPENED ON 12.21.19

2019

—for Georgia Pearle, on her birthday 4/13

Like many of our days together, that day—12.21.19, the winter solstice in the 44th parallel, the calendared day shortest and bleakest—did not go according to plan.

Our day before was busy, the last of the event center holiday rush. We'd cleaned all day with the kids upstairs, put away a wedding in the ballroom and vacuumed and mopped, then surprised the kids with their Christmas presents—new cell phones, not hand-me-downs—and took off in the pickup for Idaho Falls to celebrate early Xmas at the Olive Garden. We'd been talking about the Olive Garden for a whole week, at least, and all had that carby breadstick crave, and I think you had a gift card. We couldn't lose. Took us a while to get in with the wait, which I planned on, and used to call Verizon and activate the two phones, and we were finally buzzed in and in short notice all four of us feasted with the starved abandon and acceptance that only family members around a table condone. So pleased, I ordered Diet Mt. Dew on ice in a tall stem wine glass. We got full and tired and drove back home, to the basement of the Loft, our beaver dam, our cellar, and we lethargically wrapped the rest of the kids' presents and then did another gift exchange, the small trinkets of our meager Christmas after the cell phones. But they were elated, and we'd once again pulled it off, and now all we had to do was follow the plan: go to bed, get up at 5:30 am Saturday, 12.21.2019, get the dogs to the kennel, then load up and get on the interstate south to Utah and be at my sister Malorie's house by 10:00 am for breakfast sandwiches, and also enjoying our first weekend away from Idaho since June, some 27 weeks.

At sunrise 12.21—7:58 am—we were still zonked out from the noodles and endless breadsticks. I got up at six and fed the beasts to shut them up, then got back to bed and warmed up next to you, in our squeaky bed, in our basement bedroom, under the quilt Opal had licked at least three big holes in. Which, my bad, because Betsy was scheduled for an x-ray on her leg at the vet, before getting kenneled, and the x-ray technician would only be there until seven, so I had to get there early, which I said I would, but didn't. Missed that. When I finally did wake up around 8:45 am, I sat up and called the vet still mostly asleep, walked down the hallway in my shorts, and the woman told me the x-ray technician had gone home, so I said I'd be there post-haste with the dogs to kennel before they actually locked the doors for holiday hours. I had until noon. I set down my phone on the nightstand and decided to take off all my clothes and get back into bed with you and wake you up with a good hard cuddle. We were so late already, might as well really start it off right, with a lot of love.

I promised to keep you warm here, but I underestimated how much energy that'd take. My place is a cold place. So it was after nine before I left you warmed up. I caught my breath while dressing, then went out the door, told you I loved you and you should think about packing, then to the kitchen and to drink energy and search the office for the dog vaccination records.

The only other stirrings in the house, other than the dogs, was Aurie, your daughter, who was dressed, packed, fully awake, on her phone, sitting in the purple kitchen couch, wearing her fingerless leather gloves and scowling my way. I had not forgotten, but again realized, that today, Aurie turned 13. It was her birthday. I said good morning; Aurie made claw-hands and hissed. I got it, no problem, I'd lived through my five sisters' teenage years, been married twice, and of course, been living with you, the mother and creator of Aurie, for over three years now. I'm a black belt in mood management. Aurie, when she is good, is so good, but oh, when she is tormented, she is a hurricane. Also like her mother that way. I have always been a dirt devil, you know that, and am at my best spinning with other natural forces. I told Aurie happy birthday and invited her to come drop the dogs off with me, saying I could use her help. She relented back to humanoid quickly and became her pleasant self and helped me snap on the leashes, her fantasy purple hair across one eye, chaotic good at rest, leading Betsy the old Labrador. I had Opal, our crazy goat-weasel collie. 12.21.19 would be our first day without this pup on our bed at our feet. That felt a way for me, especially after losing Roxie the cat, who was in my life 13 years until this one, 2019, and a sliver of me didn't want to kennel the dogs at all. What if they got sick and died, or ran off? What number of Idaho farm dog was Opal for me—9? 10? Doomed like the rest, I feared with little faith.

I had the pickup warmed and idling because I started it with the app on my phone. I know I tell you that every time but let me remind you we live in utterly unprecedented times. The phones, the apps, the maps, the networks—how did we ever live so disconnected before? So remote? We walked down the sidewalk to my white pickup, chuffing clean exhaust and melting all the window ice and warming up the front seats for us like a good robot. There was snow everywhere. These miracles of human ingenuity make this cruel world inhabitable.

Me and Aurie, we summoned the dogs out of the snow and into the backseat. Was she wearing her green spiky cosplay wig? I can't recall.

I know she wore a zip-up hoodie that had most recently belonged to me. I got behind the wheel, Aurie buckled up, and I backed out into the parking lot and turned around to face the highway. More chilly winds from the north.

We got driving down the slow road to town, the farmhouse chimneys puffing gray smoke, and across the road black-blue ice in patches and big sheets, the mountains east and west visible and frigid and looming. I asked Aurie how it felt to be thirteen, told her I couldn't remember that long ago for me anymore, even though I could.

She responded: "Age isn't what changes you, not so much. What changes you is growth and experience." I was floored, impressed, really, you've raised an incredible young person. I drove one-handed and fished out from the console a piece of paper and a carpenter's pencil, and had her write down her words for me. What a gift, worth putting up on the fridge. She scrawled it down and handed it back.

I flipped over the paper and saw she'd written her quote on the back of one of the parking lot warnings I leave on vehicles left on the property: Hi! You've left your vehicle here illegally and without permission! This is a private parking lot for customers only! If this happens again, you'll be towed, as posted! If you have any questions or concerns you can call! In the future, please be respectful of our private property and business endeavors! Thanks, The Management.

Seems like we're a cellar-full of smart apples in our house.

So me and Aurie dropped off the dogs to the kennel, which, by the end, we were all fine and went our separate ways. I realized I wasn't too worried. Our mutts were survivors, just like us, stubborn stoic salty water dogs, and I realized I was pretty sure I'd see them again— tomorrow, when I was supposed to pick them up. But then, we'd see about that ... In the truck, their absence bummed me out. To cheer up, I drove to the Rigby Broulims so Aurie could pick out some healthy road food for the drive, something to offset the Olive Garden family-style state of regret we were all digesting. Aurie handed me fresh sushi from the deli, and sashimi, and a bag of tangelos, and I added granola bars, jerky, peanuts, bottles of water. Ran me over fifty bucks, which didn't bother me a bit. We had a solstice Xmas birthday to fete, an entrance into teenagerhood to boot, and miles to road-trip before we crashed and then send the kids to Alabama. We'd need all the hearty stock we could get.

We paid and drove home and got inside the house and all of the sudden I really had to go. I hadn't been feeling a hundred percent. None of us had since the Olive Garden. All of the bathrooms in the basement house were ocupado, as apparently we all had the same urge. I went upstairs, crossed through our ballroom, entered our bride's room, and took the private bride's throne to evacuate and scroll. It had been a long dogged six months of event and farm labor, and my best version of a vacation was to drive four hours to my sister's house and have family dinner there. Many days I wished I could do better than this, knowing so far I never have.

When I came back downstairs, you were ready and had your knitting bag, maybe the one I gave you an Xmas in the past, needled-up, yarn-locked, tea in your travel coffee mug. Phyrex, the seventeen-year-old, cuddled their cat Mordecai and set out food for the long solo night. Then Phyrex got their leftover chicken alfredo out of the fridge to bring on the road in case they got hungry for something other than sushi. This offended my sensibilities, and I argued against it but ultimately relented. Phyrex was a debate pro, and often, like with their mother, I found it wiser and quicker to negotiate for less. Phyrex said they'd take extra care and not spill. Ready finally, we all wheeled our gear out to your rig, my mother's golden Jeep that she lent us to drive while she was on her mission, and let me say it weirdly suits you. Reminds me of that old POS Jeep we started hanging out over, down in the Texas swamp, that one I tried to fix and did more harm than help, but also got me sweaty and greasy, just for you.

It was after noon before we were all in the Jeep, about to head south. I texted my sister Malorie to confirm we'd be there in four hours. I also apologized for having slept in. She said no worries, my easiest-going sister, unless you count taxes and recipes and card games. I said a prayer in my heart and belted up and got us out on the winter roads. Aurie and Phyrex ate their sushi trays and so did you, maybe, but then Phyrex started telling us about the Chapo podcast guys, which, he'd gifted me their book for Christmas and I promised to read it but hadn't yet, and how they did a bit about nuggets. Or maybe it was a YouTube taste test series? This happened maybe fifteen minutes down the road, on the south side of Idaho Falls, Phyrex telling jokes about dank nuggs, meaning chicken nuggets, but making us laugh on the PG-13 level too, and he was really riffing about dank nuggs on the train and dank nuggs with honey and suddenly, as happens often in Idaho, we all wanted fries. Who cared? It was Xmas, and we'd all put on a bit of potato weight in six months of Idaho living. Starchy, well-insulated, even skinny svelte Phyrex had some cushion. I thought we all still looked pretty darn good in our respective forms and layers, no matter what we ate. I exited down on that truck-stop exit with the Love's and the built-in McDonalds, and we all went in and used the bathroom again. We moved okay as a herd, better than most, at least none of us so far have been eaten by wild lions or packs of mad dogs. I think we had to buy you tissues and hand-sanitizer? Maybe this was the beginning of your month-long quitter's flu? I remember we were both still on the biggest nicotine patches, 21mg, taping them to our shoulders every day, promising this was the last of the last of the last. Phyrex was wearing their gaudy purple NYU hoodie, black slacks, black combat boots, also hair in their eyes, natural blonde, moody and clever, proud and cocky as they were recently accepted to NYU's 2020 Freshman Class, the Tisch School of Game Design. Heck yes I'd been bragging on them too.

A few locals rubbernecked Phyrex's purple college hoodie. I told Phyrex to tell them it stood for North-Brigham Young University, and they'd get confused respect. Phyrex rolled their eyes, which was what I'd been going for the whole time. Haven't we all in this family just lucked out since we got together, none of us related or legally bound, making the most of the best? Wasn't this what the best was supposed to feel like, what we'd kept looking for? We strutted through the store to the McDonalds counter and ordered. Burgers and fries and dank nuggs, to go. We stepped out of the way, near the condiment bar, and I waved you over and told you that the ketchup dispenser was hand sanitizer, and you could wash your hands there. That made the kids laugh, nice work me. I had done it the week before too at the movie theater, we saw Knives Out and all liked it to varying degrees, and before we went in I tried to get you to wash your hands in the popcorn butter dispenser. Didn't work then either.

We got in the Jeep, distributed food, and got on the road again, eating and speeding across the volcanic snowy desert stretch. The food sure hit the spot, as it always did, because American food science and agricultural ingenuity and postmodernism and greed and gorge. That's one reason this works for us—we're all in on the joke and paying for it every day. Honestly, I was sad to see the kids leaving—who else would I use as an excuse for fried family food treats and a mini-lecture on the wonder of the Idaho and national potato industry?

Feeling fat and magnanimous, I asked over my shoulder what we should listen to this drive. Phyrex offered the Chapo podcast, episode 376, "Imagine a World Without." It was all about the Bernie buddies teasing on animatronic presidential candidate Pete Buttigieg, former Indiana mayor, also our age, 37 years old. I listened, thinking it was okay in parts, taking pleasure in Phyrex's giggling at insider banter, rooting for a guy like Bernie to really come in and offer just one alternative option to the spectacular contemporary political circle-jerk. I appreciated Bernie's authentic persuasive insistence and dissent. I liked Mayor Pete too, and thought the Chapodes came across shallow and harsh when it came to our peer. Mayor Pete got me thinking of what I had done with my life in 37 years. I wasn't fit or motivated to run for President, that's for sure—I'd given up on that dream in the mid-Eighties. I was pensive driving this Jeep I didn't own down a road I've driven down my whole life, from the Snake River Mountains to the Wasatch Front, through the heart of the potato dirt to Zion, I-15 three-and-half hours just about every time, four if we stop for gas, and now I carry you and your kids on it, after three real diplomas and one fake one, kicking my own butt for never having directed my creative energy to anything other than the unpaid page. Maybe I should've started a podcast. Too, I thought about the layers of myself making this drive so many times before. Other rigs, other people, other family, other women. How many books did I think I was going to write? How many did I dare?

Our reality had felt like a dream, a blessing, somehow unreal. I drove and watched you knit a hat, or a sock maybe, and you winked at me, and knitted on. I couldn't hardly believe you and your kids.

Aurie took her turn to DJ, and we put on the Melanie Martinez album K-12. As we crossed the Idaho/Utah border doing 80 mph, I thought Martinez was onto something catchy. These two kids of yours, they are smarter than they should be, and that's your fault. They also have good taste. We listened to "Drama Club" twice, and that popped. We were all car-grooving, you were making those lips and rolling your shoulders, knitting needles in your dance fists. I too tapped my left foot, getting loose as a Mormon boy gets. Then, before we got to the heavy Utah traffic, I put on a birthday song dedicated to Aurie, and turned it up. A song from Dirty Bourbon River Show called "All My Friends Are Dead." It came up on a Spotify list while we were taking the dogs to the kennel, and it pleased her newly blackened teenage heart. The chorus was peppy, infinitely chantable, and harmlessly inappropriate. It was a fist-bumper, and Aurie looked pleased in this depressive generational angst. We were all seat-dancing and singing the chorus, engaged in a real-time organic family jam: EVERYBODY'S COMING TO MY PARTY / EVERYBODY'S COMING TO MY PARTY / EVERYBODY'S COMING TO MY PARTY / BUT I'M NOT EFFING GOING TO THAT PARTY.

I pulled off at the Maverick in Brigham City to fuel and caffeinate and offload, and I texted BC that we were in his hometown, by the bird refugee, and also to get Aurie and Ellie connected on the celly-telly phones. Ellie, who you called your extra daughter, and BC, another Doctor of the Good Words. All of us had been tenants in a Houston genius house we called the Intermountain Tabernacle, now demolished and flipped into luxury three-story stand-alones. BC was from Brigham City but now lived in Vegas, teaching classes online. He texted back with directions to a chocolate shop and happy birthday wishes, which was a nice gesture but a detour we didn't have time to take, though I made a white-lie, and told him we did.

Then it was back on the road, through the brutal grays and flames of industrial urban rock-face Utah. The air force base, the gravel pits, the refineries, the open mines. Nothing like the fertile rows of my Idaho heritage, this terrain has always stayed generally displeasing to me. This was our promised land? My Zion? Our Salt? I always had my doubts, which made for most of my problems. I wondered what you made of the sight, your southern poet sensibilities applied to this dry windy alkaline experiment, and I asked you what you thought, and your eyes got wet and distant, and all you could talk about was beauty, beauty, a setting to make belief in God imaginable. Oh the poems you could make ... Made me tear up too, this deep and abiding pleasure to show my world to you, your eyes and heart seasoned, your poetry sound.

We finally got off the highway and followed the map directions to my sister's new house, down the second cul-de-sac, not the first, which featured a front yard with a brass sculpture of three life-sized brass kids on a slide, no other shrubbery, very spooky. There was no snow down there, but the wind was brisk. We pulled into my sister's driveway just after four in the afternoon, eight hours late, just like we'd always planned to do, according to our third best plan. Their driveway faced east, and we arrived in the house's shadow. It already felt like the day was done, and we'd missed everything.

But the party was just getting started now that we were here, as I announced packing in bags and pillows through the front door. There were Malorie's three sons, all younger than seven, all in matching but different combat pajamas, and Trevor, her husband, in shorts. They made a very nice and effective family. The oldest son insisted we all take our shoes off. This was the third home they'd bought since they'd been married, fiduciary wizards. Proudly, Malorie gave us the tour of it all, and I was impressed with the corner lot backyard, the varied fruit trees, all producing. We went upstairs and downstairs, saw the boys's rooms and laundry and basement office/gym, and we all ended up back in the living room, wherein also were Katie and Deantre and Little Deantre, in from New York City for the holidays, and staying with us, riding back in the Jeep once we had the kids to the airport and on their plane tomorrow, we'd come back and taxi them north. It was great seeing them again, these newlywed parents who had traveled to Houston to celebrate our doctoral graduation last spring. The ceremony had been rained out, with Houston's monster monsoon floods, a bummer, but they'd made the most of it with us anyways.

Phyrex, Trevor, Deantre, and the oldest boy James all took up the living room couch and had Switch paddles, ready to destroy each other in Smash Bros. We watched for a while, and talked with Malorie as she started to make supper—chicken cordon bleu—and with Katie, about her new therapeutic work. Little Deantre had the saddest, most pathetic and adorable croup; he kept sneezing and wheezing and sighing those big boi sighs. You kept saying just looking at him gave you baby fever. He too wore combat pajamas, but these with footies, just a tiny tyke. At some point, you went downstairs with Aurie to situate our things. I'm pretty sure you both ate it going down the stairs.

Katie, her purpose still unclear to me in many ways, wanted me to collaborate on a rewrite of popular hip-hop hit "Shoup" by Salt-N-Pepa. Except she wanted to parodize it into a song about Little Deantre's croup. I told her I couldn't help her, but that I championed her nonetheless. She started to pencil out the ditty, then quickly she darted off with Little Deantre in front of the gaming TV. I read Katie's lyrics: Croup, Croup A Loup, Croup A Loup, Croup A Loup A Loup ... Oh my goodness, girl, look at him! ... ... He's the sickest baby in here, and he's coughing our way ...

Outside, it was night dark, but the stove clock said 5:10 pm. The chicken finished and the potatoes got whipped, and we all squeezed in at Malorie and Trevor's table and someone said a blessing on the food, maybe one of the boys, a child's prayer, and then we feasted on homemade stuffed gerbils, what they always looked like to me, something I told the table more than once. It got a courtesy laugh one time and no more. When I went back for seconds and all the hollandaise sauce was gone, I said that it was okay, I'd take my chicken dressed or nude, I liked them both the same. Not one adult at the table laughed at that, not even you. It felt good to be a family in the greater sense, to nourish and strengthen each other, and also to josh, celebrate, cringe.

Before Malorie would allow herself to cut the cake for Aurie's birthday, we went downstairs to play the interactive Jackbox party game where everyone uses their smartphones to compete. There were eight of us all down there engaged in word games and phrase battles, arenas in which I always considered myself above average, played out on a 70" flat screen as big as a wall. I won the first game no problem, but the second game I caught you reading over my shoulder at my semi-constructed answers. I felt busted, en flagrante dictato, like you'd spied my simplicity. Exposed, I froze up. It cost me the round, which was okay, just to keep the peace. It's important that I lose every day to maintain some humility. In this life I've been spoiled, had it that good, so I take my lumps. Then I won the last word game by a country mile.

Back upstairs we went to the kitchen. Malorie produced the celebratory dessert, a twenty-inch-high s'more cake with graham cracker crust and crumbles and marshmallow creme and homemade chocolate icing. It was all homemade, by my sister, who loves to make cakes for people she loves, for your daughter, who loves to eat marshmallows.

Who would have thought we could have all this cake and make room for more?

Remember Malorie's second son, Liam? The one who reminded me a lot of me, speech impediment and all? How he decided to volunteer to be Aurie's servant for her birthday, and was spinning her around in the office chair, and then running to the far end of the kitchen only to spring back and power slide at her on his knees? Utter rock-star devotion, and not bad gyrations, but so bound for heartbreak, that kid.

About then my parents—missionaries far far away in the Pacific Island micronation of Kiribati—called me on Facebook Messenger. They had not been anywhere but the islands since June, in charge of the Mormon mission force there, and were a day ahead of us, their moment in 12.22, that much closer to the first long set of holidays that we were not spending together. And wow, this tech. Keeping families alive and together through the toughest international time-zones. It was too loud to talk and too tough a connection to have a conversation, so I turned the camera outward and showed them the family parties— the group dancing, the wild goofy hair shakes, the power-slides—and they just grinned and beamed on the video chat, mostly because they were glitchy and freezing, as the reality of that connection goes. It was an act of faith, this relationship with them, and us, and nice to sort of have them there, at least in pixel and spirit.

At some point most of the women and children retired to their sleeping lairs, yourself included. I listened for you to tumble down the stairs again, but you didn't, you conveyed yourself with safe expertise. Aurie went downstairs with you, and also didn't fall. I stayed up playing some no-holds-barred rounds of Smash Bros with the in-house pros: Phyrex, Trevor, and Deantre. Me, I hadn't been into a video game since Excite Bike, and hadn't been good at one since Mortal Kombat II. I backed my characters off the board to their deaths for most of the matchups. Once, by sheer accident, I came in second of four, and quit then knowing it would never get better. As always with Phyrex, I was proud of their intuition, their ferocity in competition, their clicker speed, their strategy, and annoyed at their unfettered punishment of me at games I did not care to know. NYU will be lucky to have them, and they will make more money in their artistry than either of us could ever dream. You did well with that one too, that kid, better than you should have given the circumstances. I turned over my game paddle and stood up, reminded Phyrex that they'd still never bested me at chess, and headed downstairs, slipping on the fourth stair, failing to catch myself on the handrail, tumbling and shouting heck.

Downstairs, Aurie was asleep on the oversized bean-bag chair, and you were on a recliner space in the big wrap-around leather couch, sitting straight up, knitting under the overhead lamp. You couldn't sleep, upset in the stomach and heart from your daughter's growing up and your children's departures, your change of station and situation, and the loss of your gallbladder. It was freezing in the basement, Malorie and Trevor not interested in spiking their power bill, so frigid I said I thought I could see my own breath but it was too dark to know. After midnight when I plugged in my phone to the entertainment center power strip and set an alarm for 4:00 am, then another for 4:04 am, then 4:05. We couldn't miss getting the kids on their flights, though we hated the thought of it. We had no time for mistakes tomorrow, which was today, and couldn't afford to make it like yesterday, which was over, and started too late. We had to be on time, this time, for once, because this wasn't really about us.

You were insomniatic under the lamp light with your needles working, alert in your yarn care, clinking violently along, and I figured you weren't going to get much sleep, but we'd be all right. I knew the way to the airport, and needed to rest my eyes like two hours max. I knew you were sad to see them go, and desired my heat. I put on my coat and got two quilts and laid myself down on top of you, and the blankets on top of us, and I put my head in your lap, and you knitted and tinked in my ear. I held you by the hips, and started to fade, thinking if what we had just lived through was really truly the shortest coldest, maybe also it was one of our warmest brightest longest best.

WHAT HAPPENED ON
6.21.18

So I wake up after nine a.m.—which is not something I like to admit but also something that happens a lot so at this point why lie? So I wake up late and I stay there in bed, which is not something I usually do. Usually, I'm up and at them as soon as my eyes are open; most days, I spring from my sheets to my shoes. Normally, I work at a standing desk in the other room. But not today, the summer solstice, June 21, 2018, the longest day of the year. The sun is out in Houston, Texas for another ten hours—or something. I relax. So what if I'm starting late today. I have plenty of time. I scoot away from the warm round backside of my bed-partner so that I can actually get some work done, reach off the bed to the floor and get my janky cheap Chromebook.

I open it up and write an email to my agent. She is in New York City, a place I have visited three times in my life. Once, the most recent, was to meet her. I've been telling her I'd have a novel ready since 2014. I'm surprising her with it today, attached as a PDF and shared in the cloud as a DOC. It is 399 pages; 107k words. I told her I'd send her the manuscript by my birthday, July 5, but I'd finished it early, could not stand to read it one more time, so I decided to print it out and put it in a binder for my own edits and to email her and invite her to finally take a look and at least get the good grace of beating my own often extended deadline.

What did I feel like, after I sent it? Glad, and proud. That email took me like thirty minutes to get right. Happy, I got up to take a leak.

About then, Pearle rolled over. It was her backside I had been lying beside. Her kids were with their dads for the summer, and we were luxuriating in these slow mornings where modesty could be relaxed and neither of us really had anywhere to be but to our desks, in our books. Except I no longer had a book to write, I'd written it, so I had nothing to do. I asked Pearle if she'd cook us some French toast.

This is also not something I usually do. Usually, I handle my own food intake, especially for breakfast. Most days, I'm a caffeine and banana kind of guy. If I have time to really cook, it's meats-eggs-hashbrowns. Never breakfast cakes. Pancakes? Waffles? Too heavy.

Those put me back to bed, and that's something I cannot abide. But the day before, Pearle and I had been in the grocery story together, and she'd been waxing nostalgic re: real New England maple syrup, which I had never tried, so she bought some, and I got a good loaf of five-dollar sliced bread knowing I would try to talk her into cooking French toast for me soon. Which I did, successfully, just then.

Pearle put on a robe and went to the kitchen and made the French toast. I piddled about, scooped the cat boxes, crapped the old dog in the backyard, brushed my teeth, took my meds. Extra naproxen, because a bunch of shoulder pain had returned to my left arm, where I had had an operation in 2017. But three weeks ago, this pain had settled on me again, left me wincing any time I reached and turned, pushed or pulled, typed, drove, washed my hair, or anything of the sort with my left. I thought I was better—I'd been pain-free for six months—but clearly I was not. I froze all my summer plans, including a trip home to Idaho for a family reunion, until I could meet with the doctor, which would happen tomorrow, which, as I told the doctor's scheduler, might as well be two weeks away. As soon as I knew what was up with my arm, I could plan the rest of my life.

Pearle and I ate French toast together. The New England maple syrup ran thin and warm and washed across the butter egg bread, tide-like. I could see why she relished this great American sap, appreciated that I'd been let in on the secret. I felt the same way about russet potatoes. There, on the plastic table in front of us, was the manuscript that took me four years to write. It was in a hot pink plastic binder, four inches thick. An inch a year—now that's what I called personal growth.

10:30 a.m. My agent had had my email for over an hour. Had she read the book yet? Did she love it? Already sent the contract? Check(s)?

I gathered up the dishes to wash them at the sink, my pleasure and gratitude after such a food gift. Pearle removed to her desk to edit and knit. I washed and dried and shined the dishes, put them up. Folded and refolded the dishtowels. Swept the kitchen floor, something I'd been wanting to do for seven months. In the bedroom, I turned on the World Cup—France versus Peru—and rooted for the Spanish-speakers. I always pull New World. I took out my empty luggage and looked inside my closet, starting to plot what I would need up north, back home in Idaho, if we were lucky enough to make it back there. Pearle and I had a secret hope and plan: if the doctor cleared me to travel, we would pack the car and leave by Saturday, be to Idaho by late Sunday so that we could surprise my mother, who was turning sixty on Monday.

I didn't see the point in actually packing without knowing what was up with my shoulder, so I hooked up the leash to the old dog and took her around the block for some fresh air. Out on Gray Street, I paced and scoped out a palm reader sign that Pearle had told me recently showed up. I had always wanted to have my palm read. I can handle the truth, and am happy to pay for it. Of course, I wanted to buy Pearle a round of hand-reading too, as a late birthday gift.

So I walked the dog past a sagging peeling slat-house on a main drag in the historic Rosemont district of Houston, with a covered front porch and a beat to frick Ford Excursion in the cracked uneven driveway, a neon OPEN sign in the window, not illuminated, and a phone number on a placard on the sidewalk. In the front window, a shadow appeared behind the curtain. I wanted to make nothing easy, no dead giveaways, no easy outs. I hustled around the corner with the dog and called the number. I wanted to keep everything I could a secret; I had no faith in the palm reader, but had a hope I'd learn something somehow, anyways. I didn't disguise my voice or give a fake name. I asked if she had time to read the hands of two people as soon as possible. She said she could at one p.m. That was less than an hour away. I said okay.

She told me to call back in a half-hour to confirm my appointment. So I confirmed something with her then: She wanted me to call her in thirty minutes to tell her I'd be there in thirty more minutes? Yes, she said. I said I'd text her at twelve-thirty, and that we'd be there at one p.m. on the dot.

The dog rushed me home. There, I informed Pearle of the plan, and she took a break from editing and fussed about the flat, changing clothes a few times, deciding her wardrobe and hair situation. I too checked myself in the mirror, wondering what the palm reader might discern and misinterpret. For two months, the temperature hadn't dipped below eighty degrees, and I was in shorts and a tank-top and a farm hat, always sweaty, far from my element. I decided not to change. The palm reader, like most people, would have no idea who I really was.

These bustling moments in our relationship when both are readying for a joint event, equally energized, are intensely gratifying, and do a lot to unify. This was still fresh, vibrant, steeped in meaning, cosmic, revelatory. As Pearle and I readied, we smiled and winked at each other, took one another by the waist, swayed a bit.

What does the future—our future—hold? I couldn't guess, and didn't need to know but was asking just because I could, just because I was with someone who wanted to go along with me to find out. I pinched her peach as she went by, kissed a cheek, said thanks and also hurry up or we're going to be late.

I texted the palm reader and told her we'd be there at one p.m. on the nostril. Which we weren't. We got there a few minutes late.

At the house, half a cigarette smoldered in an ashtray. Oh, how peppery and lovely that smoke smelled. Cigarettes, those paper plant sins, had not been present in our lives for 84 days, according to Pearle's stop smoking phone app. I had finally stopped coughing long enough to want another cigarette. I didn't pick it up and smoke it, though. I was past that point. I simply longed for it, reminisced about the good old bad days. I stamped down the nico-urge, knocked hard on the thin front door. Above me, a diamond window card-boarded from the inside shook against the glass.

A little girl opened the door. Younger than eight, for sure. Cute kid. Looked a lot like any one of my nieces, Raleigh. Pink clothes, long hair, a few missing teeth. I asked her to go get her mom. I didn't really think about it. Retired Mormon Missionary reflex. A young short woman came to the door and shooed back the kid and her little brother, who had been in the shadows of his sister the whole time. The mother, who was our palm reader, called herself Luna. Luna brought us inside and shut the door. We stood in an empty living room with thin path-worn carpet over a bowed floor. Luna, chewing gum, speaking English Italian Chicagoan, set the kids up and explained she'd be in the other room, working. Once they were settled, Luna led us into another front room, behind a white door—her palm reading room.

A large pink lounger, in front of which Luna stood, centered, at the back wall. In front of Luna, center of the room, was a table desk piece, altar-like. Facing this desk were two fabric covered chairs, nice enough, but with stains. I took the far chair, and Pearle took the near. We sat down once she did.

Luna reminded me of my youngest sister Abby, and my first ex-wife Renae. Luna was twenty-four, twenty-five. Poised, serious. Wise but unrefined. No pushover, but easy to confuse. Luna, who was wearing jeans and a shirt, had three burns or scars on her sternum. They looked surgical, earned, unfortunate, designed. We discussed what services we were looking for, and landed on one in which we could each get our palms read, a tarot reading, and the opportunity to ask any questions we could come up with. That ran me sixty bucks a piece. I paid Luna through the Cash app.

Transaction sent and received, phones down and away, Luna crossed one leg over the other, interlocked her hands, mystic-like, and asked who would be going first. I looked at Pearle to see what she wanted, and I could tell she wanted me to go, so I said I would. Luna got out a deck of tarot cards from the desk. She warned both of us that regardless of what we were to each other, who we were in each other's lives, things might come out in a reading that could damage a relationship, so she invited Pearle to leave the room if I was uncomfortable. I said I'd like her to stay. I could trust Pearle with any bit of information, any transgression.

I was disappointed with Luna, incredulous—she was trying to figure out who Pearle and I were together; she was reading us. Which I knew she would do, but didn't anticipate it being this obvious. Maybe she wasn't psychically inclined; maybe this was all just jig.

"So she can stay?" Luna asked me.

"Yes, absolutely," I said, again.

Luna flipped over some cards and arranged them on the table. Then she took my palms and looked at them. She leaned back and interlocked her hands again.

"Okay, so before we start, I have a message for you. I don't know what it means, but I have to give it to you from the other side. Did you recently lose a child?"

It was a strange whiff to start with. I'd never had any kids. I considered my very much alive mother and father, my living breathing five sisters and their husbands and children, Pearle, her two kids, my cat, their cat, the dog—all, all good.

"No," I said, "Not that I can think of."

I looked back at Pearle. She had this look on her face like: Are you kidding me?

"Who then?" I asked.

"Evalie," Pearle said.

Duh. I realized I had been thinking too narrowly about Luna's question. Selfishly, I had only been considering my immediate family. But just a few weeks before, the family of my second wife Mallorie Noel suffered the catastrophic loss of their youngest member, Evalie, a little girl just about to turn three. I had not been in contact with this family since the divorce, but once I heard the news, I texted Mallorie Noel and let her know that if there was anything Pearle and I could do, we would. Mallorie Noel took us up on that, and brought over her two cats for us to watch so she could return to Idaho for the funeral. She had just retrieved the cats the day before, and was actually coming over to have dinner later tonight because she needed some good company and a meal. Pearle had offered to cook.

I said to Luna, "Yes, there is one person we lost much too soon, but my connections are now fraught."

Luna hushed me. "Here is the message: Celebrate her in her time of death. Don't blame anyone. Celebrate, and love, only love."

I nodded and said that I would pass that along, which I planned to do, but didn't yet know exactly how, or to whom.

That gravitas delivered and leveled, Luna reviewed both my palms again quickly, roughly, and set them back down on the table. She sighed. She told me I led a simple, but complex, life. I agreed. She said it would be relatively long, which brought a lot of relief and pain. She said I was happy on the outside and sad on the inside. She was so right that deep down this made me weep, which made me mad. That was all my hands had to say about me, and so I took them away and she turned her attention to the cards.

She told me to think of three questions I wanted answers to. This gave me pause. I was not prepared to think while at the palm reader. I looked at Pearle. Was there anything I wanted to know with her? She was as solid and beautiful as a person as any I'd been lucky enough to be with, and I felt we would be together for a long time, one way or another, and since we spent all our time together anyway, I'd had all my questions answered, whether she knew it or not.

I told her I had them. She told me to tell her two. So I did.

What would happen with my book?

Where would I move next?

On the book, Luna said I'd be fine, on all counts. I asked her how fine. She said just fine. I didn't want to jinx anything, so I left it at that.

And what about my next home?

Arizona, Arkansas, or Colorado. She said any of those places would be good. Also, I'd have a house for once in my life. A home of my own.

I trotted out my third question, too, this about Pearle, about us and our future, but I cannot write it here. I listened to that answer, and felt good about everything, and had nothing left to ask.

Pearle and I swapped seats, and she and Luna got right down to it; it would not be my place to go into all that was revealed. You'd have to ask her. As for me, I was feeling pretty glowy and golden, having a message to pass on, knowing I still had some life left to live with a person I loved, and a just fine book situation on my hands.

Pearle's future all came back good too. I can at least say that. Luna made some mistakes on that one, reading her, flubbed a bit. But who doesn't? Pearle's a tough nut to crack, and one of the kids had started crying. We could hear through the wall. We left through the front door, saying thanks to Luna and adios to the kiddos, time and e-funds well spent.

We talked about everything on the walk home, and for an hour at the flat. It was 2:30 p.m., and once we had rehashed everything a few times, we shut up and got back to our desk work. We had a lot to do if we were ever going to get out of Texas. Pearle edited. I paid all of my July bills and budgeted the rest of my summer money. Transferred cash over from savings to cover the travel and upcoming doctor's visit. I walked to the bank and took out some road cash, went to CVS and bought heel Band-Aids for Pearle and toothpaste for me. Returned to the flat, read the news on my phone.

Around seven, Pearle started cooking chicken curry, and I made some watermelon juice Mexican-style—watermelon, lime, a bit of sugar, water, some ice, blended it up in Pearle's awesome Ninja blender, served in a pitcher. I set up the table in the back driveway. Soon enough, Mallorie Noel showed up and we hugged for a while. Sad day back at this house where she used to live with me. Together and apart, we'd seen a lot of death. We went inside and dished up curry and all three of us sat out back and ate like we were starving and talked about Mallorie Noel's trip to Boise. She got to sing at the funeral, cried part way through the performance. The *Coco* song: Remember Me. Evalie's favorite. Made us all cry too, just imagining it.

Our upstairs neighbors and their daughter came down and joined us. BC and his Utah crew. I hadn't seen them for two weeks, as they'd been in the Beehive State on summer vacation. I'd been sitting upstairs twice a day, taking care of their birds while they were gone, a cockatiel and two budgies. Sarah caught up with Mallorie Noel, who had lived in the flat with me for a month or two, and had started a friendship but paused it, and now wanted it again. We kept after the catch-up. Stories were traded, and we all laughed about the north country, which everyone had been to that summer but me and Pearle, and we were pining for it. But it felt like after Luna the palm reader, we both knew our plan was a good one, and we'd be leaving Texas for Idaho soon enough. We squeezed hands in the dark.

I told Mallorie Noel of the message of love from Luna, and she could hardly believe it, asked if I was kidding, but insisted I relay it to Chad and Crystal, Evalie's father and mother, so I said I'd contact my friend and ex-bro-in-law, and let him know to celebrate, and love, and not blame. Evalie was beautiful and a miracle, here or there. So much of life is out of everyone's control. I missed all of them deeply.

Mallorie Noel was in great spirits, too, after having come home, because she had met a new man, a twenty-five-year-old ex-BYU mountain man, all sugar and spice. Made us laugh; reminded me of funny sweet things Mallorie Noel used to coo about me, back when we were in love. I was happy for her in this new flu. I looked around the table. We all were.

Then a disaster happened: ████████████████████████████
██
██
██
██
██
██
██
██
██

Mallorie Noel left ████████, and took off with leftovers, and drove home alone.

Then it was just the four of us who lived full-time at the Tabernacle.
██
██
███████████████████████ The glory of repentance is that it is repeatable.
██
██
██

Eleven-thirty, it was just Pearle and me, out in the back drive, staring up at the new builds looming on three sides. What a sad wonderful joke this neighborhood will be in the future, we thought together, when the palm reader and us are long gone. Pearle and I will be in Fayetteville, Show Low, Trinidad. But where will Luna be? Can she read her own palm and know? The truth was in the backyard, Pearle knew my future, and I knew hers—what else could be said? We were smug, satisfied, content. ████████████████████████████
████████████████████████████████

After midnight, Pearle and I ███████████████████████████
████, we got up and went inside and—technically, what occurred next was on June 22, so I probably should just shut up about that.

DOGMAN:
A NIGHTMARE

2018

PULL OVER AND SLEEP, my late ex-wife used to say to me, at night on the long hauls, YOU'RE GOING TO KILL US ALL. I'd squint at the road, stay vigilant, say, I can't; I feel it deep; death is nigh upon us, looming up ahead. She'd say: SOUNDS LIKE SOMEONE NEEDS TO GET BACK ON HIS MEDS. I'd say, Drowsiness, to me, is a side-effect worse than death. In this way, we'd claw through the miles, chew up the time, stay the road. She kept me alert, I appreciated that, and missed it after she took the cats and split. // I recall her now as I drive the long stretch across the desert to make it back home to her funeral. It stinks, driving alone in the car like this; it reeks mephitic and rich, burnt match, spent shell. This is the last time, I swear, I'm ever driving home. // I have not slept since getting the news about my late ex-wife. I can't close my eyes. I can't say her name. I can't even spell it out loud. Her death, I fear—I feel—I know—is all my fault. Let me explain. // This all started on a slick misty October night in 1999; my junior year of high school; I remember it with trepidation and ease. After school, I'd been breaking out a new piece of ground for my father up in the bench hills—a big swath abutting the edge of a reservoir. In my days and nights plowing this field, I encountered no one. Prairie dogs galore, and the scavengers that hunted them. Occasionally, I'd spot a moose making it down for water. One day while exploring I found some cliffs about thirty feet above the reservoir water. I told the gang—my girlfriend, my best friend, and my other best friend—about it, and they decided they had to see it for themselves. I told them I'd pick them up. // Then, I drove a maroon Chevy Silverado, just one bench seat. My girlfriend rode love-gun, my best friend sat biddy, and my other best friend got the window. It was dark out. I drove slow through valley fog until we got up on Bench Road, above the mist and cloud. Then, after a few miles of bad pavement through the empty wheat fields, the road gave way to gravel. That stretch slowed me down to forty-five, but I could do it in my sleep. So I drove it cool, with the windows down and the wet air slicking my elbow. October. Sage-stink, overpowering, chilly. I could tell the gang wanted a thrill, so I gave them one. I gassed it over whoops and through hairpins. They cried out Bench Road was a dirt-coaster. I felt that flutter in my gut too but I knew how to hold it in—I knew what was coming. I anticipated the steep stuff, gassed it, fishtailed. I kept it up until I had to slow down to make the farm-road that ran east for eight miles through sagebrush, across lava and shale, and skirting our section of plowed earth, until it stopped at the reservoir cliffs. Once we were creeping on two tracks, well off the gravel, my best friend said: "That gave me a hoot." My other best friend said, "It tickled my taint." My girlfriend said, I'D DO IT AGAIN, MAYBE, IF I COULD DRIVE. On the farm road, I could only do fifteen, so I bumped it along, bleak dust rolling in the cab through the windows, and took in the gauzy black strip where the headlights no longer reached. What was out there? The darkness enclosed us in a cipher, all around. // My best friend leaned up and squinted into the expanse, on point. He was staring dead ahead. He asked if we believed in the Dogman, part-man, part-dog, a creature that on four legs ran as fast as a vehicle on the night highway and looked like some crazed desert mutt. But it wasn't. You knew it was the Dogman when it'd look over at you, and you'd lock onto its yellow eyes, and then the Dogman'd rise up on its hind legs and sprint along with you at eighty, ninety miles an hour, locking eyes the whole time, waggling its tongue, slinging spit, scowling. Try to run you off the road. If you didn't, the Dogman'd lean back and howl, then veer off and disappear into the sage, full speed. After you saw the Dogman, it was pretty much guaranteed you'd die. All through this story, my girlfriend squeezed her nails into my thigh. I said, Yeah, well, I've been out here all alone for weeks and seen all the beasts out here, and that one doesn't exist. My other best friend was struck mute, a big guy, but a wimp, and he found the state football radio broadcast on the dial. The Cavemen crushed the Diggers on a violent punt return. The announcer gasped. One kid broke his femur. My girlfriend whispered in my ear: HOW LONG TILL WE GET THERE? I HAVE TO PEE. I told her, Soon, safe, sound. She squeezed my hand. I knew right then I wanted to marry her. I decided it and put it in my mind, and that's exactly what I did—and she eventually became my wife, then my ex-wife, now my late ex-wife. Some kind of drive, this life. What a bad trip. // The cliffs were more tenuous than I'd anticipated. Through the night and fog, none of us could make out the surface of the water. I knew what was down there, because I'd been here, and I'd seen it in the light. I stripped to my boxers, but my friends wouldn't budge or unbutton a fly. My girlfriend took one look at the setup, said I DON'T FEEL GOOD ABOUT THIS and got back inside my truck. Abandoned, I surged with anger—flared, as I do—and decided then that I'd dive off the cliff head-first, just to prove to the gang that I could be brave when they refused. I was crazed. I took two steps back from the edge and dug in. My best friends hollered for me to hold up; my girlfriend started screaming. I could hear her from inside the Silverado as I launched head-first off the lip: WHY ARE YOU BEING SO DUMB? //

I fell through states of matter: —gas —semi-solid-cloud —liquid —plasma. I could not feel up or down, top or bottom, saw nothing. All black, my eyes wide open. I gritted my jaw and stifled my panic. Then I slammed into the water sideways and, on impact, blacked out. // I do not know how long I was unconscious. I came to against the base of the cliff, and could her the gang yelling out for me from the sky above. The impact had ripped my boxers clean off me; on the rocks, I was naked, bruised. I caught my breath, yelled to them that I was alive and fine, and scrambled up the stone wall. At the top, they shoved and hugged me, punched and loved me. I had never been naked in front of a woman before, but I was that night. My girlfriend turned her back as I put on my clothes, then held me as I shivered. My teeth wouldn't stop chattering. I was soaking wet. I got behind the wheel and the gang loaded up and we started to haul back to the valley. My girlfriend put her hand on my knee, no nails, all care. I entered a stage of complete disbelief that I'd survived. I was gratified and elated, on an empty stomach, hot, clear-headed. I razzed my friends for being cowards, my girlfriend for losing faith. I flared—gunned it across the sagebrush twenty, thirty miles an hour. I hit the tops of the whoops and felt my front tires leave the ground. I really had them all bucking, but held the truck in complete check and control. YOU ARE BEING INSANE, yelled my girlfriend. "Dude!" both of my best friends yelled. I howled: Come out, Dogman, I'll break ye neck and skin ye hide! No one laughed. They all were bracing, cussing. I came up over a whoop and—this was where the night turned—there was a man standing in the middle of the road, waiting for us. I'd been checking time on the dash clock—11:39 PM—and snapped to attention to see him in my headlights. // My girlfriend saw him too, screeched: IT'S HALF-MAN HALF-ALIEN! The man had the slouch of a truck-jockey, and wore a Dallas Cowboy pullover jacket, a straw hat. I had one foot over the brake and one foot over the gas—a driving trick I learned from an old pro: coast?—stop?—go? The man reached for his belt buckle, so I gassed it. He didn't even have time to put his hands up. I didn't swerve, hit him doing about thirty-six, felt him go under the bumper and against my feet, slapping and cracking. I got over him, coasted twenty feet up a hill. He was back there, folded up in the dark. I put it in reverse to see if I could use my reverse lights to show me something and just then, out from the sagebrush, pulled another pickup truck. Four square yellow brick brights in my side-view, coming for us. // I dropped it into D and spit rocks. Whipped the truck through the sagebrush and to the gravel and beat it down into the fog of the valley once more. The truck kept up until the pavement—I was doing seventy-five through the fog on Bench Road. No way in hell that demon was catching me with me on my known straight-and-narrow. // We didn't speak in the truck. We couldn't process language, our mouths, all dust and mote. For twenty minutes, I drove us through the fog too fast, and then, out of the corner of my eye, saw a car, parked, lights off, in the barrow pit. I'd missed it by inches. I said, Did you guys see that? My best friend said: "That old dude in the gutter?" And my other best friend said: "That old lady in the pasture?" ALL I SAW WAS BLOOD, my girlfriend said, ALL OVER THE ROAD. // So I whipped it around and went back to the scene and saw it all in my headlamps: a big rusted black sedan, an old man in irrigation boots and a denim jacket and a feeding cap, and an old woman, out yonder, wandering. Gore and guts across the pavement like it'd been swept with a push broom. // I rolled down my window and asked the man what caused the mess. The old man plucked a piece of grass from near his feet, and stuck it in his mouth, said, What'd ye hit, a pack of coyotes? I peeled off without hearing more—another witness was the last thing I needed. Through town, I drove the speed limit, but when I got out on the desert to take my girlfriend home—she lived fifty miles away, in Mudville—I was doing eighty, all the way. She hadn't touched me since the collision. She kept her hands woven together in panicked prayer. I could barely even look at her, I felt so rotten and low, kept my hands at ten and two. // So, jeez, I sort of just went word-vomit then, trying to corroborate a story. Tied and twisted everyone with my words. By the end, they admitted they had no idea what had happened, and that was our story. I made the gang covenant to keep the secret. We would never speak of it again. Eventually, I got everyone home safe and sound. // At the house, I checked my truck. I didn't have a headlight out, and I couldn't find any blood or dents or hair. Had the mist and fog wiped them clean off my hood? That made little sense, but it was my best guess. What I did know for certain was that I'd killed a man, and I should be in jail, and I wasn't yet. I deliberated my few possible moves. Inside, I showered, went to bed mumbling, Where would I be without my friends? My family? My best girl? // The next day at sunrise, I returned to the bench to do tractor-work. These details I have never forgotten. At the scene of the collision, I found what I thought I would: beer bottles, tire tracks—and the body of a man. I was right—a Cowboy's jacket. He carried no identification in his wallet, just a few paper bills that looked like board game money and a paper flyer for a C.D.L. course. His poor body was wrenched and purple. I knelt in the dirt and wept for what I had done. Then I loaded him into the bed of my truck and took him to the field, near the tractor. With my shovel, I dug a deep hole in the soft plowed dirt. There, I threw him in, interred him. Then I got in the tractor and lightly plowed over the section two or three times, to cover my tracks, and pay my respects. // The wallet, though, I could not bear to bury. There was a photo in there of what looked like his wife and daughters. At the top of a lava outcropping— an island of rock in a sea of dirt—I found a natural tomb in the stone, protected from water and snow, and deposited the wallet in there. I marked its location in my mind, knew I'd never forget it. Then I let the truck driver flyer blow away in the wind. No one else ever needed to see that. // I worked in the tractor, spent the day feeling thousands of eyes out in the sage as I went back and forth. Watching me. Condemning me. Cursing me. I deserved it. I quit that night before it got dark, and in my haste to get the hell back to pavement, left the tractor door open, which I knew would cause problems. I was too scared to return and close it. I told my father I was done with the job but not the work. I couldn't go back. He was confused, displeased. That night, a blizzard set in that lasted all winter, and by the time my father got back to the tractor in the spring, the hunters and snow-machiners and weather had broken out all the windows, popped the tires, put some slugs in the motor. Needless to say, the batteries were dead. We had to junk the tractor. I take the blame for that too. // I never returned to that bench farm above the reservoir. My father sold it the following year, the year 2000, the new Millenium. The gang and I all moved on with our lives. My girlfriend and I got married. My best friend worked at the tire store. My other best friend became a county cop. I stayed on the farm. Those were good, steady years. We lived clean, upright lives, built houses, broke out more dirt, served God and our neighbors, et cetera. My friends had kids and mortgages and riding lawn mowers—my wife and I didn't, but that's another story. We were all established and happy, well beyond what we needed. Ups and downs, whoops and turns, sure, but at the end of the day, none of us lost the road. // But then, a few years ago, the gang got together all around a bonfire in my backyard. Chopping up the glory days. Things had gone so well for all of us, I thought it was time to get our secret out in the air. For one, I could not believe I'd gotten away with it, and that fact gnawed away at me. Sometimes, it stabbed at me too. Often, I would not sleep because I could see the man's face as I saw it over the hood, eyes wide open, yellow—it was all too much. So I told the gang I wanted to break my own pact, get it all out in the open, once and for all. I went first, reported every relevant detail. When I started to describe how I'd found the man and buried him—a part of the story the gang didn't know—I realized no one was listening to me. They were all looking at the stars, poking at the fire, toeing mud off their boots. // Finally, my best friend said, "Dude, you didn't kill anybody. You hit your head on the lake." I said, That's not how I recall it; we're all entitled to our own story; but here's the truth: I have the proof; I stashed the wallet; I still know where it is. My other best friend said, "There is no wallet because there was no body. You got to get over it." I shot up to my feet and started pacing, saying I could show them the wallet if they dared go to the farm with me. My wife tried to talk me out of it. I would not hear her words. Eventually, she acquiesced, walked to my truck, said, LET'S JUST GET THIS OVER WITH. We loaded up and drove to the Bench Road, to the sage-heath. // The land had changed, though there weren't any more humans up there. There were four-hundred new turbines to catch the south wind, and heavy-duty power lines that fed the valley. The stars were out, and the scarlet eyes of the turbines blinked in unison every nine seconds, for aeronautical safety. // The farmer who owned the land had developed it, fenced off the dirt road, gated it, posted a No Trespassing sign. That wouldn't stop me. I got out and scaled the gate, telling the gang to follow. We would walk if we had to. I tripped on the loose dirt on the other side. // In the moonlight, from my hands and knees, I could see that all the sagebrush was gone; all of the lava was buried; all of the hills had been developed, planted, plowed. // I understood that the wallet could never be recovered. I no longer had proof. // I stood, cussed at the black sky of the east, kicked dirt clods, jumped up and down on my hat. // My wife and my best friends came over the fence to put me back inside the truck. I fought them, running circles around them, and they didn't catch me, but we all lost our breath because none of us were in good shape. We stood there in a big circle, panting. // Out ahead of us in the field, clear out there, four yellow lights appeared. One by one, we all affixed on the lights with our eyes. The lights grew bigger, accelerated across the whoops of the earth, growing into bricks of light that were coming right for us. My best friend turned to run, and tripped over my other best friend. They tangled in the dirt. One of them screamed. My ex-wife closed her eyes and pinched her nose, as if she was dunking. She hated water, and couldn't swim. // Unlike the rest of the gang, I faced the light-bricks, didn't blink. I wasn't scared, even if they still were. I never had been. I squared. That light trucked through my chest, heart, lungs, and I wanted to puke and scream but couldn't do both, so I did neither, just watched it happen. The light passed through me, accelerated, whipped the wind turbines, disappeared. I loaded the gang into the pickup. Guys, I said, I don't think I can die. My best friend said, "Get out, I'm driving." My other best friend still was catching his breath. My wife said: I AM SO SICK OF THIS NONSENSE. // I got jaundiced, depressed. I was convinced I should have died by the lights, but didn't. That's all I'd talk about. My wife took me to the hospital. The doctors started me on a battery of drugs, pills, psychotherapy. When I dreamt, I saw the stars of cowboys, headlamps, running lights, the man's face, the embroidery of red thread in his leather wallet. Vivid dreams where I'd be driving, and the accelerator pedal would stick, and I'd keep picking up speed, unable to slow down or stop. // Faster, faster, infinitely, until I hit a wall. // The last time I told my wife about a dream, she said, I LOVE YOU BUT I AM SCARED AND OFFICIALLY MOVING OUT. I could hardly blame her. I was worried about me too. I stayed in the hospital, for my own safety. // Soon after, she became my ex-wife, as I learned through her divorce lawyers. I guess I signed off on it, someway, somehow, though I don't recall seeing the paperwork. // Things got foggy once I was checked myself out. I quit the farm and moved two time-zones away. // Lost track of my friends. // Lost track of my family. // Lost track of my meds. // Time: a dark dirt road that only I drove. // First, my best friend died. That brought me home. He was at work after-hours putting a lift on his Ford Bronco. In the tire shop were a few other rigs; particularly, a big yellow Kenworth semi that was in getting new drums and air bags. The security camera showed it all: my best friend walked behind the semi and then slipped. Went head first, then heels. Cracked his skull on the shop floor, drowned in a puddle of oil and blood. My other best friend, the cop, had the security camera footage and showed it to me. He says he slipped; to me, though, it looked like the truck bumped him. My trust in the world had shifted, slipped a gear. We both spoke at the funeral. My ex-wife sang a hymn. I got back on the road as soon as I could flee the cemetery. // Next time I heard from home, it was the news that my other best friend had been smashed. He was on the highway at dawn, helping an old lady whose radiator had blown. A big rigger hauling hay bales was texting, saw them too late, pulled the wheel hard, jackknifed, flipped the trailer, dumped all the bales. Undetermined if my other best friend had been killed by the trailer or the hay. He, the old lady, and both their cars were decimated. I drove back home for that funeral too. Closed casket. My ex-wife, who never liked my other best friend all that much, did not attend. // I returned again to my new life, alone, and cycled. Where did I go wrong with my life? What sinful choices had I made? Had I surrounded myself with all the wrong people? With my best friends gone, with my family far away, who would I tell my stories to? Who would listen? Who would care? // And I also thought: I've cursed the people I love. I've damned them. These deaths are truly all my fault. // A few days later, I got the call about my late ex-wife. She'd been coming back from visiting her new boyfriend in Montana, at night (like how I always used to drive her) and swerved to dodge a deer in the road, left the roadway, dropped a cliff, entered a frozen lake, broke the ice, sunk straight down. It all happened so fast and hard, she probably didn't even sense it. Just sound, and lights out. // That poor woman, who put up with so much of my crap. My good friends, who tried. Without them, who am I? // The end. The end. The end. // When I could grieve my late ex-wife no longer, I packed a bag and loaded my rig and got going on the trip towards home. Stopped at the gas station, fueled up. Put in a tank, then filled ten jugs, loaded them into the trunk and backseat. Enough juice to stop a semi, or a demon wall of dark or light. // Then I deadhead across the desert. // Now I am in speeding through the expanse. Stars out, roads empty, no fog. I will not make it to my late ex-wife's funeral—I plan to hold my own. I drive to finish what I start. I am sleepy, but will not stop. I am angry—and want to be. I scan for the lights, chase the brights. I pin it at ninety-nine. // I AM THE DOGMAN, I think, and, THESE FUMES ARE GETTING TO MY HEAD >>>

THE DRIVER

2017

0

Hello. I'm your driver. Please get in.

1

So the other day I'm way out in this swanky Texas suburb and get a ping. I route up to this gated, brick, lush condo-scape with fountains and hedges and a vigilant guard at the shack. Inside, I start sharking for my fare, someone waiting phone outstretched, looking down and up and down—tracking me, watching my every move, judging me, constant evaluation, high stakes—when this couple, both in bathing suits, stumbles out from between two parked cars and halts right in the middle of the road. It's a July Sunday in Houston, so sweaty. I usually don't drive in the day because of the heat, so I'm annoyed and squinting and trying to see if they're my ride or what and a beamer or something foreign and shiny is right on my bumper, and the woman, this petite young thing with big loud hair and a tiny bikini, takes a seat on the hood of my white hybrid American sedan and crosses her legs and perches on that steaming piece of sheet metal without even flinching. I put it in park, take my foot off the brake, roll down my window, call out the name on my phone. He's my fare all right, the dude in the boardshorts with the tuffet of chest hairs. I tell them to get in. Dude, gently, deliberately, coaxes the woman off my car and loads her into my backseat.

I wave traffic around; Dude comes to my window and tells me he's not coming with—he's got clients at the pool—but she's got to get thirty miles upstream to her two kids and her job at that club by the airport. I tell him I know the one. It can only be one of nine.

From the backseat, the lady stretches her legs alongside me on the middle console, waggling all ten little piggies, tickling my arm. I don't like that. No touching, in my car. Like a cruel sister, she pinches my arm-skin with two toes, bemoaning the redneck tunes, demanding I put on Mandrake.

"So what's your name?" I ask, changing the Optify station. I like to know who's in my car. Otherwise, all I've got to work with is the app handle, which is often fake, or the Dude's.

"S-Y-N," she spells.

Before Syn, it'd been a smooth Sunday afternoon. Caught an extra-wide t-shirt couple leaving the Strokes matinee, drove them way out to a ranchburger that looked like all the other ranchburgers in one of those ranchburger-burgs, proud Americans who spoke proudly about sons, flags, huntin, fishin, guns. I know where the money is, played right along, got a twenty for a tip. Scooped a couple of girl-dorks from a mall, ferried them to a McMansion with a dock on a fake lake. We passed a lakeside gas-station, an upscale Exxxon, and one girl got excited: her brother'd seen Scott Travis fueling his Lambo there yesterday. Scott was cool, let the kid snap a blip. I'd never heard of him, so when I dropped them, I put him on. Made me dizzy driving, so I parked and just listened. That's what I'd had on with Syn, before Mandrake.

Now that Syn's got her jams on, she's alive and rattling, chickened up, frenetic, flipping the vent sliders. I'm sure she'll bust the plastic, and I'll pay for it.

Then Dude gets in the front seat, which is weird, because before he said he wasn't coming. He's trying hard because he knows he's wasting my time. I don't make money unless I'm moving. Tips me two crisp fives, says we just gotta get her stuff out of his room. So we roll around to his place. He's buttering me like a kiosk cologne salesman, complimenting every visible scent and sight in the car, saying he needs to maintain a good rating on the platform, saying: "You feel me, bro, you look cool, you know what's up."

"All right," I say, parking. "Just go grab that stuff then let's see."

Once he's out, I catch Syn in the rearview. She's pretty, dainty, early twenties, baby marks on her little belly. Ten years younger than Dude, and me. Clearly messed up. I ask her if she's going to puke. I have airline-grade puke bags in the seat slip, in case.

Syn slurs a tirade about her man, then nods back on the headrest and starts snoring. I decipher: she and the dude had some words by the pool, he said it was time for her to go, and then I showed up.

Dude derps out with a purse, a romper, sandals, all in a bundle. He creeps around to the opposite door, opens it ever so gently, places the things on the seat beside Syn. He backsteps, closes the door. No goodbye, no nothing. My door latches shut, whisper-quiet—domestic design and ingenuity at its finest.

Traded the best pickup I've ever owned on this. Vertical move, too.

Dude pats the roof, mouths-mimes in the window: "FIVE STARS, BRO, FIVE STARS."

So no problem—other than all of it. My job is not to judge, but to drive. So I zip for the gate, and leave the dude on the grass, scratching his crack, and Syn, out in the back like a sack of spuds. The map shows her destination twenty miles north, most of it on the Interstate, and I'm happy I waited because now I'm in the fast money, and the quiet money, if I keep operating smooth.

Because of a few rattles across the swamp-holes—those massive rubble crevasses—Syn jostles awakes, sits up in a bolt. I hear her going through her purse. Cash swish swishes swishes behind me; her nails clack while she counts. A pause, muttering, and a second pass through. She dumps out the purse. Counts counts counts.

That dude, that friggin fudge nugget. He'd shorted Syn a hundred and fifty bucks.

I worry the count is off because of the substances. I don't say anything though because I know no one knows her money like a mother.

I ask her what I can do.

Syn says, "Boy, you need to put that Son of a Bishop on the phone!"

So I call the dude. It's really easy through the app, and most often, I do whatever my passenger wants. That's a problem of mine—I say yes too easy, I agree too much. To my own detriment, I like to be helpful. Usually, I don't even think twice.

Dude doesn't answer; I get his gilded, professional, vacuous voicemail. He sells solar panels and personalized pro-grade cutlery. Affinity sales, door to door. I know the type, I was one once. Makes me queasy, annoyed.

I ask Syn if I should leave a message or what?

Syn says: "Boy, turn this mother fracker around!"

I'm no boy, I'm thirty-six, living dollar-by-dollar, just like her, just like you, and a freeway ride is about the best thing that can happen to me. So I consider for a split second flooring it, busting the yellow light, and making the feeder ramp and getting stuck in the cash.

But I don't do that. A hundred and fifty bucks is a hundred and fifty bucks. It's clear her problem's bigger than mine. So I don't tell her no, but I don't say yes either. The fit response to the fit request is silence and the act. I slow down to whip an inside U-ee. I floor it, let the motor kick in and thrum and growl and torque us. Syn gets excited. We're going back.

At the condos, I park under a shade tree, tell Syn I'll be chilling. I've had bad experiences leaving my ride unattended. Once, I even had a truck ripped off. As a rule now, I stay in it, or keep it line-of-sight. Heck, I sleep with my keys.

But Syn demands that I not be alone with her purse in my car, which, given her situation, is reasonable. So I get out, lock up, crack an energy drink, one of a few in my trunk. My car is too hot to lean on, so I pace. Syn walks wobbly figure-eights around the parked cars, unable to see the pool directly to her left. She's got wild eyes, not knowing what to do or where to go, and, like a petulant kid, she inches down her bikini briefs until a puff of pubic hair shows.

"Whoa," I say. "Syn, pull it together. Hitch those back up. Compose thyself. We're out in public."

Syn hears me, takes a few breaths, gets herself and coverage in shape. Together, we walk over to the pool. Syn sees Dude—he has no idea, focused on stacking another empty on a pyramid—and she marches over, straddles him, pins him to his chair. Dude takes off his glasses and, the whites of his eyes, my heck. White as snow. I'm clear across the pool and I see that. The wide bright whites of the transgressor. Dude gets Syn off him and stands and goes through a backpack and shows empty, upturned hands.

I finish one energy drink and get the second out of my back pocket, glance at the too-blue sky and strange ghost trees and get some gulps, say a little prayer to get us back on the dang straight and narrow.

I turn around and, Dude and Syn are coming my way. A few goons follow, chests high. I think about pouring out the can and getting ready, but then, I finish what I start, keep glugging.

Dude arrives, locks eyes with me. Our relationship has changed, clearly. He barks: "Why'd you bring her back?"

"I called ahead," I say, "check your phone."

Syn yells, "Where's my flicking money, Brigham?"

Dude says to me: "She says I stole cash from her? Bro, why would I steal? I make six figures a summer. Serious. That's how I roll. That's why she's back. She wants my slick rich baby, but I won't give it to her. I'd pay you two hundred bucks right now just to get her out my face."

I say, "One fifty should be easy for you then."

One of the goons, chinning at me, says, "Who's this effing guy?"

Now, would I fight? Sure. If I had to. I knew I had guardian aliens to protect me. Did I want to fight? Not particularly. I try to use my words. What did I want? I wanted Syn to get paid so I could get paid. And I wanted Dude to pony up, because I'm telling you, he was a real scum bucket, a skeezy coyote, degrading her publicly, defacing her motherhood, acting like a real dirt bag.

"I'm her driver," I say, staring into that thick idiot's wrap-around sunglasses. "You don't want me leaving here without her."

Dude breaks in, says, "It's not my fault I can't find my stupid phone. I'd vend it if ... "

All of us stand there looking at him, thinking, well, go find it, or at least pretend.

Dude is frat boy drunk, eyes squinted, focusing on the big words.

"You should put him in some shade," I suggest to the goons.

Dude, in his boardshorts, opens up one eye and drills it on Syn. He says, "Do you think I need this dip? I just got promoted. I just treated you like a princess. Look at this freaking pool! It's not my fault you don't know how to drink! You're embarrassing me in front of all my friends! You're embarrassing yourself! You're an embarrassment! Get out of my face, go back to your kids!"

Syn—arms crossed, hip canted—doesn't even blink. She says, "You got sixty seconds to give me back my money, otherwise I'm calling your mom."

Driver asks the grass, "Am I really paying for this horsepucky?"

Then he turns on me, says, "Driver, cancel this. I'm done. I'm out."

Now, I have a mother, seventeen aunts, three grandmas, five sisters, who knows how many female cousins, two ex-wives, all still very much alive. I never would've left Syn marooned out with these buffoons. I know what men can do. Like I mentioned, I am one.

So I tell the dude, "I don't cancel. I drive. It's your ride. You do it."

"You don't think I'll cancel?" Dude feels around in his trunks for his phone that isn't there. "Seriously? Where is it, guys? Where's my witch bass phone?"

So I lie and say: "I think I see it there, floating in the hot tub."

Suddenly everyone flexes, ready to punch something, hard. There's a squabble, a moment of high intensity. A lot of jostling. No hard fouls.

Long story short: No blows are thrown. Dude and his posse retreat to their condos and lock the doors. The money is never recovered, or the phone. Syn and I make it to my car, jump in, blast the AC, get back on the ride. I'm sweaty, on-edge, embarrassed. I try to keep my shiz together, feel like a real nimrod.

Right outside the gate, Syn sprawls across the backseat, writhing, weeping, swearing men are all pigs! dogs! maggots! muckers! metards! cheaters! hoes!

"Those are boys," I interject. "Boys still."

This soothes Syn, and she thanks me, apologizes. She declares we need to hang out more, and decides to come front-seat via the consul. She starts head-first, but then sits and pivots and swings her legs up over my head—and knocks me in the melon, my hat and sunglasses go ski-wampus, and I swerve into the next lane.

Syn crashes into copilot, slides off, climbs back on, all good. Finds the radio dial.

I'm in a cold sweat. When I swerve, I get this pump of adrenaline in my shoulders and my forearms; my glutes twitch; my feet itch; my eyes go wide; I intensify; I brace. I've crashed plenty, and they usually start with a swerve. So far, I've walked away from everything. But I know that's only a matter of time. The swerve is my downfall.

See, I don't want to die in my car with a stranger. I don't want to die in my car. That is my worst nightmare. I am on a mission from God, with so much more to accomplish in my time.

We're fine, though. None of us die. It's Sunday traffic. Empty roads. Not a lot of people go to church anymore, myself included. It's just me and her out here, trying to be decent Christians.

Syn's all banana in the front seat, cranking the music, her hair skinning the cab ceiling. I am hands at ten and two, sitting up, checking my mirrors, ignoring her, skittish, on-edge. The freeway looms ahead. I turn down the music from my steering wheel, announcing paternalistically that I need to hear if I'm going to get us home safe.

Again, Syn ratchets the tunes. The stock speakers crackle at top volume. One blows. Which miffs me, because I can't afford that mess.

About then, the dude finally finds his phone, because he cancels.

The ding interrupts the music. Just like that, and it's over. I don't even get the satisfaction of rating his dumb butt.

The navigation closes out and shuts off. The screen blanks, cycles to home. I have to go under the freeway, coast ahead. My new reality: Syn and I, complete strangers, are trapped in a car in a ubiquitous suburb, unsure of north or south, freewheeling. She's got her gross bare feet on my jockey box, and painted fingernails in her mouth.

I mute the music, ask her directly, "So where you wanna go now?"

She directs, sober as a loon, and mad: two blocks up take a left then look for the gold SUV on the river-side. She crawls into the backseat and legs into her romper. All the while, Brigham This and Brigham That and Brigham Can Snack Her Bits. I spot the SUV and ask if she's good to drive. She doesn't respond, just clicks her key fob and unlocks her wagon and bangs doors together and hucks her things from my rig to hers. Syn's about to jet when I realize she's left one shoe, so I holler at her. It's on the back floor. I lean back and pick it up.

It's not a shoe at all—but a personal-security stun gun strong enough to stop a grizzly bear.

Syn crawls in co-pilot, grabs the device, takes me strongly at the nape. Her long purple fingernails give me goosebumps. I am concerned, but don't blink, reminded of my childhood books.

Syn looks me deep in the eyes, calls me three different names—none of them mine—and says: "But you, you're not like him. You're one of the good ones! You, Sweety, I just love you!"

Then Syn plants one on me. Right on the kisser. MUAW.

The whole time, I'm sweating a lightning bolt to the neck-meat that never comes. It's my lucky day, and I'm thankful. Syn releases my neck, gets out, slams my door. She jumps into her car and slams that door too. She shifts it hard into gear, tears off doing thirty, tires chirping, cuts off right, no blinker. Then a left at a light, and I lose her through the green Texas foliage, shadows abundant.

I park it, wait there a few, count my blessings. I made two fives, cash. Syn's kiss felt like a punch to the shoulder, a backside slap. Good game, Hustle Town. Meanwhile, I was out a vent slider, a speaker, a half-hour of my life.

Still, my big dumb Scout Boy instincts kick in, and I deliberate if I should follow Syn home, make sure she arrives safe. Her address is in my app, on my phone.

But I stay put, lean back, sit in safety and shade, get out my pocket knife, clean my fingernails.

See, every day, that day, my job is to stay alive. Y'all get in with drama, y'all get out with drama. My job is to shut up and drive.

I wait two minutes and get the next ping, and get right to him. He's a large old man, with a walker, late for dialysis.

2

On the day roads, in business prime-time, its stop-and-go amateurs, people yapping on speakers and headsets and Redtooths, trying to bust four lanes to not miss the exit that, three days out of five, they blow. Teachers and lawyers, dentists and delivery people, sensible folk who work proper hours, always driving and yapping, rushing to and from parking spots. Anxious. Distracted. Dangerous. They slam on their brakes, drift, drool, drink their caffeine, blind yap, do all they can to make me swerve.

Who are they yapping at? I wonder, as I dodge them. To whom?

I prefer the cloak and cover of darkness, six pm to six am. That way, it's just me and the pros: truckers, meat-hooks, cops, robbers, pimps and hoes, cattle, chattel, the herd. At night, we throttle the inspired roadways of our fathers, grateful to the engineers and civil servants who mapped them, to the immigrants who paved them, to our rich and diligent fathers who needed them and funded them for their transport, like powerful men do.

It's the right way to learn the city, if you ask me. Hit the grit after all the cheap talkers prattle home to streaming content; get off and garage before they get another chance to swerve and send me dead into the shipping channel.

Too, I work nights because I'm ducking some people. Past familiars. I mentioned the many wives, yeah? It's easier to sleep the days and not answer my phone.

I'm not from Texas, heck no. I come from the last American still-developing continental dirt-patch: Idaho. My people, experts in cultivation and proliferation and irrigation, communing, blooming the frontier. Full of pioneer spirit, and procreation. High desert, less than ten inches of rain a year. Born and raised on a second-generation potato farm.

Still a lot of dirt and gravel roads. Hardly any people, comparative, though that's changing. Snow four months out of the year, followed by three distinct seasons of mud, dust, wind. I miss that. And my family's all there. I miss them too.

All different in Space City, one long day, all the same day, inner and outer loops. It all circles and connects: the freeways, the tollways, the Beltway, the Inner Loop, same temp, same loads, the same dark miles and pot-holes and fares. Me and my hybrid sedan and six lanes coming and going. Me and my Stroks cap. Me and my weird beard. Twelve hours. Sign out. Eat. Garage. Hit the sack. Wake up. Fuel Up. Glasses and cap. Get out there.

Sometimes, when I'm really questioning, wiping up a fare's booze puke behind a dumpster at a truck stop at three in the morning with my back pocket bandana, and remember some of my life's previous titles: son, brother, elder, poet, husband, farmer, hypocrite, husband again, heathen, apostate. I refocus myself, say: Now I am the driver. Without a car, there is no driver. So wipe up the mess and get on with it. I report the pics through the app, and collect my $250 service fee. I throw the ruined bandana under my tire, slam some go juice, think about getting right with the Word of Wisdom someday.

The HTX nights are hypnotic, futuristic, dreamy, the fracture in the infinite loop. Tail-light lasers, great orange orbs, tracers and faders of white and blue buildings, the dark shadow of a real person, alone, alongside the road. Or am I always alone? Who is in my backseat?

I've screwed-up my internal perceptions, from night-driving, the pain pills. Circadian rhythms shot to hell, my inner compass compromised. Voices, too, internal, external. I should probably take less, but no one sees, no one knows. In the car, in the city, day is night is night is day, it is always hot and light. Strangers get in, strangers get out. They are mostly voices, interrogations floating from behind.

What are you? They ask me. Jewish? Mexican? Canadian?

Generally, my rule is I don't speak unless spoken to. I rarely tell people I'm from Idaho. They respond the same way: "No, U-daho." Bad joke, makes no sense. Instead, I say, "I'm not from around these parts." Same thing about me being Mormon, or once having been, and the same goes for marriages, and divorces. I keep it vague, like a true driver would.

I wouldn't be blabbing so much tonight but something happened that's got me rattled, and I have to tell someone. Might as well be you. We're all here for a reason, right?

See, last night, a voice came over my shoulder that was squeaky but sure of itself. A voice that had never missed a fare; never blown a light; never caused an accident; never made a scene. A voice of compunction. A truth-speaking voice that said yes to the right things, a voice confident in its indictments. A 401(k) voice.

Immediately, I didn't like it. Put me on edge. I felt guilty, judged. Sounded like my oldest sister, bossing me. Shes a redhead. I hate being told what's-what, especially by the younger and older crowds.

That apt, controlled voice asked me if all I did was drive.

I was insulted. All I did? Drive? Did I have to explain the myriad machines, simple and complex, I've operated, starting with my infantile rolling chair? My big wheel? Should I map out the geography of my youth—the basin, the mountains, their roads and veins? The twenty personal vehicles I've owned and driven? The combines in the barley? The tractors in the spud fields? The snowmobiles? The back-hoes? The skid-steers? The pavement rollers? The dirtbikes? Cement trucks? Four-wheelers? Three-wheelers? The cattle trucks? The boats? Skis? Ice Skates? Roller-Blades? Snowboards?

Or should I go on with my sob story, my aching crack, my broken parts?

So I didn't tell her about my driving history. The voice'd never understand the thrill of the road, the emptiness of it, the addiction.

Nor could she envision the yard-full of machines I once drove, all in my mind, and how it was an art to operate them all, in the family dirt-patch two thousand miles away, growing food.

I replied, instead, "In thirty-six years, I've learned I'm a natural at two things: driving, and picking fresh produce. What about you?"

"I'm in oil and gas. Actuary."

"That pencils out," I said.

She quipped back: "Sharp. What's your favorite fruit?"

"Peaches," I lied.

"Hey, me too!" she exclaimed.

I listened to her go on about the sexy efficacy of numbers. Yuck. I'm a word-man. I just need numbers to get the next meal.

At the drop, she tipped me a cool ten bucks and her business card. I flipped her my own, saying, "I also walk dogs, if that's a need, or I'll sell your stuff, or teach you about the One True God."

That was the end of that. She said No thanks, and so I left.

The Actuary hasn't reached out—which is fine by me, I tossed her card out the window at the stoplight, with an empty slender can—but the exchange bothered me, being forced to self-justify.

How had I become the driver? Why had I become the driver? Didn't I have anything better to do?

3

Tonight, you get in my car and ask me the same question, more or less. Serendipity. Synchronicity. Synergy. You seem cool. I like you. We have miles to burn. And I finally have a coherent answer.

How did I get this way? Well, let me tell you. It involves this cousin I have. He's the one that taught me everything I know, or at least that's the fricking lie that Satan hoodwinked me with there for a few years …

HERE COMES
THE HOTSTEPPER

2017

Late one winter night, January 2017, working alone in my bedroom/office in Houston, Texas, I listened to "Here Comes the Hotstepper" for the first time as an Adult (though technically I am still Young Adult until July 2017 when I hit 35 and thus set adrift across the decades of adulthood doldrum; I'll make peace with the fact that I'll paddle my raft alone, no partner to spot for sunburn or suspect moles or call my misplaced iPhone, no one to scuttle and cull; I'll mutter about the inevitable forecast: MORE OF THE SAME). I report now that Ini Kamoze's 1994 chart-topping reggae-rap anthem did nothing but annoy me, like it had always done.

That night, I was too country: I'd lost my money, my pony, my woman, and my path, and wandered the wilderness, down the RX bottle, barking at—and trying to bite—every visible, extant thing. Over-dramatic? No doubt. I am a first-wave American Millennial watching the gloaming of my youth b. July 5, 1982, Idaho Falls, ID 2:55 pm; graduated Rigby High year 2000.

R.I.P., J.D.F.

January 2017, a prime example of my dysfunction: during my PhD studies, my wife of four years (her first marriage; my second; she, seven years my junior) informed me that a separation was imperative, packed her things, moved out. Strapped double to make bills and rent, student-loan money long gone, no T.A. paycheck until the end of the month, I pawned my BMX bike and Herman-Miller Aeron chair. Other than my ten-year old cat Roxette—the most successful relationship I've ever had; a decent history of animal husbandry, at least—my rig was my remaining asset: a Nissan pickup with 209,466 farm miles on it, patched with duct tape and zip-ties, and, scratched into the passenger side (from some smartass vandal's index finger, the crime perpetrated in the parking lot of an Idaho grocery store after a day in the fields): I Wish My Wife Was This Dirty. I put the truck up for sale, priced it way too high, knew it wouldn't sell.

I looked for another job. ... well, I asked the Internet, at least ... dragged my feet with a shelf-stocker app because they wanted a drug-test ... I was too old for this sewage, I realized. So I got sad, drank a Red Bull, and read on my phone about the Superbowl. One million unique visitors to Houston, America's Third (or Fourth) largest metropolis!

That night, I completed an application with Uber and found a car to buy. Next day—with thirty dollars in my bank account, and two credit cards, maxed out—I traded the truck on the car—a 2013 Ford Fusion hybrid sedan, gloss white—and financed the rest over sixty months, the whole ordeal taking less than two hours. What A Country! Where a guy with sand and a data plan could still hustle wheels and a gig!

But I didn't drive off into the sunset, no. A check engine light came on. I was sent home in a loaner. When my car was delivered, the check engine light returned, and Uber wouldn't certify it. Second opinion said there was $4000 damage under the hood. I returned the car; they sent me in another loaner and promised to expedite the repairs. Finally mobile, I went out for groceries and cat-litter. While inside, a crook broke the window out. Five loaners and ten business days after I turned over my truck—and a $450 insurance claim on the loaner window—my Ford was collecting dust in some lot.

On top of that, my wife moved back into the apartment. She, too, was broke-up and broke-down and just plain broke. As a loyal, peacemaking Cancer (ascendant sign Libra) and, per Meyer-Briggs, Extroverted iNtuitive Feeling Judging, and a former Missionary for the Lord Our Savior and Eagle Scout, I didn't turn her away. Cosmically, I never could refuse her. Naturally, I was dejected and sullen. We divided the flat.

Car-less, careless, pathetic, indignant, wired—in this state of delicate mind/heart/wallet—I could still hear her singing the Halfway House heartbreak blues—I accessed "Hotstepper" and turned it up. Sat with my face in my hands and viewed it seven, ten times. As a child of the Nineties, this should have at least filled me with some warm Care Bears nostalgia, that deep Rudy rally. Nope. I was put off by the mesh tank tops, tassel bikinis, open windbreakers and CAT boots, white dreads, myriad unfortunate hats. The peppy lime, the gross tangerine. Refused to hear the lyrical savviness: Bo Jackson and Mack Daddy, N.W.A., the sampling, "Money to burn, Baby." What a bummer. All of that decade's pureed, gauzy pop culture foo foo only existed now for fodder, fuel. I did my research on the artist Ini. Read the wiki, at least.

Decoyed as an exercise in evaluation, I showed "Hotstepper" to my seventy-five writing students. What was a hotstepper? Juice like a strawberry? How did we get on a train? Where is this three-walled abandoned—but newly painted—shack? Who did this cocky, pudgy, slow-strutting rhymester think he was, anyways? Who writes a four-minute thirteen-second song?

To my surprise, the students liked it. Catchy intro. Good beat. They'd heard it at Rockets and Astros games. Hotstepper meant fugitive in Jamaican Creole (Wikipedia), or could be an allusion to AIDS (Yahoo! Answers). Take that for what it's worth. He's no killer, they answered, he's a lyrical gangsta—he slays rhymes. The set? Metaphorical—Kamoze blew off the roof. I couldn't get them to naysay or deride.

So I told my friends—during classes and at gas stations—about the song. No one recognized it by title; folks shook their head at the artist's strange name. I would sound the hook—nah na na na nah na na na nah na nah nah na na nah na na na nah (also a popular Google search)—and they'd acknowledge it. I complained about this to my parents, friends, the cat. The world no longer made sense to me. I was at a loss as to how I'd make it through.

"Be a beaver," my father said.

Victor promised my luck was gonna change.

Kendall texted, simply: Get a Win.

My mother encouraged prayer.

No duh, guys ... but then, advice from three steady businessmen and a genealogist? Not sure they could solve my problems. For one, they'd never been dumb enough to get in them ... soon, I was pacing, vexed, thinking ... You don't know me! ... You can't judge me! ... Don't tell me how to live!

I kept hustling, teaching, studying, eating Ramen, busy busy busy. I texted the car salesman every morning for updates on the Ford. SUPERBOWL WEEK—LOSING MONEY EVERY DAY. Finally, seventeen days after I'd signed my name on the dotted line, threatened arbitration and the BBB, the Ford was done. I picked it up, shook the salesman's hand, told him I hoped we never saw each other again. Drove straight to Uber HQ and squeezed into a three-hour line. The waiting room was crowded: people of every language and pigment, mothers with babies, grandfathers, pairs of balding men, on and on ... Hip employees in their twenties—matching t-shirts, their common uniform—completing the work via tablets and phones. Dinner arrived: single-wrapped tacos in pizza boxes. It was a sullen, downtrodden, ravenous crowd. The food got snarfed. The house games—bean bags, Tic-Tac-Toe—remained unused.

The Ford got certified, and I started driving that night. It took all of Thursday and part of Friday to get my bearings, but it wasn't a steep learning curve. Having come up in the Nineties, I found the tech intuitive, game-changing, disruptive. As for driving, I'd been doing that since I was fourteen as the farm's parts runner, using paper maps, gas station clerks, and sketches drawn in dirt. By eighteen, I'd operated spud trucks, John Deeres, Case Magnums, skid-steers, back-hoes. I taught myself to drive semi while delivering pallets of sod at twenty-three, I can man most watercraft without sails, and once took the stick of a Cessna and drove it 200 mph through the Teton air. Sure, I suffered juvenile accidents. Nothing fatal, but enough to learn how to crash.

I can't remember the first fare I showed "Hotstepper" to. By then, I'd Ubered over twenty hours, made twenty-five trips ferrying bobos and yuppies and Up North Yankees, Screen Babies ordering

McDonalds via Post Mate, nice boring couples, bougie med students with vocal fry, Gen X event workers, packs of stray dogs. I never talked in the car unless the fare initiated, and I made sure to be the first to cut if off. If the fare was racist or drunk, I didn't encourage conversation at all. None of them had much interesting to say about the song: The Beach. The Houseboat. THE CLUB. It stayed that way—steady, mostly uninteresting—until Saturday. I punched out midday to get some sleep—my teeth stung from the Red Bull—and when I woke saw a text from Uber that the next twelve hours would be the busiest in UBER HISTORY.

I shook it off, inhaled caffeine, moseyed out to hit the grit. Picked up a dork on a pizzeria date who told me I had five stars. He was astonished, floored. He'd never experienced five stars. I was his first. As a rider, he had 4.94 stars. Which is pro level, gave me a thrill.

"News to me," I said, perking. I hate authority, but love assessment.

... Rate me. Do it. Badges. Stars. Thumbs. Hearts. Shares. Votes. Views ...

Next in a swank hidden condo-plex: two slender women; two men—world-worn, tatted-up, ten years older—all in workout gear. Sketch? It raised a brow. Uber (and my mother) had sent warning messages to lookout for cases of human trafficing.

When I asked if they were visiting, one of the women squeaked, "It's top secret—we're FBI."

The man in the front seat, sleeveless hoodie, goatee, 80s sailor tatts, said, "We travel with people to crud like this."

"So you're the guy they call when there's trouble?"

Dude paused: "People call us to find trouble."

Was he a handler? A fluffer? A pimp? Were these L.A. strippers, or East European Escorts?

"Did any of you come up in the Nineties?"

They all did, the women clearly on the shady side of the decade, in hospitals still, but I showed them the song, and before even the Nahs, Dude said:

"Ini Kamoze! Dude, I'm just saying...damn, man. Miami, 1994."

Dude closed his eyes and raised his fists and started rolling shoulders. I could see him, white silk shirt flowing. "Here Comes the Hotstepper" held the Billboard Hot 100 one-spot for two consecutive weeks, December 17 and 24, sandwiched between two Boyz II Men superhits and following songs by Mariah Carey, Bryan Adams/Rod Stewart/Sting, Celine Dion, All-4-One, Ace of Bace, R. Kelly, and Lisa Loeb. I dropped that crew at the gym next to the popup where I'd taken an NFL linebacker to the night before. Texted myself: HTSTPR transportative?

Later, because of traffic and parking, I had a bad start to a ride. Caught one that was NOT FROM HERE and unaware of concepts like COOPERATION and TEAMWORK and NESW. I had to park and find her (and her friend)—two tall, side-shaved women—and walked them back to my car. They carried their dresses in bags for the Playboy party and were dressed down in stretchy clothes. Their disinterest was visceral. Traffic was awful then, and we had ten minutes, so what the hell? One loosened up and told me about her dad who would play only "Hotstepper" and AC/DC "Back in Black" on the way to soccer practice. He was her coach, and apparently a deadbeat—they no longer talked. I dropped them at a hotel, texted: HTSTPR equalizer?

But that was the last text. As soon as I dropped a fare, the next one pinged. The afternoon got hairy—loud Yankees asking me for drive-thru and happy ending recs. Graduated SEC frat brothers, the ugly sidekick promising his handsome bud that "Bro, basically I'd never let you bang Erica tonight." A sixty-year-old father bragging to his forty-year-old son about the stripper who grabbed his junk. "You coulda nailed her, Dad." More than one clever scumbag asked taxicab confession questions: Had I seen one yet? Had I got one yet? Seriously, bro, what would you do if that went down in your car?

I did not show "Hotstepper" to these fares, not because I had given up on the song. I was finally having some thoughts about it, and wanted to talk. No, these buttfaces did not deserve humanizing common ground. I put on soft jams for them.

The sun set. Houston finally dark, misty, traffic surging all around. I avoided it, stayed on the fringes. Downtown, visible to the east, a nocturnal emmision of patriotic team colors that saturated the sky. The stadium, where there were choppers and crews and a three-story decal of Tom Brady and Matt Ryan—helmetless titans, so handsome American white, every moment of their lives leading to this one, THE BIG GAME, tomorrow night, soon to be over and done.

... Elsewhere in the league, grunt players you've never heard of are shooting themselves through the heart for further studies ...

This mess, these brutes, had me down on life. I stopped, ate two chili dogs. Drank a Red Bull, stretched, phoned a friend. Then I got my head right back in the Uber game. Ping, one minute away. High-rise apartments, all soft light and glass.

The woman took her time. Came out, looked around like she was lost or confused. Stood by the trunk, as if I were a doorman, tucking things into her scanty blue party dress. I waited, not realizing she expected me to open her door. Eventually she figured it out. Got in, asked for a phone cord. She was on her way to the Maxim party and had to call her boo. I turned off the music, as she was using speaker phone. Well, the guy was not that interested. She played cute, coy, then cruel. The guy said "WHY YOU EVEN CALLING ME?" and hung up.

I checked the rear-view. She was fine. Not a wince or tear.

"Can you get me some air?" she asked. "I know I'm barely covered but I'm all sweaty back here."

I did, and offered music, her choice.

"You DJ," she said, "turn it up."

We merged onto a highway and started south. Sugarland. All the traffic was headed in, which mean six open lanes. I put on Run the Jewels 3 ("Hotstepper" felt off-mood) and got right to eighty mph. Why not? I was a five-star driver. All the cops were downtown; the road construction equipment had been cleared. A princess was in distress. I was a de-crowned prince, a high-borne from a low hinterland caste, my skill in the saddle, at the wheel.

Uber kept chirping about speed.

"Want me to slow down?" I asked.

"You're good. I trust you."

That perked me up. Arrived six ticks too fast. We sat in a drop-off line, ahead of schedule. Stopped the music, chatted. She was Russian, transplanted first to L.A., now Texas, modeling. She lauded my driving. I queried about her career.

"I used to be busier but not right now, not with these curves."

I talked my way to the VIP Entrance. Jumped out to catch her door. She took my hand and I helped her out.

Told her: "Tonight's your night. Tear it up in there."

She re-situated her dress, hugged me, and tipped me a crumpled ten.

Back downtown, party ebb and flow. Did that a few hours. Picked up a couple dudes headed to League City, forty minutes away. They slept. I listened to "Hotstepper" and mused:

Does one-hit mean easier ... lesser than ... if you can do it once, can you do it again, and again ... does Ini love "Hotstepper" ... did it curse him ... did he sell-out ... was he never-should-have-been ... Worth it +/- ... OR WAS IT MORE LIKE that one time Ini got off the island ... That one time Ini was on MTV ... Those two weeks Ini mattered ... OR WAS THIS NOTHING MORE THAN a time, a thing, a moment, a beat ... a series of syllables, sounds ...

League City was lights-out. The kids peeled themselves from the backseat, loaded into a Dodge pickup, and drove straight home to San Antonio, two hundred miles in the opposite direction.

Midnight, stuck in B.F.E. I waited around for action. After a while, I got a request from a rider named Thor. I wanted Adventures in Babysitting but got instead a boat mechanic with his young Tejana bride. Thor rejected the app's instructions and took me along Coward Creek to show me Hurricane Ike's flood line but to also keep me from running into pigs. Actual pigs, not cops.

I dropped Thor at ten till one AM. I was torn about what to do. The bars would close at two, and then everyone would want to go home. And then it would be dead, and regardless of songs and conversation, I would still be mostly broke and down-and-out. Should I finish out in the suburbs? Or jet back to the city? I limped along in economy mode. Something pinged, eight miles closer to the Gulf. I accepted, turned my back to Houston, and whipped around.

Four young people stood out front of a Mexican Cantina, three boys and one girl. She got in the front and the three boys jumped into the back. None looked old enough to be drinking, though the acted loose and laughy. What was the big deal, I thought, it was Super Bowl Weekend, an International Holiday, a day when laws barely applied.

The cantina had been a bust, and they were puddle jumping to the next bar next town over. They asked about me, joked around. Their arrangement started to shake out. The loud dude, a minor league baseball player, had been dating the girl since high school back in Corpus. The other two dudes—the quiet lug, the pipsqueak—were his best friends and couldn't find dates. Not that they needed them—they were out to hang with each other. The pipsqueak had turned 21, and the friends were treating him right for a first night out.

But that was not all, the pipsqueak had been in the hospital. His doctor had given him permission to go out.

"The hospital," I said, double-taking him in the rear-view. He was thin, down to his bones, with oversized elbows and protuberant wrists. His t-shirt fit him like a tablecloth, and he probably weighed all of a hundred and twenty pounds.

The boy scooted up—he was sitting middle-back—and occupied space between passenger and driver seat, and he talked, at first right in my ear.

"You want a story? Here's a story. Last year—last year! 12 months ago!—I got diagnosed with cancer."

"Oh dear," I said.

"So I got diagnosed with cancer and they did the chemo. Think of me, twelve weeks sitting in the chairs, chemo in my arm. I feel worse, really, but they say that's normal. So I take it, whatever. And after twelve weeks, 12!, the doctor regrets to inform me that they diagnosed me wrong, and used the wrong chemo, and had to start over."

"Oh lordy," I said. "So you got that done, right?"

"Yeah, another three months later, and nothing changed."

The pipsqueak was loud and gripping, and his friends were roaring. They thought it was hilarious. Clearly, they'd heard this one before, had been hearing it all night.

"So then what happened?" I asked.

"Oh, my parents mortgaged their house and I moved into this big ass hospital in Houston."

"How's that going?"

"Oh, they haven't done nothing either. I mean, I'm still getting chemo. I'm on like my fifth round. All my hair fell out and now new stuff is growing back. I feel like a human baby. They have no idea what to make of me over there..."

It was then that I could see they were all here for him. The friends. The pipsqueak was laughing, so his friends laughed. Can you believe this cosmic crapfest! Lolololol!

So I'm waiting for the turn. Clearly, he's in better shape now, right, if he's out with friends? There's a happy ending to the story? Or was this the last hoorah?

"So what was it?" I asked. "What do you have?"

"THAT'S WHAT'S SO FUNNY! NO ONE KNOWS!"

R.O.F.L.O.L.O.L.O.L.

Then the kid said, again, right in my ear: "You don't believe me, but my hair's soft. Touch it. Seriously, feel it. It's pretty much exactly like a newborn's, I swear."

The friends joined, cajoled, prodded, backing up their friend.

I considered not doing it, briefly. But—maybe this is just me, or maybe it is where I was born, and who I was born to, and the techniques under which I was raised, or just my own adult predilections—but I am not a person who likes to disappoint ... I am philosophically opposed to the D.A.R.E. program—I never Just Say No ...

My left hand on the wheel, eyes on the road, in total control, I reach back and palm the guy's delicate head like a Nerf basketball. His hair felt like—what? A chinchilla? The perfect peach? The body, at its conclusion? The soul? Pipsqueak's crew was right: his hair was and is the softest thing that these fingers have ever touched.

I dropped them at some strip mall sports-hole. The lug hung back to tip me five dollars, patted my shoulder, thanked me, wiped a tear. Shoot dang, it was 1:40 in the morning. I parked to wait until the bar closed or I could try and make it back to Sugarland and the Maxim party before two. It would be ending and maybe I'd luck into Curves again.

By then, I was in a reckless, depressing mood, thinking about all the friends that I'd lost, who'd died or killed themselves since the Nineties, how many in the last three years alone, and I put on an album that reminded me of all of them and turned off Uber, got on the Beltway. I pushed the Ford to 99 mph, empty, deadheading, Lucky Numbers Nine, HIGH SCHOOL NUMBERS, and I poured it.

Made it back to Maxim. Got a ping—not Curves—and moved up inch by inch. Who was I kidding, about her? We couldn't/wouldn't/didn't understand each other. We'd never meet a second time, like predestined Google pins. It was fleeting, unreal.

I saw my fare before she saw me. Black dress, shoes off, standing at the curb. Eyes up, not glued to her phone. I hollered her name through the open window. Our eyes locked, and then she got in the car. She was astute: my first fare to pick out that I was Mormon, or at least still reeked of Boy Scouts. She'd left the church after Prop 8, had already been married and divorced. Reminded me of a girl from Sunday School.

It was after three when we got to her spot. She wanted to keep talking. Sure, I'd take a caffeine break. We shuffled in the gravel. I showed her the song, at least the first minute, but then shut it off. She wanted me to take down her number and call her sometime, for a walk in the park. So I did, we hugged, and I got in my car and shut the door.

I thought about quitting then, for the first time all night. I'd put in a long day—ten hours so far, hardly any stops. Been all over the city, two-hundred plus miles. I could feel good about going home to my empty apartment, taking my meds, boiling some noodle water, petting the cat. I got a phone number, even, from a woman. That exceeded expectations. Why not go out on top?

I pulled around the block and drank Red Bull. I stayed trucking, keeping the music low and the rides smooth. Two more hours scooping up wanderers, couriering them home. Worn out, ornery, pukey looking pukes. Cognition way down. I got to an office building at five and pulled right up next to my fare. He wouldn't get in. He wandered down the street, hugging people at the bus stop.

"Brother,"—he kept calling me that, Brother, Brother, as I walked him to my car, like he knew me from my home ward.

Once inside: "Brother, I have never seen so many beautiful girls."

I pronounced his name, poorly.

"Brother, call me Bomb, brother. Brother, can you take me to get some food? I have never felt such hunger."

I routed Bomb to Whataburger. He was a PhD student too, and based on his male-pattern baldness, older than me, I hoped. He'd been raving all night, and boasted sexy drug allure. Back there? Where I picked you up? I hardly believed him.

The drive-thru was twenty cars long, spilled out into the empty street.

"Take me home," he said, "I will make eggs there. And here, here,"—he fidgeted with his cuff and then handed something up. "Go back, brother, it's VIP. You will not regret it. You will not."

I put the purple paper band in my cupholder and thanked him. I vacillated on the rave as I took him the rest of the way home. But as soon as I could, I turned off for the night and routed right back to the building. Parked, watched the windshield wipers, then wrapped my wrist with the band—I'VE JOINED THE CIRCUS, it read—and fastened the loose ends with chewed gum, drank some water, exited, and followed the music inside.

A huge cavernous space in a receiving bay, or some sort of shipping business. Couches, makeshift bars, tables with empty liquor bottles. The sound pulsated, bumped, and debris—paint chips? asbestos?—pinwheeled from the ceiling. Water dripped down. Stage in the middle, a DJ at the turntables, laser lights—green purple orange blue—through fog machines below. A chill-out corner where couples and singles crashed out in hammocks and bean bag chairs. Maybe fifty people day-breaking in front of the stage. It didn't look that different than the Uber office, really, other than it looked like you could smoke anything inside.

I went and stood near the people smoking the good stuff, stared at the lights and the crowd. A tall slender man in a jacket and jeans and chains on his boots. A woman in capris and bobbed hair. Denim abounded, such high-waisted jeans. It was the Nineties again. What the heck? I danced all by myself.

On the stage, three women made silhouettes like a Bond Girls collage. One was different than the rest, looked like a Cowboy's Cheerleader, reminded me of my first love, my square-dance partner from fifth grade Idaho History class. I watched her feet. I was all sorts of sentimental, tripping over my youth. 34, tired, lonely, and sad ... I was going to do something about it ... I went around backstage ... plotted something clever to say.

She came past me, and I caught her attention, and asked her.

"What?" she asked. "I can't hear you!"

She was a little unsteady—me too.

"TEACH ME HOW TO CLOG?" I shouted.

She hugged me around the waist and said, with a tickle, "You know you liked it.I remember too."

She bolted immediately. I wandered around peacocking until I grew bored. I planned to leave, but the three women came out. I could tell in the yellow halogen that the clogger was older than me by the way she handled her phone, complaining to the bouncers that she needed an Uber.

I went over to her, opened my phone and showed her my rating. Still five-stars. We both turned on but couldn't connect. So I took them, free of charge.

Lady was rolling, or worse—kept mentioning the last drink she'd had. She rode shotty, the two ladies—DJs who had performed earlier— rested on each other in the back. Lady laughed at my jokes, put her hand on my arm. Pleasant, short drive. When I got to her condo, she sent the girls inside, said she wanted to talk. She was from Colorado, or had come up there. We lamented flat Houston, waxed for cold mountains snow. I told her that my favorite first photo is me on skis, ready to descend the front-yard flower garden in the front yard of my childhood trailer home. I was four--the year I peaked.

She told me a beautiful thing: she, too, was a skier, and her father had taught her by putting a hula-hoop around them both, so she'd have something to hang onto, so she couldn't zip away. I imagined her and her father, big S curves down the hill, encircled, and that was a beautiful sight. I got homesick, choked-up. Pizza, sniffle, french fries.

She had to pee, but instead of going to her room, she squatted in the shrubbery and kept chattering. Nbd—I had five sisters, I knew the drill. When a man passed by on a bike, I made sure he kept his eyes on me.

For a minute, I thought she'd invite me up, but in this case, I planned to decline. I didn't show her the song. That hardly mattered anymore. We both had wanted reminiscence, and having completed that, were hungry and tired. I stood there waiting for it, curious as to how this would go.

A text came. Weird number.

Can you come to Harris County Jail?

I had no idea who it was ... I replied ...

Is this my wife?

It was the preppy Dallas snot, the freestyle rapper. He needed a ride home.

Lady freaked. Had he smuggled in his phone? Was I his only call? Holy Crap What Was I Going To Do???

Told her I guessed I better go—someone else needed saving. Played it cool on my way out. Sauntered. Really, though, I wondered how much gas I had left in the tank. I was road-worn, weathered. There was a dude out there in need ... I texted him ...

... off the clock, bro, good luck ...

Dawn. I pulled into Jack-In-The-Box on my way home. I turned off my music, ordered a Munchie Meal and, what the hell, two tacos for dessert. There was only one young dude, manning till and grill. He took my money and started frying.

I anticipated this was almost over. Soon—after I'd driven home and my wife's car would not be there, and I'd watch cartoons and eat alone; after, in a week's time, I'd lose my five stars to an unknown fare (a drunk with a fat thumb? the women I wouldn't let hotbox?)—soon, I could shower and power down.

"Here you go, Boss." Young Dude hung my food out.

Oh, what relief, what joy! The caffeine in my gut percolated. I salivated at the smell. Finally, I was happy, proud. Sweat for bread; sacrifice for gold. I was finally something—a driver. I took the bag and set it on the floor. Shifted to D, coasted ahead.

Almost to the main road, I realized the radio wasn't on—but there was sound. It came from me. I was singing, nodding:

... .
nah

...
nah na na nah

...
nah na nah na nah na na nah na na nah

...
nah na na nah

... ...

MY FATHER KEEPS TOUCHING HIS HEART

2016

My father keeps touching his heart. We are sitting in his church pickup at the Rigby Pioneer Cemetery. He lifts up his tie and undoes a button and runs his fingers into his white shirt, patting. I go to say something but he puts his left hand up, WAIT, WAIT, he motions with his free hand. So I wait, quietly. What's the point of talking when he can't hear me? Finally, he snakes out the Bluetooth dongle. It hangs on a lanyard around his neck, and controls the new hearing-aids he's trying out. One big button he depresses a few times seems to solve his problems.

"Stupid wind," my father says, and means it. "Had to shut them off. Couldn't hear a word of the prayer. All wind." He laces the tube around the cauliflowered crest of his ear and better into his canal. The pickup shifts and rocks in the gusts.

This is autumn October 2014, a crop year disaster, the fall work done and the wind thirty miles-per-hour. The coldest summer in the last hundred years. It rained three days on, two days off the whole month of August, never got above eighty-two degrees. That first rainy day wasn't so bad. It was joyous, actually. We were changing oil in the combines, polishing mirrors, greasing, whistling, etc. We were ready to cut that golden beer barley, our second-favorite crop behind spuds, we were chomping at the bit ... but rain clattered on the tin roof of the shop, and we all stopped what we were doing and opened the bay door and watched the rain come down. For this gift, we could wait two days. We had spent all summer irrigating—no small toil— and to see these natural puddles tinged with the rainbow of runoff motor oil was satisfying, to say the least. The spuds were happy. But then it rained three days straight, and the barley started laying down. We knew it wouldn't—couldn't—stand back up, but we prayed that I would against all odds. It did not. After a week, the gold was sucked out of the stalks, and took on the tombstone gray of hornets' nests. Then one day instead of rain it hailed pea-sized pellets, which knocked the kernels out of the heads. We were all out in the muck of the spud fields, digging diversion ditches so the cash crop wouldn't get washed away. We did it all by brute human force—it was too muddy to get a back-hoe in or out—men with shovels can still solve problems. But after two wet weeks of it, my father sent everyone home, including me. Ultimately, our efforts were lame, and ineffective. 95% loss on barley & wheat; 60% on potatoes; the hay, black as tar. But we had to harvest all the crops, for insurance purposes, so we picked up the damaged harvest without all of the typical enthusiasm. No one waved on the roads. No lighthearted group-texts, morning jokes. Scowls, all of us, growls. The guys from Corte Primero ganged up on the two from Jalpan and someone popped a tire on a truck, bent a rim. I covered for them, because my father was in a firing mood, and all of us were expendable, and we knew it. By October more Idaho farms came on the market than had since 1982, the year of my birth. J.D.F.: b. Antelope, ID (camping trip) July 5, 1982.

My father, B.S.F.,—Rigby High School graduate year 1976 (important, he thinks, in regards to our Nation's history) — now sees his entire livelihood is in flux. He has been in Burley, at emergency potato meetings, instead of attending my best friend's services. Ever since my grandfather died when my father was fourteen, he's been farm-busy for plenty of funerals. I—Rigby High School graduate year 2000 (interesting, I muse, all those zeroes, like a broken odometer)—I am 33. I know, or sense, rather, that at some point over that span of 365 days, now more than ever, that I will probably die. I tell my friends: this is our Jesus Year. If I die, I might resurrect, I figure, I hope, I doubt. That's what I have planned to do, me and my new wife: get out of here and make something before we keel over in the dirt.

But this is 2014. I am not a dumb thirty-three. I have seen some horse-apples. This is not my first trip to the cemetery. This is my place, my people: I am comfortable here among the stones. Across the grassy flat quads, the short stout practical markers, the pine trees, to the lone maple where lies my paternal grandfather D.C.F., buried alongside my grandmother Melba. There are the eight burial plots that await me, my mother, my father, my five sisters. Beyond our still-empty graves—through the chain-link fence—are the church softball fields. The greenest thing in the valley, what with all the rain, the white foul-lines growing wild. Those are called D.C.F. Fields, named such in memoriam for my grandfather's service as a Mormon Stake President, Farmer, and Peacemaker, b. 1928—d. 1972.

The Mormon Stake Center across the parking lot—it was once white but now so yellowed, like coffee-ed teeth, as I see it on this windy October Saturday, 2014—was where my father baptized me when I was eight years old, in 1990; where I received the Holy Ghost and the Priesthood by the laying on of his hands that same year; where I delivered my missionary farewell speech in 2001 and where I delivered my homecoming address in 2003. It's where I learned, and was taught, all my life. Where I had my first and second wedding receptions. It is where my father served as first, my bishop, and later, my stake president, where he counseled and guided me spiritually, or at least listened when I had the courage to tell him my problems, and explained the repentance process to me once again. He was my Scout Master, my boss, and my private wrestling coach. Sometimes, when I had to cut weight before a match, we'd come over to the church in sweats and grocery bags and run up and down the stairs. It was the dead of winter, so we couldn't run outside, and really, the stake center was the only two-story building all around. It had a hardwood basketball floor too, good for wind sprints, and a stage we would grapple on. Pinewood Derbies, Stake Dances, Scout Camp, Co-Ed Softball. I could go on and on about the church ... though I hated going inside it now. I did it for Graig because I had to.

"Go ahead," my father says. "Talk to me. I should be able to hear."

"Okay, what do you want to know?"

He taps his heart, under his tie, ups the volume.

"Say again—"

"It was a nice service for Graig."

Graig B., b. 1982, d. 2014. Testicular Cancer. I lived with him, before I got married a second time, and in college before that, and for a few weeks once he came to live with me, in Oakland, but then, the last time I lived with him, in his upside-down rickety-built condo on the sad side of town, he only let me pay my rent by mowing the lawn. That kind of guy. Then one day, swollen nut. No problem. He wasn't married; hadn't even really ever dated, after his mission, and he could freeze some for the future. After all, he was only thirty-three. So, snip, tuck. One round of chemo. After two months, all his markers disappeared. Last week, finally, we all release that sigh—the three surviving friends, his four brothers, his mother (widowed), his many cousins and in-laws—that communal sigh, where we all pull at our collars and say, phew, that cut close, seems that Graig's gonna be okay.

We all look away for one day—all the ruined crop harvested, all the machinery tucked away, all the Mexicans gone back to Mexico, Graig going back to work at the plumbing shop—and I get a phone call from his little brother saying they just found Graig dead on the lawn of Rigby's only chiropractic office. Cause of Death: brain aneurysm, I guess caused by some unmonitored side-effect of the treatment? He never signed anyone to have access to his hospital documents—no one, not even his mother, really knew what was going on.

Of course, when I got the call, I was five hours west, in Boise, with my new wife's family, doing new family things like barbecues and movie nights. I had to take this entrance exam over there anyway, and just ended up staying, for the fun. I was pretty sure there was no future for me in farming, what with the year we'd just had, and I had to have options, after all.

In fact, it wasn't ten days ago that I told my father and mother, in the presence of my new wife, that I might never come back. Things were undecided. I was unsure. But I left and didn't say goodbye then, but then once I got the phone call from Graig's little brother, he asked that I relay it on to all the crew. So I went down the list, and that was tough sledding, let me tell you, because my friends are big starchy tough guys who try hard and lead clean lives and have families and see plenty to make them cry but they don't do that often, nor do I or my father really weep, except when reality sets in, and no one else can see.

After the phone calls, and making a plan with the new wife and new family at a pumpkin patch near the airport, I caught a bus back home. I couldn't sleep, knowing Graig was gone, texted his phone anyway. Julius picked me up at Dynamo's where we ate gas-station hotdogs and Red Bull, and Ralph brought me his deceased brother's missionary suit, which was too long and big, and Milo spared me a black tie, and we all went to Me & Stans and ate biscuits and gravy across the street from the funeral home and wrote out a eulogy for Graig—we were all pallbearers along with his brothers, and his mother had asked that we share some thoughts—and within five minutes I was writing everything down in a text message to myself. I remember it all in a fog, after the food we walked across the street for Graig's viewing, which lasted that night, and reconvened at the stained Stake Center this morning, for more viewing, and official funeral service, burial, more casseroles to come.

Had I been up for two days or three? Three days, or four? Existing on canned caffeine and borrowed pharmaceuticals? Now here I am with my father, exhausted and tripping, and he's grilling me. What had we even said, the three of us, hulking at the pulpit?

"I bet you all did a nice job." My father nods solemnly, looking off across the steering wheel, out the windshield, to some unknown. Then he reaches for his heart and readjusts. "For Graig. I bet Graig was proud. He and his dad."

What strikes me, then, are the ruts of my father's sheen head. They have grown more pronounced. This crop loss has taxed him. He has the gaunt eyes of a desert shephard. He loosens his tie, undoes his top button, wipes his eyes, puts on sunglasses. The ruts are not weird; but their pronouncement is sharpened ten-fold. My father is either aging, stressed, or that pill I took is finally kicking in. My father's overall hairlessness has made him glisten, even though it was cold and dry. Hair. No hair. It's always been a thing my father and I have differed on. When D.C.F. passed away at 44 years old of acute kidney failure (he'd bounced himself to death, literally, on the tractor), my father lost all his hair. Catastrophic Alopecia, it's called. It all fell out, and it never grew back. Fourteen years old, the year 1972, fatherless, and hairless. Of course, my father was angry; he was jaded, and driven, and deeply reckless in ways stubborn men in my life seem to be. He was a repeat Idaho State Champ in the 172 weight class, bald as a beet and ears beat stiff to hell. This is the reason for his protuberant, cardboard-like ears, cauliflower ears, all around the outer rims of both sides. He refused to wear headgear. That has nothing to do with his hearing loss. That comes from a lifetime of working all the jobs a farm has to offer—shop work, mechanic work, outside work, clangs, bats, falls, yells—and never wearing ear plugs. Every year, I see him do unsafe things he shouldn't do around the farm just to pace the guys to go faster. Everyone loves him for it, and they trust him as a leader, mentor, friend. My father is one of those rare people, folks say, that leads by example, and he does. I, on the other hand, am a lousy long-hair who tends to avoid hard labor, anymore. My hair grows like weeds. And one time, back when I couldn't wring more pounds down for a freestyle tournament, my father got out the electric shears, and readied to shave my head. I easily had three pounds of mop and bangs. I refused, flat out, and he twisted my arm. What was I willing to give up to win? Would I give it everything, my all? I clutched my head in both hands. Clearly, I was not. Then you should quit, he said. If you're not in it all the way, you shouldn't be in it at all. Fine, I said. Say it, my father said. Tell me that you quit, and I won't shave your head. I wouldn't say a word, and walked out of the garage. And that was that. I never said it, but I never stepped foot on the mat again. But that's not true. That's what I planned to do. But around midnight, my stomach aching, I got a second wind, and I put my mother's Jazzercise ankle weights around my legs, put on three layers of ski gear, and went out and shoveled the snow off both the driveways, and my aunt's, who lived next door, and at the deaf neighbors' ranch. At five am, I was a half-pound away. My father woke up and said nothing about sheers and we drove to Pocatello for the tourney, me spitting into a Dynamo cup, and I made weight and entered the tournament. As exhausted and dilapidated as I was, I quickly lost both my matches, first and second round.

"It was good seeing all the boys," I said. "We're gonna get together more, we all agreed."

My father touches his heart once again, mashing the control button of his remote with his flat calloused thumb. A soft blue light emanates from the white plastic, and my father nods his sheen head, smooths his tie over the glowing LED.

Blue light through his white shirt, radiating from his chest, which I guess means it's functioning finally.

"Yeah, that's not gonna happen," my father says loudly. "You and your friends are not getting back together. Nice to think about, but life goes on. There's no time. You guys are old."

Not much to say back to that. Sooner or later, I ask, "So where are we going now? Graig's mom said there was grub at the church."

"The farm," my father says, driving out of the Pioneer Cemetery and D.C.F. Fields, and turning east towards the mountains, away from the Stake Center, towards the fields. He touches his heart, turns me down. "It's always just feel-good food at these things, and I'm almost out of battery."

TELL ME HOW YOU REALLY FEEL: A ROMANCE

2016

I shake awake in the driver's seat of Q's brand-spankin-new Buick LeSabre. Q is my wife, my second wife, my new wife, my sugar. She ordered the deluxe luxury model painted Honey Gold. A ray of light from above, and silver slivers flash across the metallic flakes of the wide long hood, like trout-turns back home. I surmise I've fallen asleep at the wheel. I am squinting in this bright light, so I put on sunglasses.

My left arm aches. I don't dare examine the pain. Last time I did that—my left hand was gone.

I am in my new home—One-Way City, Texas—the #powerhouse of this great grease-griddle America, parked in front of a stud- and piercing-shop. I'm shirtless; my belly paunches above my belt and jeans. I am sweating, slick enough to slide right off the leather upholstery. Q is not with me, off warbling elsewhere. Q is a songbird, a siren. She is a singer in a band. She is always gone. I am always wrapped up in some adventure.

A shuttle bus parks broadside and boxes me in. The bus door opens; young female twenty-somethings disembark, all are dressed in the same thin, form-fitting gymnastics leotard. But no costume matches another in color; the women become a gradient chain, light refracted through prism. Some of them link to another by the arm, and the sleeves of their costumes blend into new exciting shades.

They clack across the pavement and into the store.

As the women seem to never end, I roll down the window and tip down my sunglasses in an effort to gain clearer vision. When I lift up my arm and rest it on the sill, I realize what has caused my pain: a tribal tattoo—geometric patterns of arrowheads and capping waves and black banded boxes—wraps from my wrist all the way up to shoulder. The webbing ends in a complicated seam above my pink protuberant nipple. I have never had a tattoo; as a rule, I don't accessorize. Ma would kill me. Embarrassed, I quickly roll up the window and hide my arm.

The ceaseless women cease; the shuttle releases its air brakes and merges into traffic; and I shift the Buick into drive. But before I can move, a small old woman dressed in flapper getup opens the passenger door. She wears a string of white pearls that loop down to her lap, and has a peacock feather tucked into her headband. In one hand is her phone; in the other, a roll of cash. I remember her—she was the only one not in spandex, and the last one off the bus.

—You Uber?

Because I don't like to disappoint people, I tell her that indeed, I Uber. And really, what with the new car and ink, I, nay, Q and I, we, need the money. In fact, I was telling Q last year that I was going to find a summer job to force me out of our dark and dreary apartment and away from its fridge full of vegetables. It is packed tight with leafy greens from crisper drawer to top shelf.

The woman sits down and fastens her seatbelt and laces the shoulder-strap behind her back. Otherwise, it would run right across her nose.

—What do you call this? The Queequeg Express?

—Exactly right, madam.

—Well, make like I'm Ahab and get me to 6413 Drum Street, fast.

I lie and tell her she's in luck, I know just the place.

She makes a little huffy noise.

I nose that big golden American canoe out into the current. The Buick's side mirrors graze parked cars on both sides of the tight road.

At the push of a button, the mirrors fold in like wings. The woman remains unimpressed. At the intersection, it takes me a six-point back-and-forth to make the corner out of the neighborhood. I'm feeling flustered. And when I'm flustered, I talk a lot, prattle.

—Don't worry. I used to drive eighteen-wheelers with loads of spuds, barley, cattle, and Kentucky bluegrass sod all over three rural Idaho counties.

—So what? I've dined with swine all over the world.

—Lady, do you understand that I could operate any machine you see on or along the road? I've driven everything from a Mexican Backhoe to a Caterpillar. Weed-whackers included. My father always said I had greasy thumbs. You sound like you're in a hurry, or I'd show you. What's the rush?

—I am a self-made woman; I owe no man an explanation.

This big American sedan floats over every crack and fissure. Such comfort should be unattainable. We stop at red lights, go at greens, and buzz through the yellows, feeling no fear.

—Actually, I'm glad you brought up selfhood. I sometimes consider myself a self-made man.

—You WASPy boys with your elongated, grandiose WASPy roadsters! A financial exercise in phallic compensation! I wish you'd all drive off a cliff! Explain yourself!

I clear my throat:

—I'm from a farm in southeastern Idaho...

——land stolen from native hard-working tribeswomen!

—Born of goodly Mormon parents...

——without 63 wives, Brigham Young would only be ears and chin-hair!

—and have five sisters, all of whom were raised on the idea that you could marry more in a minute than you could make in a lifetime, and so they skirted chores and rarely came out to the fields. Once my oldest sister beat me with a broom handle until it broke and my father watched for me to see if I'd lose my temper, which I didn't, didn't even yelp or shed a tear, and now all of them own houses and have families, and here I am, some boy in your eyes ...

——so you're the prodigal son of a wealthy, conservative, religious, land-owning man, you were once a prince of a place!, and now you're three-thousand miles away from the home place, playing chauffeur. Such a tough life you've lived! You've sold out your heritage and bastardized others, most recently the noble Māori tradition, all to spackle over your own existential fears. You are the postmodern man: hapless, neutered, solipsistic, helpless. You are a spoiled millennial brat addicted to Red Bull and pornography. You are either experiencing your first adolescence, or your second mid-mid life crisis. How many women have you ruined already? How many children? You're General Custer reincarnate! You're a conquistador ... You sound just like my fourth husband ... Now, HE was a boy!

I realize, then, that I am parched and starved. The conversation has, for various reasons, served as a numbing agent for the tattoo. The flapper prattles on and on. Who knows, really, what she says? I look ahead at the various restaurant options. A brick building for TexMex tagged with purple aliens and blue spray-paint; four Subways; a shotgun house advertising comida Italiano; three gut-trucks; and, luckily, through some trees, the Golden Arches. I slow down and shift the car into park but leave the motor running for the AC so the woman doesn't boil to death, or dehydrate. I find my t-shirt on the car's floor. I put it on, then engage the emergency flashers.

—So what do you do, Lady?

—It's complicated, so I don't expect you to follow, but I'm a connector. People come to me, and I connect them to other people and places and things.

I am hangry, like the wolf, because I do not know how to rebut the woman. I snarl and bark as I walk across traffic and under tangerine trees. Being inside the restaurant, however, calms me. I recall a time my father argued with my mother over not having meat for dinner. I was fifteen, cutting weight for wrestling. Sort of. Nothing too serious. Pre-season training. We were all eating chef salads. My father ordered me to accompany him to Eagle Rock, the nearest town with fast food, where he bought us six cheeseburgers and two super-size fries at the drive-thru and then we parked and ate every last sesame seed and half-fry. We dipped each bite in a pool of ketchup, twenty packets worth squeezed into a soda cup he'd ripped in half. We both puked it up on the side of the road before we got home.

I order a double-quarter pounder meal—large, to-go—and pour a Mountain Dew and, thinking of my passenger, fill a cup of water. Bag of grub. Back out the door.

But Peacock has the Buick wedged from white line to white line, stopping traffic completely.

I bump her across the bench seat, but her necklace catches on the gearshift and snaps—a hundred ivory balls clack like marbles across the dash and floor; a few roll into air-vents and rattle inside the defroster. She's fallen over, and I don't know if she's hurt. She shakes, convulsing. I scooch over and tilt her up. She is laughing hard enough that she has tears.

—Get your grubby mitts off of me!

Honestly, I am unaware that I hold her at all. I let go, annoyed that she has misjudged my actions, angry for being clowned. No longer jovial, she irons out wrinkles with her hands. She opens the food bag and starts eating my fries.

—Why did you touch my car?

—More to the point, what kind of high-hatting spoops leaves a car parked in traffic with no explanation of where he's going or how long he'll be!

—Oh, woman! Are you so blind? I am not the Savior; I am his cousin, raised in the wilderness, wandering an irrigated desert that millennia ago was seafloor! I am as bitter and gnarled as sage grown in sulfur! I am stocky, like the bull calf, and have matted, unkempt hair, and jumpy eyes that always spy the downed fence, the open gate! I grub on processed meats and cheeses and tubers, never having tasted anything sweeter than a tomato! And even now, look at you, scarfing my fries, enjoying the tubers of my labor, and mistaking me for some dolt! Verily, my loins are girded in horsehair; I don't want your sweetness—I am here to lick honeycomb! I have not come to cry repentance, but to cry, and cry, alone!

The woman checks the food bag and says, over-dramatically,

—Tell me how you really feel.

Then

—What, no nuggets?

She sounds just like X. That was something she'd say sarcastically, pouring it on, after I'd ranted. She'd say that, and sometimes I'd laugh at myself, and calm down. That changed, towards the end. I'd only get more focused, and argue her into a chicken-wing.

—Do you really think my father's only son is a vegetarian?

—You jack-nasty, I bet you count diet soda and masturbation for exercise!

I shout, shifting from reverse to drive, aligning the car, and speeding ahead.

—These roads were built for King Ranch livestock! It's herd migration—get on a path, stay on the path! Alongside every road are bogs and hungry gators!

—This heap drives like a mattress.

I review the Buick. Naked threads appear from the seats. The leather has deepened in shade and wear. It is darker, dingier, and there is weird play in the steering wheel. The Check Engine light is on steady. Deep breaths, I think, but don't do.

—Lady, I'm sorry for raising my voice, but I didn't say you could drive.

—I'm not the type that waits for directives.

She unwraps my burger, remove the buns, rolls up one patty, and finishes it in four bites. She asks me, again, how much longer.

—Up here, I'll turn left and then go straight for a while, then another left.

—That's why I don't ask questions; no one gives a straight answer.

—Would you rather me bleat and bear my soul?

—Fool Boy, do you expect me to lean over and wail with you? I have three daughters. One's a Painter, one's an Accountant, and one's a Lawyer. They are a continental pain in my ass. But they handle my investment portfolio and legal proceedings. The artist has rendered me in over thirty self-portraits, all while experiencing different psychotropics and other mind-addled states. They are the fodder of nightmares, and I find every single one breathtaking in its own particular way.

—I recently dreamt that I'd rolled my old farm pickup into a ditch and, in the crash, had my left hand severed clean off.

—Did you find it?

—It was in a pile of garbage alongside the road, about fifty feet from the crash.

—So you went to the doctor ...

—No, I picked it up and placed it against my bloody stump, and tendons fused, skin regrew, and, though there was a pink wound that was raised and tender around my wrist like a cicatrix watch, I regained total control. The hand worked just fine. I spent the rest of the time going around Jay County, running into my friends and family. There, everyone knows everyone else. People go to church with my father, and so they nod hello to me. It's a stoic and friendly place. With every person I met, I felt an overwhelming desire to roll up my sleeve and show them what had happened to me. My miracle hand. But I never did. Not once. Never showed a soul. I was ashamed, or something. By the time the dream ended, the scar had totally disappeared.

I wrote it all down and emailed it to an online psychic. She thought it showed my capability and resilience; the power to heal.

Peacock disagrees. She says,

—The dream merely showcases your inability to experience anything alone.

—Once, on the farm, this was back when I was 22, I got into an accident with an auger. I almost lost three of the four fingers on my left hand. The blade stopped at the bone. Sometimes, when I'm journaling, I fold down my pinky, ring, and middle fingers and imagine what it would be like if the metal had gone all the way through. I stare at the L-shaped claw. I hold the L up to my sweaty forehead, as if I'm in Junior High, when we did this to stand for LOSER.

From her loose blouse, Peacock produces a skinny, bedraggled joint, and a lighter. She puffs thrice and fills up the car with smoke.

—Peacock! This is not a legal state!

I roll down my window and hold my breath and wave fresh air and coast the car to the edge of the road. The woman is holding her left hand in L shape and staring at her wrinkled knuckle. So I say, feeling funny:

—Excuse me, but I have to drain the main brain. I will return in seven minutes, tops. Please keep the flashers engaged and the doors locked. Don't try to drive.

I walk around the corner to a new-build, four-story townhome with corrugated steel siding. This row looks like my father's granaries along the Jay train tracks. I knock on the door and stand on the welcome mat that reads Furry Friends Preferred.

My mother answers. She is wearing a purple Sunday dress with a full apron, and is as barefoot and short as she's always been. From inside, the waft of cold air and pot roast. She looks me over and then calls me by my full name, emphasizing all seven syllables, something she does when she's righteously peeved. She's spotted the tattoo.

—Shame on you! Your body is a temple!

—Ma, listen, this isn't what it looks like. I've been reading about the Carthaginian empire. I guess I got curious. Henna. And sharpie. Come on, Ma, you know how I get. It rubs right off.

I go to the kitchen sink where she keeps a pumice stone. I wet it and rub my left forearm until the skin peels away and the ink and blood blur. I blot my arm with napkins and change the subject.

—I have something to tell you, Ma, but I'm scared it might offend you.

—I've lived with your father for 36 years. Do you think I'm weak?

—I might have to kill off you and Dad.

—Oh, that's okay. We'd understand. How do we go?

—Small-plane accident as your fly back from Lewiston, somewhere in the River of No Return wilderness area, likely at the bottom of Hell's Canyon, during a lightning storm. Dad didn't factor the weight of the organic wheat seed into his overall load.

—For your dad, fine. He's been promising a plane-wreck since the Eighties, but you've got mine all wrong. I want to pass right here in my front room, surrounded by my children and grandchildren, all of us together singing hymns. Do that for me, and I'll love you forever.

—Ma, let me be honest, I did this arm-art to commemorate dad's mission to Auckland, if you really want to know.

—It makes my only son look ugly. I hate it. And it's made you lose your manners. How come you haven't yet introduced your friend?

Peacock sits, perched, at the breakfast nook.

—This is my fare. I stopped for directions. We are late for some such thing.

Ma says,

—It's nice to meet you. We find your city pleasant and charming.

Peacock says,

—Thank you, but I'd never live in this feedlot.

Ma says,

—Tell me, what did you think of my only son?

Madam Peacock chews her lip.

—Maybe he'll turn out, with decent women influences. As for the ride, two-stars.

Ma:

—Did he give his little John the Baptist speech?

Peacock:

—Ha! I thought that was Piggy from Lord of the Flies!

Ma says,

—You're staying for dinner.

I say,

—Ma, I'm on the job. I'm broke, remember, again?

Peacock pulls out the cash, sets it down, gambler-style, on the table.

That settled, my mother turns to me and explains:

—Your sister has locked herself in the bedroom. She and her husband and child are not acclimating well. They are demonstrating in hunger strike. Go, talk her out of this, and take a little paper encouragement.

My mother hands me a stack of hundred-dollar bills, bound with a shamrock paperclip.

—And wake up your father! And put on one of his shirts! I don't want your youngest sister or your brother-in-law or nephew to see you like that! You bet Q won't be pleased, and X, well, X would have twitched a flip! And trim those nostril hairs! I can see right up there and it makes me nauseous! You should think about other, shorter people occasionally! And hurry! Supper is almost done!

Once I'm upstairs and out of her sight, I count the money. Enough scratch for three months' rent! I pocket it and take off my shoes. I hear my sister's wails and her husband's sobs. The baby, it seems, must have a wet diaper, because it isn't happy either.

So strange such sadness could come from a change in latitude.

Sly and light, I bypass the sister problem and sneak into my parent's bedroom.

My father is in his hospital bed. Propped up at a forty-degree angle, he doesn't have on his shirt, and his left arm in a sling. A big tuna-can bruise over his left eye and all around it. His top left lateral incisor is broken, gums inflamed. He gives me an emphatic thumbs-down.

—Pops! You go down? Did I do this to you? Is this, somehow, my fault?

He struggles to talk but asks:

—This is just a dirt bike spill. Don't tell your mother; she thinks I sold the motorcycle. And would you mind texting Lou? Tell him I'm not going goose-hunting.

—You got a punctured lung? What else?

— Lots of stuff but let's not worry about that. Right now, I need my meds.

I go into his bathroom and see, on the counter, a Halloween-sized candy bowl full to the brim with pills. Norcos and Oxys and all-day Adderall, Vicodin, white round ones and blue and yellow in pastel. It is enough to stop me in my tracks, drop down, and say a prayer of thanks. I take a handful of pills out to my father and he selects the one he wants.

—A drink of some sort, too.

Back in the bathroom, I put away the pills and look for a cup. There isn't one, so I make a bowl with my hands and fill this up with water and quickly go over to Pops. He is the type of man who drinks out of creeks and brags when he doesn't get Beaver Fever. Pops puts the pill, ten milligrams of Lortab, onto his tongue, leans up, and drinks, like a horse, from my hands until the water is no more.

—Flush the rest. I don't need that crap. We gotta plant spuds tomorrow.

—Dad, you're in One-Way City! You need to rest! Relax! The spuds will plant themselves!

—I see you've already forgotten everything I taught you.

To prove I haven't, I ask about the planting conditions, and my father and I discuss the weather history of the Snake River Basin from 1954 to current day. After about twenty minutes of this, Pops explaining the abnormal thaw of '95, I go into his closet and put on one of his white long-sleeved button-up shirts, the Uniform of the Priesthood.

—What happened to your arm?

—Ma wanted me to dress up for a Family Home Evening lesson. Missionary work in the Pacific Islands.

—I mean the blood.

The left sleeve is maroon and pink and fuchsia—the open wound from the pumice stone oozing through the fabric. I shrug and say nothing.

—What is it you left home for to do again?

The Great and Spacious? The Pride Cycle?

—Keep that shirt. It looks good on you. I don't want it back anyhow.

—It's too big.

—Don't look a gift-shirt in the mouth.

—Right.

—Come to work with me tomorrow. We need to swing past the

FSA office, then we'll get Molinas. Or Morenitas. Or Mongolian Grille ...

My father continues listing his favorite eating establishments, so I know the pill has taken hold. Around here, I do as I see, so I go back to the pills and take a few straight down the gullet, just because, then go back down the hall. Downstairs, there is the commotion of people seating themselves around a long table. I edge across the hardwood in my socks. At the ornate front door, I reach out for the knob, and the oak is smooth. No handle. I cannot leave. I set down my shoes and return to the kitchen.

Everyone is seated at the table: my sister and her brood, Madam Peacock and her children and grandchildren, Ma. Everyone but my father, and me. There are our open seats—the two spots on the piano bench. I sit down for the prayer, and my mother blesses the food then proceeds to be thankful for over four generations of ancestors. It takes many minutes.

At amen, it is chaos, forks and knives clanging. I reach for the butter and my sister snaps. When it's all over, there are no leftovers for my father and me. The table is carnage: remnant lettuce shreds, gravy driblets, smashed potato sandwiches, fat-flecks, corn-silk, dozens of dinner rolls (torn in half), so many naked cobs. Most of the women, the ones wearing pants, have unbuttoned the top button and lay catatonic among the mansion's many couches. Those in dresses take throw-blankets and fill the floor.

I make my way quietly, backwards, to the stairs ...

Ma, from the mantle, where she's curled in front of the fireplace, fuzzy slippers:

—Hey! Dishes, Mister!

So I march into the kitchen and break all the dishes. I chip them on the granite countertops; I drop them onto the Spanish tiles of the floors. A scree field of ceramic and glass crunches beneath me. Silverware gets tossed into the mangled recycle pile. I am salty, pragmatic, sweaty; there is no celebration or aplomb. No discussion. I clomp around the kitchen, slamming cabinet doors, intent on putting everything in its place. No one stirs except Peacock, who crochets a sock, and harrumphs.

Upstairs, I blow through my parent's door. My father is ranking his favorite Taco Bell drive-thru locations, from Tombstone to Helena, his favorite in Brigham City, for the bonus KFC. He waxes on about specialty craft Mountain Dew, handmade cinnamon twists, cheese.

—Pops, tonight, I'm springing you. We're eating out. I got wheels.

I sprint across the room, and punch out a window. A large shard of glass falls like a guillotine and lops off my left hand.

I get a clear look at my stump. As clean a cut as any, more obsidian than rusty saw mill. I'm not worried. I'm up to date on my tetanus shots.

One-armed, I scoop up Pops and put him over my shoulder. He

wasn't heavy, just a hefty old boy. But then, I suppose, so am I. I take three long steps to the window hole. I warn Pops to hold tight and keep his mouth shut. But he doesn't. We go flying, and he's mumbling about gravy fries, all the way down.

NATE BOZUNG: MORE SPIN

2015

26 JANUARY 2015

When I answer my phone tonight from an unrecognizable Utah number, I hear Nate–in a subdued, melancholic monotone–mumble into my speaker:

"What up. It's your long-lost cousin, calling straight out the fuggin looney bin."

This came as a surprise, seeing how one of my last interactions with Nate was from June 2014:

[PHOTO REDACTED: NATE BLACKED OUT / FACEDOWN IN NYC ALLEY]

Who took this? I texted back.

Idk just showed up on my Insta

A few months passed. I followed Nate as he globe-trotted from SLC to NYC to Russia and back to SLC. When my profile essay on Nate reached print in Tin House magazine, we had another interaction. He wanted me to drive to Salt Lake–4 hours from my home in southeastern Idaho–and, in what Nate described as "a fuggin sign-my-yearbook" scenario, I'd sign his copy of the magazine, and he'd sign mine.

I tried to set it up. He dodged my contact, though, and when I'd text instead of call, his responses were:

Im wasted

Im wasted

can't talk wasted

Meanwhile, online, he posted crap like:

[PHOTO REDACTED: NATE SMOKING & SKATING DOWN SLC HILL WHILE HOLDING TWO BOXES OF BEER]

To heck with him. Salt Lake's rowdy snowboarding son could bottom-bottle his way to oblivion. I signed a copy of the mag and stuck it in the mail. If he wanted to talk, he had my number.

Of course, the day after I'd gone to the post office, I see this show up on someone else's feed:

[PHOTO REDACTED: NATE STANDING ON SNOW AT A REHAB FACILITY, TWO PEACE SIGNS]

Two weeks sober? What was this? More importantly, who was this? Nate hadn't been sober 3 days in 15 years.

I started sleuthing to find out just what had happened in his life to encourage this change. Couldn't tell much.

I put a call into the rehab facility and waited for Nate to hit me back. Meanwhile, I scoured his online profiles...

[PHOTO REDACTED: NATE GETTING AN IV AT REHAB, ONE PEACE SIGN]

and waited...

[PHOTO REDACTED: NATE IN FRONT OF CARTOONS HE'S DRAWN IN REHAB]

and waited...

[PHOTO REDACTED: NATE ON SMOKE BREAK AT REHAB]

Then I heard some awful news about Nate's mother, my Aunt Susan, having received a cancer diagnosis. Then I started to really worry about them both. Here they are at Thanksgiving 2014:

[PHOTO REDACTED: NATE WITH HIS MOTHER IN FALL UT BACKYARD]

Then Nate called me late one night, January 16th. I missed it, my dumb luck, but he left me an energized voicemail full of positive vibes and big hopes. Rehab was working, he was on the mend.

I stayed in touch with Kate, Nate's Russian model love interest, as she visited Nate in the facility, hoping that she could connect us. I wanted to offer encouragement, support, love, and set up a day to come see him. She said they would call on her cell phone at noon. I took lunch early from the drywall job I was working and sat alone in my pickup, checking my phone every two or three minutes. When a half-hour came and went, I returned to work. No call. Kate texted and said Nate had been super busy that day and that he'd call me later that night. And again I waited, and again no call came my way.

Same old story, same old Nate.

[PHOTO REDACTED: NATE IN FRONT OF REHAB, TWO PEACE SIGNS]

He did call two nights later, it rang twice and, by the time I picked up, went to voicemail. This new voicemail was markedly different from the one left on the 16th. He sounded lower and more downtrodden than I'd ever remembered hearing him. I called and left messages for him Friday, Saturday, and Sunday, the phone nurse scribbling down my number, but never did connect until that Thursday.

Then he told me the whole story: he'd bailed on rehab, hadn't been there for three days, and was now on a mandatory 3-day hold for his behavioral and mental health. Some state facility that was so awful he already wanted to go back to rehab, and by the end of the call, promised he would. He'd let me know. He'd call again. He hung up.

5 FEBRUARY 2015

"I'm an alcoholic but I'm the best one you've ever met."

"The more I learn about life the more I lose respect for a lot of things. It's a whole different world than what I imagined, and I'm just trying to keep from drowning."

—Nate Bozung, 2008 SNOWBOARDER MAGAZINE interview

[PHOTO REDACTED: NATE BOARDSLIDING A TWO-STORY PARKING GARAGE, PHOTO BY ROB MATHIS, CHICAGO, 2001]

Nate finished his mandatory 72 hours in the behavioral hospital but, due to factors both financial and personal, decided not to go back to the rehab clinic. This, to the chagrin of his therapists, concerned friends, and family who had worked hard and fast to make the arrangements.

Instead, his sister picked him up and he stayed the night on his brother's couch in Orem. I talked to Nate again Wednesday–he was great, sober, playing with his nieces and nephews–to plan a rendezvous when I reached town Thursday afternoon.

Nate finally reached out Thursday around 1:00pm, calling from a number I didn't recognize. Apparently when he arrived back at his SLC pad from the BHC, a party of concerned individuals were there waiting for him. They believed that Nate needed further medical evaluations that rehab and the behavioral hospital had not offered, including CT scans and detailed MRIs to search for any problems that might exist due to past snowboarding concussions and injuries.

So Nate went with the posse to the University of Utah Emergency Room for a triage. Those third-party members weren't allowed back due to medical privacy laws, so they went home. Once Nate tested through the initial stages and came up clean, sober, and (relatively) healthy, the doctors asked him if he'd voluntarily check himself into the U's psyche ward.

As Nate had told me over the phone, the behavioral hospital had "scared him straight–just like the TV show." He vowed he wouldn't drink again just so he'd never have to return to a psyche ward. At the U, Nate heard the words "psyche ward" and promptly bolted. He walked to his house in the middle of the night. He didn't have a key–his place was still buttoned-up for his rehab stint–so he kicked out the wood plate covering the doggy door and crawled through the back door. There, without heat or water, he slept fitfully, thinking that he'd be hauled back to the U, this time by police and EMTs. Thursday morning, he jettisoned from the house on his mini skateboard, sans phone or cash. The only place he could think to go was Milo Sport, his first snowboard sponsor way back in 1997. His trajectory looked something like this:

[SCREENSHOT REDACTED: NATE'S 10 MILE SKATEBOARD TREK ACROSS SLC]

He skated/walked approximately 10 miles to the snowboard shop. He figured I'd be in town by then (per our conversation 2 nights before) so he dialed my number from the store phone. I happened to be home packing when he called, so I told him to hang tight for a few hours and I'd be down ASAP (which, at its fastest, meant a trip of 4 hours). He warned me not to tell anyone of his whereabouts–I didn't–and I asked him to stay put–miraculously, he did. By 7:15pm, I had Nate loaded in my pickup and he filled me in on his situation.

"So what do you want to do now?" I asked.

"Let's go to Park City. It's Sundance right now. I know lots of people."

Was I nervous? Not really. I've known Nate my entire life and felt like my whole role in this was to keep him safe and happy, and to serve as a second opinion off which he could bounce scenarios. I could tell he wasn't going to drink.

Here's the two of us on Park City's Main Street before getting dinner.

[PHOTO REDACTED: NATE AND THE AUTHOR, SELFIE, PARK CITY MAIN STREET]

We found a seat at an Italian restaurant. Nate, full of energy and charisma, colored on the tablecloth until his Utah Trout over rice arrived. He pounded glass after glass of hot green tea.

The waiter, a young ski bum, drummed up a conversation with Nate. The waiter told Nate about Egyptian Licorice tea, his personal favorite. Nate ordered one but then the waiter informed him that the restaurant didn't actually serve it. In retrospect, there was a good chance the waiter was high. He was a nice guy though, and tried not to interrupt as I asked Nate a battery of questions, most concerning the thing I knew the least about Nate: his pro career.

[PHOTO REDACTED: NATE COLORING ON PAPER TABLECLOTH]

Nate finished high school early (at 17, a 3.4 GPA) in order to go pro. He's sharp and witty, has a plethora of stories to swap, and easily makes friends.

In fact, when I pay the tab for dinner, the waiter waves me to the back of the restaurant and asks me to wait. A few minutes later, he returns and slips me an Egyptian Licorice tea bag.

"It's from my backpack," the waiter says. "Tell your friend it's really good. I hope he likes it."

When I relay the commerce and tale to Nate, he just laughs. "Story of my life. People have been good to me all over the world. That's just how it rolls."

We walk down and up Main Street–where, 6 days prior, Park City policemen found Nate barhopping and arrested him. We're passing by the screening of 1 of 3 James Franco movies featured at Sundance this year when from behind us I hear a man's voice yelling out, "Boz!" "Hey Boz!" "BOZ!"

It's a Bozwreck fan, a handsome man about our age, who knows Nate solely from Instagram. Lex, an actor from LA via Philly, compliments Nate on his girlfriend, his tattoos, and his life in general. When Nate mentions that he just got out of rehab, Lex sings praises to sober living—he's been clean 2 years running—and the two of them swap war stories for 10 minutes. By the end, Lex and I exchange phone numbers and tentatively plan a Friday rendezvous at The Canyons, one of Park City's sky resorts.

We bail on Park City and head back to Salt Lake to try and find a place to sleep. I talk Nate into calling his mother to let her know that he is safe and sound. The conversation escalates, as one might imagine, and I drive and listen and try not to interject. We find a hotel room for $40 a night in downtown SLC, in what Nate says his fellow rehabbers call "Heroin Block." Nate is pretty excited to be out of rehab and ecstatic to be miles away from what he calls "The Nutty Prison."

[PHOTO REDACTED: NATE STANDING ON HOTEL BED, SHIRTLESS, HOLDING PILLOWS ARMS OUTSTRETCHED]

The night at the hotel is free of drama. Nate catches up on his social media consumption while using my phone. At one point, a woman screams uncontrollably in the parking lot for a solid minute (when I look out the window, she is nowhere to be found), and around 2:00am the man in the room next to us starts doing vocal warmups and then runs start-to-finish 4 times through an original R&B number he's perfecting. Nate and I both konk out in our clothes.

6 FEBRUARY 2015

Nate's mom calls, hooks up the gear, and for the first time in our lives, Nate and I snowboard together. We've been waiting for this for 20 years.

[PHOTO REDACTED: THE AUTHOR, NATE, AND SUSAN AT THE JEEP AT THE GAS STATION]

[PHOTO REDACTED: THE AUTHOR AND NATE IN FRONT OF MILOSPORT]

[PHOTO REDACTED: NATE SELFIE IN RED WHITE BLUE PULLOVER HOLDING SHOTGUN SHELL BOARD]

[PHOTO REDACTED: THE AUTHOR AND NATE SELFIE AT BASE

OF THE CANYONS, EACH FLASHING PEACE SIGNS]

[PHOTO REDACTED: NATE SNOWBOARDING AND SELFIEING HIMSELF, LEX, AND THE AUTHOR, ALL SHREDDING]

[PHOTO REDACTED: THE AUTHOR, NATE, AND LEX, SELFIE IN THE GONDOLA: THUMBS UP, TWO PEACE SIGNS, DEATH HORNS]

[PHOTO REDACTED: SIGNED COPY OF THE AUTHOR'S ESSAY: LOVE LIFE 2 MY BEST KUZ! LOVE YA NATHAN BOZUNG MUCH LOVE #KUZIA #BOZWRECK #DUHLIFE]

CLEAN UP, 1997

2014

What I remember about '97 was that people dumped a lot of trash at our farm that year. Dad blamed this on the weak winter and the awful holdover '96 crop. Too much of everything, and nobody in eastern Idaho moneyed up enough to care for excess, so the extemporaneous got ditched. Osgood got Os-bad real fast. An inordinate amount of garbage littered the borrow-pits. Mattresses. Refrigerators. Stoves, sinks, toilets. Black trash bags full of the unknown. But when Dad found a toothless horse hitched to the gate of the Steel farm, I sensed this year would be worse than ever. Along with his elk rifle, Dad took the horse out to the cinder pit and put that sad bag-of-bones to rest. This act left him ornery for most of January, and I thought I understood.

The next animal abandoned at the farm was a big black lab dog. Dad spotted the blip 400 yards out in the stubble field behind the farm yard—what we called the area behind where sat my family's house— the farm repair shop, the workers' cinderblock bunkhouse, and two earthen A-frame potato cellars. Dad looked through the gunscope and declared it was no coyote. I stood with him on the back porch and squinted, trying to make out the dog. Dad shot and, I guessed, missed. The lab ran free and, two nights later, left its ghostly scat as provocation on the front lawn.

Dad stepped in it next morning, erupted: "I guess I'm expected to clean up everyone's messes, solve everyone's problems!"

"What's next," I asked alongside him. "A snapping turtle? An ostrich? A flipping rhino?"

Dad didn't laugh, blew air through his nostrils and grumbled, scanning the field and beyond. I never did see that mutt again, and knew why.

At the end of March, eight arrived from Mexico: Poncho, Memo, Armando, Victor, and four new guys whose names I still needed to learn. This added to the yard's already large population. We had the Brothers D (Dan, Darrel, Dick) employed year-round to mechanic and truck crop-to-market, always in the backyard. Together they carpooled the 14 miles from Rigby, but joked about pulling out a camper and living in the shop. There was my mother, taking care of the banking and bills. My six sisters aged 13, 11, 9, 7, 5, and 3. Dad. And me, Jonny Stirl, 15 years old. I had applied for and received a farmer's driving permit; otherwise, I would have had to wait until 16 like all the rest. The laminated card was a formality, as I'd been driving the 3-speed '65 Ford pickup out on the washboard desert farm roads since I was 12.

In fact, I was driving the Ford back from an FFA meeting one muddy March day, making the sharp curve around Cinder Butte, scanning for new garbage, as Dad had given me the job to keep the road clean, when I spotted a cardboard box up ahead. It sat in the road dead-center, and was too big for me to safely straddle or hit. I pulled to the shoulder and planned to take it to the shop dumpster. When I bent to pick it up, whines emanated from inside. The box was duct-taped shut, so I fished out my bone-handled Glory West pocketknife and sliced through the tape. The ratty box contained a litter of five beautiful black and white kittens, their eyes wide and terrified, their bodies huddled and pressed into a one corner mass. Not newborns, they were alert, and hissed at me.

I'd never been around kittens, Dad loathed cats. I picked up the box and carefully slid it across the Ford's bench seat and drove home with caution. I let them out in the garage and prepared a saucer of milk. They didn't take to that. They wanted meat. I opened a can of tuna fish, and they feasted. After, they flexed and scampered, roly-polied all over each other—happy, satisfied creatures—until they tired. I sat and played with them between my feet. They returned to the overturned box and fell asleep in a pile, at the foot of the garage deep freezer.

When Dad came in that night, he was pissed. He'd seen them in the box.

"Cats serve no purpose, climbing everything, clawing everything. They sleep wherever they fall over. They don't mind anyone. Even if they mouse, they torture them, kill them, and bring guts to the back door. Cats are cruel, vain beasts. Get them away from my pickup, you shouldn't've swerved."

"Dad, these are pretty sweet-looking," I said. "You'd like these."

"I don't like cats, I don't want cats. Cute kittens become cats."

"Jeez, Dad, they're babies. Should I drown them in the canal?"

"Jonny, don't be so dramatic. Get them gone. Now."

He had that stern look; embers smoldered far behind his pupils. Dad was not an intentionally cruel man; if he expected me to kill them, he would have said so. He probably sensed that he'd have to do that anyways, as I didn't enjoy hunting or fishing or, in general, causing pain.

I interpreted his command as one of practicality, and got moving. I put on warm clothes, grabbed a flashlight, gathered up the kittens in their box, and, through the dark and wind, moved them to the woodpile behind the cement bunkhouse. I made a den from split logs and end-cuts of plywood, and inside piled up clean shop rags for warmth. When I freed the cats, they timidly looked about and read the air with their noses. They looked cold. I shined the light to the entrance, but they remained at my feet, clawing up my knee-high boots. One by one, I placed each inside the hovel and held the box against the entrance until they settled down.

What would keep them here through the night? I didn't leave until I had to. I hurried back to the house and, from the dumpster, fished out the remnants of a roasted chicken from two nights before. The kittens alerted to the scent of flesh, and picked and clawed at the sinewy ribcage in a frenzy, then all really fell asleep hard, in a soft pile. Inside my own bones, I felt I'd done a good thing, proud of my animal husbandry. I walked off home and went to bed.

It wasn't until the next morning, checking the woodpile, that I realized my mistake. Bones and skin and fur everywhere, black and white and red. Guts. Skunks had come for the chicken—and the kittens. Not one heartbeat out there but mine.

BRING ON
THE SPINS

2014

January 2011, late Saturday, and a heavy winter storm parks over New York City. Compact cars are white mounds against the curb; the subways, slick wet messes. I am twenty-eight years old, bundled in a parka, scarfed and gloved, dressed more for my home—the sweeping, hilly potato farms of southeastern Idaho—than for NYC. I pick my way through puddles and over ice patches and finally under a Williamsburg overpass and when I feel that I've found where I'm supposed to be, I text my cousin Nathan Bozung (known as "Boznuts" to the snowboarding industry, though I simply call him "Nate") to let him know I've arrived. He appears on a stoop, sprints down the black-iced sidewalk, and embraces me full stride, nearly knocking me off my feet.

Despite the cold, Nate has no coat. He wears a T-shirt that hangs to his knees, tight tapered black jeans, throwback Nikes, and a neon-lime lanyard that holds his keys and Blackberry. He is a jittery, skinny critter with bleach-gray hair to his shoulders and a scripty OOPS! tattooed above his left eyebrow. His bony arms are still strong; he holds me up and squeezes me. His timbre is as familiar as my mother's, and he laughs with that same escalating giggle I haven't heard in over a decade.

"Holy fugg," Nate yells, "I can't believe this. My best cousin is here."

I nod and grin. Even in the cold, his body stinks ripe and fetid.

We go up the flight of stairs to his second-story pad. We are alone; his three roommates are waiting for us somewhere across the bridge in Manhattan. The white walls of his apartment have been graffitied in every color imaginable, the mediums ranging from aerosol to Crayola.

"You got to sign the wall! Everyone signs the wall. We need to get to the city. Fugg! My phone's blowing up. I got twenty bucks till Monday, we can cab it to the city. Oh man, my super hates me. Fugg, I'm gonna treat you like a king!"

I scan the scrawled wall scripture. Above the door in hot pink: "Pride . . . never even crossed my mind." Elsewhere: "Down with the ship." "Don't tell my girlfriend." "Did I really ██████████?" "██████ savez life." ████████████ cookie sheets and ██████████████████

litter the tiny kitchen; the sink is full of plates cemented with the rock-hard remnants of Hot Pocket innards. "I quit quitting" is written on the door of the fridge. I enter Nate's bedroom. He's shirtless, spraying cologne over his tattooed midriff, coating scent across his stained canvas. He yanks a hoodie out of a waist-high cardboard box—the room's only furnishing but for the twin-size mattress on the floor—and pulls it over his head. He takes it off, finds a pair of scissors, and cuts off the sleeves before putting it back on.

"Nate, you getting enough to eat?" I ask.

"Duh. That's my munchies pile over there." With his toe, he motions to a pile of saltine crackers stacked on the floor near his mattress. He rummages around in the box and retrieves a button-up long-sleeved flannel—pink, yellow, orange, and green, emblazoned with his own snowboard apparel brand—and tells me to have it because, "Dude, you're a farmer, right?"

This seems to be the extent of what he knows about my current life, that I'm a farmer, something he knew when he was fourteen and my aunt would bring him and his siblings to my house for the summer. Though we are first cousins (our mothers are sisters), Nate doesn't know if I'm happy or where I served my two-year Mormon mission or what I studied in college or where I'm living now. ████████████ ███ ███ ███

"So you got any tattoos yet?" Nate asks. He's back in the box, looking for different swag.

"No," I say, though I think to add: "Just a lot of scars."

"So you're married, right?" Nate asks. He knows I am—he promised he'd make it to my reception, way back in 2003, and didn't. He has dodged my calls until now.

I last saw Nate in person in 1999. It was in weather not unlike this New York weekend but two thousand miles west in the foothills of Salt Lake City. Nate had turned eighteen and dropped out of high school to become a professional snowboarder. I was seventeen and in town with friends to see the Utah Jazz. Once everyone had gone back to the hotel, I took my mom's Suburban and found Nate's new place. I pounded on the door. Finally, he opened, fresh-faced, smiling ████████████. We didn't stay upstairs long. He wanted to show me his bedroom. In the downstairs living room, we passed ████████████████████████ ████████████████████████████who watched TV and ignored us.

In Nate's bedroom, he explained everything: his rail board, his big air board, his pipe board, his trick stick. This was from his watch sponsor, a goggles sponsor, a sunglasses sponsor. Against the wall, he had skate decks leaned up one against another, and brand-new shoes in a spectrum of styles stacked three deep. He gave me a black T-shirt with his new snowboard team logo ████████ emblazoned across the front. His mattress was bare but for a small blanket and a pillow.

We talked about the future. In a year he'd be eligible to serve a Mormon mission. He told me he'd play out the snowboarding gig, save up some money, and turn in his church-required application after he turned nineteen. That was a good plan, I said, as his parents had recently divorced, and ████████████████████████████████ ██ ██████. Nate's younger brother and sister needed a role model.

"I got a story for you," Nate said, "promise you won't say nothing to the family?"

██Our mothers came from a traditional Mormon family with twelve siblings, and our cousins were plentiful and ubiquitous and impressionable. Nate was my family's purest athlete, idolized by all. In the morning, Nate could drop a fifty-foot cliff while spinning a 720, then shoot scratch golf that afternoon. Nate had chosen me as his protégé. After a visit from him in sixth grade, I convinced my mom to loan me money for a skateboard. I spent the summer skating outside the junior high but—in Rigby, Idaho—couldn't go more than five feet without hitting a piece of gravel. That winter, I started riding snowboards.

Nate started in ████████████████████████████████████ ██ ██ ████████████████████

Growing up in the Mormon Church, we both knew this was contrary to doctrine. ██████████████████████████████████████ ██ ██ ██ ██ ████████████████████

"You ever ████████?" Nate asked me.

"No," I lied and ████████████████████████████████████ ██ ██ ██ ██ ██

"Good, man, so good," Nate said semi-solemnly. "It's better that way. Straight-n-fuggin narrow all the way."

Nate then seemed antsy to have me gone and ushered me back to the entryway upstairs. He held me under the disco ball and examined me from head to toe, preparing to say something revelatory.

"Cuz," he said, looking down at my five-foot-eight-inch frame from his six feet. I waited for him to impart something brotherly, perpetual.

"You're the perfect height. Man, if I was you, I could really spin."

The car Nate ordered from a private service arrives. We hurry downstairs, jump in, and shoot across the Williamsburg Bridge, suspended above the black East River, surrounded by mist and cold. Nate is on the phone the entire time. He asks me if I want to go to a Saturday Night Live after-party with his publicist. Of course. Nate tells the driver the after-party address, the driver reminds Nate he only paid twenty dollars. Nate bails on the SNL plan, saying he never really wanted to go there in the first place.

We end up at a club, and there's a line like I have seen only in movies. Nate and I bypass everyone and walk up to the bouncer, a burly man wearing a T-shirt with Nate's label. The bouncer marks Nate's hand and lets him in. He eyes me and stalls.

"This kid!" Nate shouts up to the man. "He's my best cousin! We rode so many horses!"

The bouncer nods, pulls me in for a one-armed hug, and marks my wrist.

Inside, every employee—the bartender, the DJ, the women serving drinks—wears iterations of Nate's gear. We are ushered downstairs to the VIP lounge. This is hotness like I have never seen: women in cocktail dresses and hot pants and halter tops, women with glassy eyes and wandering hands. I wear cheap jeans and Nate's obnoxious multicolored flannel. The lounge walls are textured and colored like adobe. Cubbies and benches are carved into the walls. Candles are set on ledges and alcoves. It is an Ancient Egyptian den of iniquities. I feel as though I'm spelunking into lusciousness.

"What ███████████?" Nate asks.

An hour earlier, on the subway headed to Nate's, I ████████ ███ ███. I do consider my wife in California, Renae, asleep after a late night of quilting (a family skill passed down by her grandmother), my father and mother resting before a long Sunday at the chapel. ████████████████ ██ ███.

"I ████████████████████████████," I answer, ██████████████ ██████████████████████████. I follow his neon through the crowd of pearls and pleats. He shows me off to packs of provocative people. With ████████████████████████████████, Nate sweeps both arms and declares:

"This kid! He's my best cousin! His dad's like the biggest potato farmer in Idaho!"

"This kid! We sawed down a tree at Scout camp and had to dig an outhouse!"

"This kid! He's like my brother! We shot so many fuggin birds!"

Strangers ██████████ and slap my back; I smile ██████. We finally sit with a group of supermodels and trust-fund kids. I, polite as ever and feeling sociable, ask them all what they do. One by one, each person in the group ignores me. Nate pulls me aside.

"Everyone does something and they don't want to talk about it. They'll think you're trying to angle them. Just shut up and have a good time."

"Okay," I say. "Yeah, sure."

"Fugg! Like that kid—his dad's an MTV exec. I need to hit him up to see if he'd throw some money in for ████████████."

Nate's oldest brother is facing ████████████████████ ██ ██ ████████████████████████████ Nate should have the money, he tells me, but of course he doesn't. The government caught up with him after seven years of tax evasion, froze his funds, and now garnishes his wages every month. Luckily, he paid a year's rent on his flat and sells clothes and snowboard gear for petty cash.

An indiscriminate man comes up to Nate and they ███████████ ██ ██ ██████████ After, he laughs, and says, "You didn't see that."

Of course not. I see only 1993 Nate, that California kid in rural Idaho who introduced me to Rollerblades. He put his on and I borrowed his brother's and we skated three miles from Grandma Edna's all the way out to Rigby Lake, the road so rough my teeth chattered. I see Nate pulling down vines out of a cottonwood tree—████████████ ██ ██ ████████████████████████████████████ but when a police cruiser stalled in front of us we █████████████████ ████████████████████████. The cop drove on. We bladed back and called my mom. When she picked us up, we repented to her then and there, Nate actually leading the confession. We both wept, contrite. We'd committed a serious sin and, for that, we were grounded from skating for a week.

Nate heads for more ████████████████████████ ██ ████████████████████████████████. When was the last time I actually ██ ██ ████████████████████████████████████ ███████████ █████████████ ███████████████████████████████████ ██ ██ ████████████████████████████████ Renae would say that I was behaving █████████████████████████████. She'd say I was choosing ██████████████. She'd say I was acting ████████ ██████. I'd say I ████████████████████.

A tall man with dreadlocks crashes next to me and asks if I'm really Boznuts's family. Before I can answer, he pulls out his phone and shows me photos of a woman, ██████████████████████ ████████████████████. She is a German with a group of other Germans at the bar, and she sees the man showing her off. She comes and covers both our eyes, hardly embarrassed. Her hands smell sweetly of Granny Smith apples.

Married since twenty-one—a virgin till then, my wife no more experienced than I—this is what I imagine Nate's dream-life to be. ████████████████████████Even as I sit with the man in dreads, a woman across the club ████████████. She is a recently retired LA Lakers dancer. Her fiancé is here too, ████████nodding out in a corner, wrinkling his tuxedo. ████████████████████ ████████████████████We'd sat by each other earlier and I told her I was a writer and a teacher, that Nate wanted me to pen his biography. She started introducing me as The Professor. Perhaps she's attracted to that—someone once told me that writers are the world's best aphrodisiacs—and I wonder ████████████████████ ██████.

This power with titles—████████████████████ ████████████████████—has always frightened me, a literalness instilled in me by my father. "If there is one thing I cannot tolerate, it's a liar," his measured voice has testified to me many times, often after catching me in a lie. For this reason, I have never felt comfortable titling myself in any real way. I am not a snowboarder, because snowboarders have sponsors and travel the world and compete in the X-Games; no, I ride snowboards. I am not a writer, because writers sell books and have agents and are interviewed on NPR; instead, I write stories. I am not a professor; I am the lottery-winning recipient of a Stanford University fellowship during which all recipients get to teach. I am not Mormon, because Mormons are cheerful and problem-free████████████████████████. And I am not ████████████████████████████ ████████████████████████████████ ████████████████████████████████ ██████████.

Nate comes back having traded some ████████████████ ████████████.

"Nah," I say. "Want some ████████?" ████████████████ ████████████ But tonight is special, and Nate is my best cousin. This, our ten-year reunion.

"I don't ████████." Nate ████████████████████ bounces to the dance floor.

A pro skater named E-Z talks to me about his video shoot that morning. He looks a lot like Nate: skinny, tatted up, scrappy. But unlike Nate, he's coherent and intelligent. His bravado seems like a façade. He's built a half-pipe in his Manhattan loft. We pull up his videos on my phone. The kid is insane, board sliding three flights of stair rails and bailing into street traffic.

"Skating and shooting," I say. "Seems like a good life."

E-Z gets close to my face, not a whiff of booze on him. "Want to know the truth? The feckin truth is with all this shite—my sponsors, my videos, my chicks—I'm feckin living by a shoestring. I'm barely alive. I'm flat feckin broke."

"What are you going to do?" I ask.

"Wake up tomorrow and shoot. What else is there?"

I've got ██ ███ ████████████████ I excuse myself to the bathroom.

E-Z jumps to his feet. "You ████████?"

I shake my head. "Got to ████."

"Hurry back," E-Z says, sitting up now, talking loudly so others can hear. "I was enjoying our conversation."

I go out onto the snowy street and trudge half a block to a hole-in-the-wall bodega. When was the last time I ████████████? About a year ago. Renae and I were living in Idaho. I had finished graduate school and was working on the farm. She was a juvenile probation officer. It was a spring Sunday and we had settled into one of those weeklong fights, the catalyst of which I no longer recall. We were cycling again, this Ouroboros of devouring and being devoured.

After church, we argued in the car, stomped through the kitchen, brooded in the bedroom, and screamed through closed doors. She started packing a bag. I ████████████████████ left in my pickup, driving east to Wyoming. Forty miles later I ████████████████ ████████████. I was ten minutes from the border when she finally called me, crying, apologizing.

I turned around. On the way back, I stopped at a ranch my family owned where once stood an old cabin. Nate and I would stay there in the summer. We thought it was haunted and cursed and loved it from serial-killer basement to bat-infested roof. But while I had been away at school, my parents had torn it down. All that remained were a few earthen mounds. I drove the muddy road as far as I could, then walked the rest of the way. I hunkered ████████████ and tried to visualize that leaning structure. It seemed like everything I once loved had shifted out of my line of sight, or crumbled, or disintegrated into thin air.

I looked down at my left wrist, at my brand. A few months before my nineteenth birthday, I received word that the Church had assigned me to serve my mission in Indiana. I'd been repairing fence on this ranch. That night, at home in my basement bedroom, I fashioned a brand out of some leftover wire. 1-0-0, just as we marked our spring calves. I heated the metal over a lighter and scalded the digits into my wrist. To remind me where I came from, who I was, what I stood for. Something only for me, covered by my watch, hidden beneath a cuff.

But when I saw the brand now, it ███████████████████████████ ██ ██ ██ ███. Then I drove home.

I give ████████████████████ on the street before I'm even able to ████ ██. For me, there was nothing spiritual about ████████████████████████ ██ ██ ██ ██. I used to assist in protecting new life. I guess I still could. I high-five the bouncer and go back inside.

Nate is in the corner with two models, a blonde and a brunette, ██████████ and laughing.

"I'm ███████████████ these chicks," he says in front of them. "I can't help myself!"

I sit and ████████████████████████. The models are stunning; they are stunned. Their eyes roll in and out of focus, and the one closest to me sways like a cat's tail. I start to feel sick, ████████████████████ ████████ and cannot tell if the models are spinning or I am.

The women invite us to meet them at their Chelsea loft, mostly because Nate says ██████████████████████. Nate's roommate Rex joins us as we leave.

I █████████████ at a stoplight. The cabbie yells at me ████████████ ██ ██ ██████████████████████████████.

Nate proclaims: "Welcome to Duhlife."

The models' place is up a long flight of sapphire-blue stairs. They've both changed from their club getups to black leggings and white T-shirts. It is a sprawling place, open and beautiful████████████ ██.

I hear one of the women ask Nate if I will be okay.

"He's my best cousin. What do you think?"

I wash my face, my equilibrium a tortuous mountain path, not unlike any one of the hikes Nate and I did as kids. It doesn't take much to imagine the purling of Palisades Creek as Nate and I climbed the five miles to Lower Palisades Lake, a runoff pond in the mountains east of Swan Valley. We bushwhacked through tall grass to a sandbar. We took off our pants and waded out in our boxers and caught brook trout all afternoon. We hid in the willows and called to girls on the path, inviting them to come join us. Until one actually said, "Tell me where you're at? I'll come find you." We were both so scared that we stayed silent until she and her friends left.

After the bathroom, the brunette leads me to the couch and gets me a blanket, instructing me to take a break. She is kind to me, aware that I'm neck-deep now, perhaps someplace she's been before. I don't have the courage to ask her name. ████████████████████ ██ ████████████████████████████████. The woman and I watch Nate and Rex ████████████████████████████████.

I wake up at 4:00 am, confused. The blonde is demanding that everyone leave. A strange guy—who wasn't with us before—is stretched out on the loveseat, his legs hanging off one arm. The blonde goes to the stranger and shakes him awake. The man throws a hand up, not hard, like shooing away some pesky gnat, and pops the woman in the nose. She screams. Nate and Rex collar the man, haul him to the door, and start him down the stairs.

Nate holds up both his arms, that universal sign of dominance and invitation for physical altercation. "That's right, you better fuggin move, reesty nobody."

The man yells from the stairs. "What you ever done?"

"I've fuggin rode all over the globe. I've partied fuggin everywhere. I own a billion-dollar company. So fugg you."

The two models rematerialize, having retreated to check the blonde's war wounds.

"Get out," the brunette tells Nate. She doesn't look my way. "We're tired."

The blonde stands a few feet away, mascara running down her face in gnarly streams. I place a hand on her shoulder and ask if she's okay.

"No, no, no," she says, each with increasing intensity. "Next week is fashion week. Everything is ruined. Everything is trash."

An hour later—after stiffing the cabbie a tip for a ride to Brooklyn—we are back at Nate's pad for the Sabbath. Rex DJs music on YouTube, flipping through music videos, saying something about Sunday Fun-day, and then nods off on the couch with his fly wide open. General arrives ████████████████. Nate ████████████████████ ████████████████.

Nate punches his Blackberry, trying ████████████████ ████████.

"You okay, Nate?" I ask.

"Better than ever. Better than you." He laughs. "Tito"—the last roommate I've yet to meet, a Colombian with whom Nate wants me to speak Spanish—"cooked us a feast on Christmas. Pork chops, mashed potatoes, turkey . . ."

"What do you think about your little brother's baby?" Before I'd arrived in New York, I'd texted the youngest Bozung to let him know I'd be seeing Nate.

Nate ██ "He's got a kid?"

"Three or four months old."

"No fuggin way." Nate █████████████.

"Are you happy?" I ask. "I mean, like, are you good?"

"Fugg yeah. I got my taxes worked out. The company's blowing up. I'm a fuggin uncle again! Tito and me are going to Colombia to open a bed-and-breakfast ████████████████████████. What about you?"

My wife and I ask each other this often, usually after long weekends when I stay in reading and she works on quilts and catches up on her sleep. And, of course, after the fights. There is the issue of being my father's only son and having abandoned him and the family farm twice in five years. Before I left for California, he had said to me in a moment of weakness, "I really thought you were staying for good this time."

I lie. "I'm pretty okay."

"You should be! You're like ████████! You're going to be a fuggin famous dude!" Nate gets up to pin a bedsheet over the window to block out the sun.

"How do you know about ████████?"

Nate stops. "What, you think I'm a poser?"

No. Never. As my father would say, Nate is dumb like a fox. He's got █████████████████ quotes all over Facebook, along with pictures of his crew titled: "████████████."

Nate meanders around his apartment, █████████████████ ██. After the OOPS! tattoo, Nate bought his own gun and has been using his body as a practice canvass. Love curls beneath his left eye. I'm looking at his left hand: X-O-X-O across his knuckles. A mediocre NYC and LA on one of his wrists. A box that represents the state of Utah, its area code, 8-0-1, inside. His middle finger displays perhaps his most ingenious and paradoxical tat: the simple outline of a Valentine heart so he can simultaneously say "Love You" and "Fugg Off." On his forearm, Isaiah 1:18: "Though your sins be as scarlet, they shall be white as snow."

"You believe that?" I ask, pointing to the scripture. Scriptures, with their promises, have begun to lose their force with me. I do not point out to Nate the following verses, how they have nothing to do with effortless absolution. No, forgiveness is contingent on behavior. If willing and obedient, the good things of the land are available. But resist and rebel, and the sword of judgment awaits.

"Let me tell you," Nate says, sitting down next to me. "The first time I ████████████████████, I woke up the next morning and had this shoot where we were dropping this eighty-foot cliff. I thought that God was gonna kill me. But he didn't. So what's that mean?"

"I don't know."

"Me neither." Nate laughs. "But I'm still here. Living fuggin large. I mean, look at me"—he leans back to display the tattoos on his arms, lifts his pant leg to show more, pulls down his T-shirt collar to point out names—"I'm like Joseph and this is my many colored coat. I don't hide anything." He mixes ███████████████████████████████████ ████████.

I envy my cousin for this philosophy, mostly because I bury my faults and failures. My pain is real. Here is the railroad track from my back surgery after my snowboarding accident, three compressed disks and shattered bone from dropping and spinning off a measly ten footer and slipping the landing and sitting squarely on an exposed rock; my foot where I ran it over with the lawn mower trying to finish Grandma Edna's yard too hastily; the knuckles of my left hand where a farm auger almost chewed off my fingers because I was careless around the machine . . . ███████████████████████████████████ ████████████████████ ██████████████████████ ██ ██████████████████████████████████

Nate hands me a marker. "Sign my wall."

I go into his bedroom and try to think of something hip and fitting to write. Instead, I print beneath his doorknob "God Damned Our Land But Lifted Our People," the title to an essay I'd written years before. Perhaps to say to Nate: Yes, we walk forsaken ground. Yes, our world is made of despair. And yet, perhaps, something special awaits. We must remember that.

Nate reads it and comes out shaking his head.

"You like it?" I ask.

Nate goes from ashtray to ashtray, searching for roach butts to re-smoke in his pipe. "Like it? I don't know what it fuggin means."

Tito arrives, and we speak Spanish. We immediately like each other. He gives me a book of poetry that his uncle wrote while in Colombia during a time when everyone was dying or being killed. The title: Visitaciones (Visitations). The dedication: "Por Nadie" (To No One). This is fitting and right and incredibly sad. Tito tells me he once ███ ████████████. The paramedics hit him with a defibrillator and saved his life. That happened at twenty-seven; he's thirty-three now.

"Did it change you?" I ask.

"Frick yeah. I look at the world in a whole new way. Every day is a gift."

"You ███████████?"

"Oh, frick no. That's what I do."

At 11:00 am, all the roommates awake and leave and return with ████████ breakfast. Two new women—an NYU art history senior and a model from Arkansas—show up. The NYU student keeps ignoring the phone calls of her study group, waiting for her at the Metropolitan Museum of Art. With each unanswered call, she grows more agitated.

But she lightens when ██ ██ ████████████████████████████████████. The student is elated ████████ ██ ██ ████████████████████████████████████.

Everyone is uplifted. Rex DJs again. Nate skips about the apartment dancing ████████████████████████████. Tito ███████ ██████. Carlos ██████████████████████████████████████. Nate █████ ████████████████. General ██████████████████. The ████████████ ███████████. Everyone starts to ██████████████████. Rex pulses ████ ███████████████████████ like Zeus.

██

I finally feel good again. ██ ████████████████████.

An hour later, when it's time for me to go, Nate calls a car, the number written in marker on the wall below the light switch. We stand by the window and wait. Across the street is a triangular park with a small but rideable ridge. The sun shines down and melts ice from tree branches.

"Man, look at this day! I should go set up a fuggin rail."

"I would have gone out with you," I say. Even though Nate got me to start snowboarding, we have never ridden together.

"Fugg that. I'm retired."

After ten minutes, the cab hasn't shown. Nate calls again. "Dude, I've got my best cousin here and you're fuggin holding him up." The car arrives in less than two minutes.

I exchange goodbyes with my new friends. What else can I call these caretakers of my cousin? Nate gifts me with more of his only currency: multicolored beanies, a coat, stickers, a baseball cap. Things I will be proud to wear; items about which I will brag.

I am out in the clear day, ████████████████████████ and already I miss Nate. Before I jump the ice to climb into the waiting car, I glance to the second-story apartment. Nate is there, standing at the window. I throw a hand up to him. Not a peace sign or a love salute or a signal to rock on. It's not even a wave. Just my open hand, my extended fingers, my scarred knuckles. Through the spiraling glare, I see Nate's pink palm pressed against the glass; his tattooed mug watching over my departure.

How can I know ███ ██ ███████████████████████████? My novel will fall in on me, as will my marriage with Renae. I will leave California divorced and jobless. ████ ████████████████████████████ I will hear from Nate three times over that span: once from Colombia, when I will negotiate with Colombian officials to allow him to leave the country, as he'll have been jumped by some local skaters he's pissed off who took his his wallet and passport.

Again, from LA, when he'll walk into his neighbor's condo ██████ ████, pick a fight, and get two molars kicked out. And finally from Salt Lake, where he's staying at a buddy's house, having fled rehab. I'll join him there and he'll ███████████████████████████████████████, my divorce having finalized the day before, me on my way back home to the farm███████████████. Enveloped in his phone, he'll ignore me when I suggest we visit his mother███████████████████████████ ███ ██████████████.

How can I even imagine that I will meet a new woman and we'll hike to the Lower Palisades? I'll wake hours before her and sneak out of the two-person tent and pick my way across the boulders to the lake's edge and sit in the dawn's stillness ████████████████████. A moose will wade chest-deep in the water, moving lethargically, and pay no attention to me. I will step into the lake—so cold it makes me dizzy—and try to find the sandbar that years before Nate and I claimed as our own, now swallowed up and submerged. And I will think: under this bright reflective surface, below this murk and moss, somewhere deep in this icy, foreboding pool, there is solid footing to be found.

BIRTHPLACE OF TV

2014

So, the envelope.

First, there was a certificate notifying me of three years of service with Dynamo. Chandra's voice sounded in my head: fancy. Gold swirls at the corners and a dignified printed font with my full name: Warren B. Fischer, and below, 15 July 2008—15 July 2011. I'd landed the job right after the Fourth, I remembered now.

Today was Friday, July 22. The Human Resources department in Helena must be on the ball to get me this so quick. A smooth operating business, Dynamo Incorporated. A well-lubricated apparatus.

I held the certificate up to the fluorescent light. A neat watermark on the paper, the company D, and the signature of the President, Deborah P. Sauer, and Vice President, Stephen Sauer Jr. As I held it there and stared, my hand trembled. It made me anxious to see those dates, as if on a headstone. Three years of my life, spent like a vampire at an Idaho gas station, ringing up Copenhagen and corn dogs and tortilla chips. It made me visualize my mother's headstone too, in the Rigby Pioneer Cemetery, alone but for her parents and the empty plots awaiting her siblings and me. My mother spent most of her life running away from her parents, Rigby in general, and where did that get her? Beside her mother and father, within city limits, until the Second Coming. Sometimes God's keen sense of irony was evidence enough of his existence.

Twenty-five years old—six years older than Chandra, but she was a mature nineteen, much more responsible than the average Millennial—and what did I have to show? A few work shirts (Dynamo supplied the first one, a pea green fly-fishing button-up to cater to the outdoorsy crowd), a steady paycheck, twenty-percent store discount, and an extensive knowledge of gas station capitalism. This wasn't how I envisioned my life, not by a long shot. At twenty-five, I was supposed to be married, have a kid or two, certainly a college degree, and be settling down into a comfortable job or advanced study. That pipe dream was a thousand miles away. So the certificate made me depressed as hell, and I kept staring at that dash between the dates.

15 July 2008—15 July 2011.

My life: a plain, flat, uninteresting line; the simplest and most inanimate mark on the page; that dash, a pair of handcuffs; that bar, a spear through the heart.

I set down the certificate—"To save for prosperity's sake," as my mother said more than once—and wadded up the envelope to fit it inside the office wastebasket. As I did, I felt something else inside. I uncrumpled it and found a small envelope that Chandra had somehow overlooked. My own name was handwritten on the outside in a sure, slanted cursive. I'd never seen my name penned so elegantly. I opened this letter very carefully, a slice along one side, and gently shook out the contents. That was a trick taught to me by my companion long ago, when I was twenty and living in Fort Wayne, Indiana. Elder Powers was his name. Cameron Powers. He worried a lot about cutting his incoming mail correctly, lest he lose his only connection to the outside.

A button, a plastic gift card, and a piece of paper fell onto the desk. The button said: 3 YEARS! I took it and pinned it to the left pocket of my shirt, where I once wore my ELDER FISCHER missionary badge. I appreciated the slight heft of it there.

I unfolded the paper.

from the desk of
DEBORAH P. SAUER
President, Dynamo Inc

Dear Mr. Fischer,

I am well pleased with your service to our company. Rarely do we have an employee meet his/her three-year mark missing less than 2% of his/her shifts. In fact, in this three-year span, you are the only employee to do so. Dedication such as this does not go unrewarded. Please find enclosed a DYNAMO gift card of $25, redeemable at any of our locations, and a commemorative button. Wear it proudly! You are exactly the type of employee that Stephen Sr. would have hired!

As well, I encourage you to continue to apply yourself. Have you considered DYNAMO management as a career option? I will make the manager application and test available to you via the DYNAMO employee portal on the DYNAMO website. Please notify me if you do apply; I will expedite the process of your documents.

Sincerely,
Deb

A cartoon of a spaceman blasting off adorned the card, one fist on a hip of his spacesuit, the other pointed heavenward. Davy Dynamo, the icon with which Stephen Sr. opened his first store. Corporate still sported the big neon marquee above its front doors, or so I'd seen in company paraphernalia, idolizing Stephen Sr. and that bygone Space Race era. Our current logo, DYNAMO with lightning bolts for the letter feet, better suited the burgeoning millennium.

I turned this note over to see if anything more was written on the back. Nothing. I liked that. The fact that there wasn't a scribble to get the pen going, or a false start, gave me solace. Perhaps this small contentment came from my expectations being met. I had the idea that Mrs. Sauer was a complete woman: proper, classy, professional, adroit, sure-handed. I hadn't known many women like that. The fact that she took time out of her day, which I assumed was very busy as acting president of a far-reaching chain of service stations—to write this personal message made me proud. Not proud like I'd finished a marathon, but proud that a woman connected a positive connotation to my name.

I tried to picture Mrs. Deborah Sauer, but I didn't have an idea of where to begin. Instead, I considered my own mother, her curly brown hair, her soft eyes, the slight lisp when she said her Ss. One of a kind, Ms. Gaye Fischer. Gaye for light-hearted, glad; Fischer for Mack Fischer, the man she ran off with when she was seventeen. Mack, a drifter who came to work the farm with W.P. and Hank, convinced my mother that true love involved risk and uncertainty. They got hitched in Nevada on their way to Tucson, where Mack had his people, and it didn't last much beyond my arrival. After a year, my mother filed for divorce and moved us to Henderson, outside of Las Vegas. That's where I had my first memories, of the gray desert, of Gaye's painted fingernails; of sandboxes that I feared were quicksand. I was loony for quicksand in those days, Saturday morning cartoons to blame. I grew convinced that quicksand would cause my demise. One Venus flytrap of a sandpit, somewhere in the desert, not a branch or a vine to grab hold of, and me, all alone, drowning in the dirt. But my mother's hands were always there for me. I'd take one of hers in both of mine, we'd walk around the edge of the sandbox on the railroad-tie border, and I'd dip in my toe to make sure I wouldn't sink. Then one foot, back to the border. Then both. My mother clapped and cheered when I finally had the courage to stay in. If I panicked, my mother's hands with those painted nails always awaited me. As predictable as the sunrise, as dependable as time. The hands, I remembered well. They were thin and pretty and soft. But the nails were a different story. I'd tried to recall the tone of her nails the last time we were together but, depending on my mood, the color morphed. Sometimes they were Coastal Surf, but then, weren't they Ginger, or Butterfly Stroke, or Snappy Sorbet, or Mint Envy? Once, in a confusing and sexy dream, Fishnet Stocking. Another, Stiletto. And the worst, a combination of Sable and Tilled Soil and Kentucky Grass—like how they probably were now, as nails grew even in the grave—and that made me sad as hell. Really low, thinking about her resplendent nails, long and curling and cracking, all while the rest of her turned to rot.

Maybe that fixation attracted me to Chandra's bracelets so much. She wore one for just about every color in the watercolor palette. I didn't buy into that horsepucky that the bracelets denoted specific sex acts. One, she was pretty much only with Zeke. According to her, their relationship went up and down, so I doubt they hooked up all that much or, at least, consistently. Two, the sheer amount of bracelets combined with Chandra's time spent at work, her age, and her location made the equation unfeasible. She hadn't had the time or population density to achieve such a vast sexual repertoire. Really, the bracelets were about show, most likely purchased in bulk at the Idaho Falls mall. The truth about Chandra was that she barked but didn't bite. She wanted people to think east when really she was west. She claimed Wicca when she'd been baptized Mormon. That rap music, for instance. She played it in the store because other people could hear her playing it. But really, she adored animated movie soundtracks. I laughed out loud when I saw that playlist on her phone. She claimed it was for Destinee, but I didn't buy it. Here Chandra was, fronting this confused gangster Goth façade, when really she imagined herself wearing sexy kaftans.

But I could hardly fault her; we all lived double lives. Take Hank, this bald, thick, staid, potato and grain farmer I call my uncle. He bought a How-To harmonica kit—eight CDs, a couple of mouth-harps, a neck harness, the whole shebang—and taught himself to play one August while cutting wheat in the thresher. He said it took him five weeks and an entire tin of Bag Balm for his lips. He played well, according to him, and even figured out a few hymns. But with Hank, I had to about get down on both knees and beg him to play. The only reason I knew about his skill was because last year I went out with him to do some research and he didn't hide his neck-harness well enough in his lunchbox. It took me an hour of cajoling, and then he only played the first few bars of "She'll Be Coming Round the Mountain." Stubborn old crow, Hank. If I had that talent, I'd be serenading Dynamo customers all night long. Or I'd move to Nashville.

I had my own obsessions, ones that didn't involve my Dynamo persona, the identity by which most people knew me. Back at my trailer, I had nine full notebooks of character backgrounds, scene sketches, plot outlines, and analyses for this daytime soap opera I was writing called We are Pilgrims, We are Strangers. The cast centered on Philo T. Farnsworth, the inventor of television, and was set in Rigby in the 1920s when he lived here. I envisioned the show to cover a lot of ground too: prohibition, loss, frontier living, Mormonism, racism, small town life, doomed love.

But most of all, the show was about genius; how hard work and a good idea could lift a person out of the lowest valley to the highest peak America had to offer.

The concept came to me before I started working at Dynamo, the first year I lived in Rigby. I was drunk, walking around town on the Fourth of July. I deviated from my regular route and ended up on the road that led to the lake. Halfway there, I decided to jump the barrier fence and walk in the gutter along State Highway 20. I grew dog-tired, like if I took one more step I might pass out and die. Too much tequila. So I hunted around for a place to sit. Up ahead I saw a dark rectangle illuminated by the oncoming traffic. I discovered a large marquee—almost billboard-sized—painted in the Rigby High colors maroon and gold, illuminated by a few small spotlights. It read:

**Welcome to RIGBY
BIRTHPLACE OF TELEVISION
Philo T. Farnsworth
Easy off—Easy on!**

I stood there and picked over the four lines again and again, and their meaning never really clarified. Maybe the sign's purpose was to catch the attention of traffic and get them to exit at Rigby? Cars and pickups whizzed by, and some blared their horns. I was getting my bearings and figuring out how to get back to town when ... in the sky. Fireworks. Idaho Falls put on a fairly elaborate Freedom Celebration, and the red horsetails and white fishes and blue spiders filled the heavens. Something in my brain sparked, the word television and Philo's strange name coupled with the pyrotechnics. That was when I felt the initial impetus for We are Pilgrims, We are Strangers. Or, shortened: Pilgrims & Strangers. Abbreviated P&S. But really, the more I thought about it lately, I called it P.O.S ...

When Chandra started in the winter, I tried to explain to her my show's concept. She wasn't interested, she said, because she hated daytime TV. Everything except Judge Judy. That I could understand—different strokes for different folks. But I was explaining fascinating history about the town that she called home. How could she not be engrossed by the fact that the man who invented a contraption—a machine found in almost every home in America, influencing young and old alike—had discovered the scientific idea for it while living in (using Chandra's misnomer) butt-zit Rigby? This floored me.

To impress her further, I told her about all the money I'd saved to buy a car to get down to Hollywood to pitch my script.

"How much you got?" she asked. "None of my business. Just curious."

"Over fifteen-hundred bucks," I bragged.

"Sheesh! How much do you make an hour?"

"Minimum wage, same as you."

"Well, it wouldn't be fair for Dynamo to pay you more, right?"

"You're missing the whole point," I said. "Pretty soon, I'm leaving this dead-end town. I have a grip of cash and a golden ticket. What do you think about all of that?"

"Heck, I'm not surprised," she said, chewing her gum obnoxiously. "Even I knew about Farnsworth and Rigby. What, you didn't take Idaho History class in Fifth Grade?"

"Honestly, Chandra. Ask me something about electromagnetic imaging, or Farnsworth's three sons, or about General Hospital! What do you care about a bank?"

"I go to Zion's Bank. What about you?"

" I manage my own money. Does that satiate your curiosity?"

"Woah cowpoke," Chandra said. "I was just asking. You know me. I got an inquiring mind." She held up the copy of National Enquirer she'd been perusing.

It took me a minute to calm down. It was not easy to bear my soul to Chandra and have it dismissed like so many date invitations.

Before she left, though, Chandra did say, "Bud, your, um, book or whatever, it sounds real good." That made me feel a little better.

All of this led me back to Mrs. Sauer's note, and her invitation. Because of P&S, no, I hadn't ever considered Dynamo management as a career option. In fact, I'd only taken the job to fund my research. I didn't want it, and the thought of another year in Rigby made me want to punch myself in the guts. Once I received my next check and paid my bills, I'd break $2000. I'd buy a car, pack up my tapes, say adios to my few friends and family, burn my Dynamo clothes, hit the road, and belt "California, Here I Come" all the way to L.A.—just like Philo did.

MY TIME
IN THE DIRT

2013

- Consider that in 1982—the year I entered this world as a complete being with hands and feet and vocal cords—a certain tract of land in the foothills of eastern Idaho, surveyed and recorded at approximately two thousand acres, was owned by seven different men: Amle Landon, Arthur Harris, Erroll Spaulding, John Wheeler, Orlando Smith, Stewart Simmons, and my father.
- Near that tract of land, up on a hill, is a small country cemetery. There are a few trees and a handful of ornate headstones. This is the place I may or may not be buried. The entrance is marked with an arch and the name "Ririe-Shelton Cemetery."
- For many years I think the cemetery sign says "Ririe-Skeleton Cemetery" which to me makes perfect sense.
- On that farm—where the soil is fine as flour, and the earth packs and blows like snow, and the dust billows up from every seat cushion and the dirt sheets down the pickup windows, reminiscent of raindrops chasing raindrops down glass—I grow dirty.
- My first work requires me to pull weeds next to the repair shop. Inside, my father plans with the men what to till, what to sow, what to bury, what to burn. I lull in the shade until the meeting is almost finished. Before the men trickle out, I rub handfuls of dirt into the thighs of my jeans, across my chest, I powder dust in my hair. All this to create the illusion that I've been engaged in the cause. But all around, red root and wild oat stand green and vibrant and untouched.
- Once, in front of the other men, my father teases me for being lazy. Rain falls that morning; work is slow. I mill about inside the shop until I ask my father to take me home. "I've got a job for you," he says. "Go out

there in the dirt and turn all the rocks dry-side up." And I do for a while, just to make him feel bad, then sit in the pickup until he takes me to the gas station for a drink.

- In junior high, I sketch a cartoon during church a la The Far Side that is titled "Strange Similarities Between Potato Farmers and Prison Wardens." The cartoon is two-paned; in the first, a potato farmer stands in his field, holding a tuber up to the heavens. The farmer says, "Partner, you're gonna fry!!!" In the second pane, the prison warden, his hand on the breaker switch to the electric chair, in which sits a grizzled mass murderer, echoes the potato farmer's refrain.

- Until the late 90s, most of the schools in the farming regions of Idaho offer their students a two-week vacation called "Spud Harvest." My friend Victor comes to work with me. We work six days a week, as many hours as possible. Only the weather, or mechanical failure, stop us. One morning driving to the farm, bouncing along a gravel road in my '65 Ford, I fall asleep at the wheel. Vic had conked out as soon as he got in. The sagebrush and gutter weed wake us, scratching against the windows. Vic pushes us out of the dugway and we make it to the cellars on time. Later, Vic tells me he'd been dreaming about potatoes.

- My uncle stops taking daily showers during spud harvest. He spreads them out to once or twice a week. "Why should I?" he says. "I mean, I go to bed at midnight. I get up at six in the morning. What's the point?" His wife claims that his pillowcase has a corona outline of dirt, that she can shake dust out of the sheets.

- I attend a local Mormon college so I can be close to the farm. I bumble through journalism and business classes, not finding much that engages me, until I take a Spanish literature class and read a story by Juan Rulfo called "We Are Very Poor."

- "And Tacha cries when she realizes her cow won't come back because the river killed her. She's here at my side in her pink dress, looking at the river from the ravine, and she can't stop crying. Streams of dirty water run down her face as if the river had gotten inside her." Rulfo, Juan. "We Are Very Poor." The Burning Plain. Trans George D. Schade. Austin: University of Texas Press, 1978. 36.

- In his career, Juan Rulfo works as a traveling tire salesman and writes two books, a short story collection, The Burning Plain, and a novel, Pedro Páramo. He is heralded as one of Mexico's finest writers.
- So when the chance arises to study in Mexico for a semester—in Jalisco, no less, home state to Rulfo and the setting for his books—I leave the farm during grain harvest and don't return until the whole place is buried under two feet of snow. By chance, I meet a University of Nebraska professor in Guadalajara who is writing a book on Juan Rulfo's life. He agrees to allow me to accompany him on his endeavors. I associate with students that, for the first time, are not Mormon. One tells me the reason he transferred from his state university to a liberal arts college was that he tired of seeing his friends share needles. On the ranch, I tell him, with the cows, we use the same needle over and over until the dang thing breaks.
- I travel with the professor south of Guadalajara for a weekend. We are to interview the prominent local scholar on Juan Rulfo in a town called Sayula. We leave the metropolitan area and surge out into the wilds. Here are men herding cattle on the road's shoulder. Here are nine children riding in the open bed of a pickup truck. Here are toothless women drinking Coke from bottles. This is my type of country.
- The prominent local scholar is the owner of Sayula's hardware store. He tells us that Rulfo lied about everything—his age, where he was born, what happened to his family. I don't believe the man. To me, it seems that he'll stroke out at any moment. I pass the time watching chickens scratch for seeds in the dirt pavilion of his home. I take a picture in Sayula by Juan Rulfo's home. The plaque says he lived there, so it must be true. But there is another, exactly the same, on a different house a kilometer away..
- Here is what I think I know: Rulfo's father was a wealthy landowner killed by revolutionaries in the Cristero Revolution. Rulfo became a child of the state when his relatives would not take him. Rulfo studied in Guadalajara, then dropped out, then went to Mexico City, then took a job working as a rep for Goodyear Rubber. While in DF, Rulfo started a literary journal called Pan. Pan, in Spanish, means bread. Pan, a Greek prefix, means everything.
- That night, back in Sayula, I walk to the local library.

There are just two shelves of books, neither of which contains anything by Rulfo. I leave once it's dark. In an alcove of a small restaurant is an arcade. Inside, barefoot girls in pink dresses play Dance Dance Revolution. The worn gameboard is encrusted with dirty footprints.

- In Azatlán, the professor and I search for a waterfall he remembers from his time in Mexico as a graduate student. We find it, except that it is no longer a waterfall. Local entrepreneurs, in the last thirty years, have dammed the creek and created a water park. Now the place is deserted. The swimming pool is half full of rainwater and run-off, sludgy and leaf-splotched. We walk freely through the buildings, behind the cash counters and soda bar. The professor explains how the creek once rushed off the mountainside into a pool of crystalline blue. He and his student friends would jump from it with the local kids. There is a photo of me next to a merry-go-round, half buried in sediment, the once-bright clowny colors faded to a transparent brushing.

- I return to Idaho and take a job at a call center for a local company that sells all-natural bullcrap. When a caller asks me a question that I know I cannot answer, I put them on hold, hang up on them, and return to reading Faulkner's As I Lay Dying, a work that Rulfo cited as an influence to his novel Pedro Páramo. I quit the phone center before they're able to fire me.

- Pedro Páramo, the novel's antagonist, is a wealthy land owner that lives in a town called Comala. Pedro has conglomerated all of the farms in the area to his own through means both dastardly and damning.

- Juan Preciado, the novel's protagonist and most frequent narrator, starts the book by saying, "I came to Comala because I had been told that my father, a man named Pedro Páramo, lived there. It was my mother who told me. And I had promised her that after she died I would go see him. I squeezed her hands as a sign I would do it."

- By the time I finish college, my father—through means neither dastardly nor damning—has conglomerated all of the land belonging to Amle Landon, Arthur Harris, Erroll Spaulding, John Wheeler, Orlando Smith, and Stewart Simmons. What once seven individuals owned is now controlled by one.

- That is how these stories tend to be going …

- Instead of going back to work that ground, I apply

to graduate school. My father does not believe I am leaving until, the week before classes start, I tell him I need time off to pack the moving van. He says, "You're really going to do that?" I answer by driving south on a Thursday morning, my father just starting in on the ripe barley out at the desert farm. In Tucson, the yards are made of dirt and gravel. They pay the landscapers to rake rocks rather than mow grass.

- On the days I feel homesick, I drive south of the city to the Tohono O'odham reservation where the mission of San Xavier del Bac juts out of the desert floor like a white dove. I climb a little hill and look over the reservation farms—those straight field lines, those muddy canals, they feel familiar even though they are foreign. I finish college in Arizona. My father offers me a job back to on the farm. I take it and make the trek back to the northern country in the middle of winter.

- The first year I am home, I help the farm manager repair an irrigation pivot—those monolithic robotic waterers. Water floods the field and I don't have irrigation boots, so I take off my tennis shoes, roll up my jeans, and walk barefoot the quarter-mile into the problem area. I feel as though I am halfway around the world in a rice paddy, tending to my mu.

- I make it through planting, irrigation, and grain harvest, and I find myself in my first complete potato harvest for the first time in a decade. My job is to stay at the cellars and make sure the trucks unload without any problems. My crew eliminates dirt: we pick dirt clods from the potatoes, we shovel dirt from beneath the conveyor belts, we scrape the dirt into a pile away from the line. When I get gear-lube oil on my hands, I wash my hands in dust and mud. I exist in a perpetually filthy state.

- One night—it is past ten o'clock, we are pushing it until midnight or the temperature dips below freezing—a truck arrives with pieces of junk mixed in with the crop.

- Twisted metal and petrified wood.
- A bent irrigation riser.
- The sole of a British Knight sneaker.
- The front half of an old toy pickup.
- A sprocket like an ancient sun dial.
- A chain.
- A septic tank cover.
- A heater grate.

- A mangled egg beater.
- A black plastic toy poodle.
- Truck springs.
- Half a dozen horseshoes.
- Where did this come from? A young kid we've hired for the harvest, all of fourteen, says to me that his father—Arthur Harris's grandson—remembers eating plums off his grandfather's tree during potato harvest thirty years ago.
- And then, like a flood, like a cascade of mud and water, the memory returns: out in the middle of the farm once stood a homestead. Arthur Harris had built a house there, a mile from the nearest paved road, where he stayed during the summer. He hauled in water from the canal and stored it in a wooden tank. He planted apple and plum trees. My father bought him out when I was very young, and we took our depreciated equipment out to the plot for our equipment boneyard. As a kid, I'd go with the mechanic out to Arthur's to scavenge parts. There, I'd eat apples and hunt blow-snakes and hide out in the windowless shack. When my father finished buying out the other men and the land became contiguous, he developed the farm for irrigation pivots and this required him to topple Arthur's place, again move all that machinery, and bury the plot.
- I stand near the pile pulled from the potatoes and think, twenty years ago, when I was seven, I crawled across this junk when it was still above ground. Is this my black toy poodle? My sandbox truck? I sit down in the gravel and measure the British Knight sole up against my boot.
- I reel with the remembering, the re-memory, of the Harris place. Now all is covered by crop rows, by ten feet of soil and rock. What other things, half-alive, did I prematurely inter? I know by now, wise at twenty-seven years old, that the undead doesn't stay buried--it works its way to the surface. Hell, even Juan Preciado, who dies on page 58 of a 125-page book, rises up from the dust, interloping, his voice warning the other ghosts. I know that, as dirty as the farm made me, I can't get clean of it. As long as I live, this mud and crust will mean something to me. I know too there are other clods that have stained me: books, curiosity, a pair of restless legs. What can be done? I stand in the halogen white of the cellar lights, holding the toy pickup.

- If I leave this place, will these memories, these seeds, cease to exist?
- If I stay, what will I never discover?
- I go to my pickup for a notebook and begin to catalog the items collected from the potatoes.
- For the time being, I am here to recall, to investigate, to report, to experience this midway purgatory between earth to earth, ashes to ashes, dust to dust, my only hope to be like Juan Preciado when I'm buried at the Ririe-Skeleton (or elsewhere) and from my back, six feet below the surface, I say to whoever will hear me: I believe the weather is changing up above.

FOUR SEASONS OF MAKING HAY

2012

SPRING

In a tuck of cottonwoods along a feeder canal stood a sandstone milking barn surrounded by corrals grayed from weather. Bales from long-ago harvests, lined with wire panels, separated the pens from the hay field. There was a small yard with dandelions coming through like bright buttons. At the center of the grass, cement steps led up to a small square stucco house.

Mildred Trafton, widowed, stood at the kitchen sink and peeled carrots. Her stare carried out the window and caught on the seedpods wafting down from the trees. Like big wet flakes of snow…or shreds of quilt batting. Either or…or both. What was it that Sheldon always said? A guy can't be worth a dang as long as he's got two choices.

Mildred figured she'd made them wait long enough. She rinsed the carrots and put them in a bowl of water, washed her hands, dried them on her apron, and turned to the kitchen table where Frank Fisher sat with his son Mike.

"How is the arthritis?" Frank asked.

"No worse, no better." Mildred pulled out the empty chair with her gnarled hands, curved and calloused from many years at the teat.

"How are your girls?"

"Like they all but forget the road home."

"Give them time. They'll come around. They still need their good mother."

"Not according to them." Mildred watched Frank chew on her words.

"Well," Frank folded his hands above the table, "let me again express my gratitude for the years I've spent renting this property. I still remember the day that Sheldon offered it."

"Me as well."

"He was a good man. I miss him. Everyone does."

"Lordy, Lordy. I've seen plenty of death."

Frank reached a hand on top of Mildred's fist and gave it a squeeze.

"Alone, it's a hard row to hoe." Mildred dabbed her eyes with her sleeve. "This was never a business meant for one."

"Rest assured that I'll help out however long you need me," Frank said. "But from your message I get the feeling it's time to move in a new direction."

"So it is."

"I've brought a check to settle any outstanding balances."

"No, it's not that." Mildred's gaze drifted to the wall. She couldn't look Frank in the eye. As if that admitted the failure she already felt. "I'm ready to sell."

"Oh."

What could she tell the bishop? That her daughters, once her very miniatures, her four sweet-hearted girls, were hounding her to move to town? That her son-in-law made a special trip out and, rather than bringing Mildred her grandchildren, unrolled the blueprint of a housing development overlaid on her farm? That her casseroles kept spoiling because she couldn't eat so much food on her own?

"What are you considering, Mildred?"

"That goat married to my oldest thinks that this place, what with the canal up front and the river on the backside, could be zoned for houses."

Frank stalled before speaking. "I'm no golf course designer, Mildred. I'm not a wildcat. I'm a farmer, plain and simple, with some head of cattle. I don't have any use for the dairy. The pens maybe, but not the barn. I could grow alfalfa if the price is right."

"What about the house?"

"It might be difficult to find a renter clear out here."

Mildred shifted and crossed her legs and folded her arms across her stomach.

"I have to justify the bottom line to Annie. She's in charge of the books. I'm sure you can understand that. You and Sheldon worked in a similar arrangement for years."

"We bought this ground for a hundred twenty-five dollars an acre. Only the front parcel was clear. Now we have two hundred growing acres, corrals, a milk barn, a stack yard, a garden plot, and a house. We done it all ourselves. So what would you give for it, all told?"

Frank took a day calendar and pencil from his front pocket and worked figures on the inside of the back cover.

"Three-hundred thousand dollars."

Mildred did the math in her head. Tithing and taxes out first, then divided by four. That left each of the girls fifty grand, give or take. At seventy-four, Mildred wouldn't need much more than the leftovers to get by. But then there was the rest home to think about...

"That's with the land at twelve-hundred per acre," Frank said, "the house and outbuildings rounded up to sixty-thousand."

"I won't take less than three-hundred and fifty thousand."

Frank erased and scribbled some more.

"That I can't do. But thirteen-hundred an acre gives you another twenty-thousand. Or we could crop share and get you cash that way."

"No. I want out. I'm done with all this."

"Mildred, you don't have to decide today. I plan to farm until I die. I've got Mikey, too, done with school. We'll be here a long time."

"If you can't meet that price, Bishop, I understand. I'll find someone who will. Not that I want to, mind you, but that I got to."

Frank leaned back and set his hands in his lap. He breathed in deeply and sighed.

"What's fair is fair," Frank said. "I can't pass it up. I'll go three five and four zeros."

Mildred went to her bedroom to get a yellow legal tablet from the dresser. A picture on the wall stopped her. Her and Sheldon on their Massey Ferguson tractor, the only one they'd ever bought new. Sheldon at the wheel; Mildred against him with her feet hanging over the well of the big back tire. Now, that tractor was parked under the cottonwoods, the paint worn off and rust circles cankering the metal panels.

"What could I done?" Mildred asked the photo. "We got a mess of mouths to feed."

At the table, Mildred dated the paper and wrote out a bill of sale. She drew lines where all three could sign: she and Frank as the interested parties, the boy as witness.

When it was all over, she bagged up the carrots in a grocery sack and gave them to Mike. She walked with the Fishers across the yard to their pickup. As if she couldn't allow them to leave.

She shook their hands. They loaded inside. Mildred waited until Frank rolled down his window. "Sheldon had a saying about land," Mildred said. "The first generation earns it, the second spends it, and the third piddles it away. I guess I just done all three."

SUMMER

Rose Moss, girlfriend to Mike Fisher, trailed her boyfriend and his big hay-cutting machine, the swather, down a dirt lane. Rose was in her Chevy Vega, hazard lights blinking, like she'd done all the way from Poplar. Rose had been on her way to work at the sandwich shop when Mike called to explain he needed her help. But it wasn't an explanation, it was a demand formed around an emergency. When Rose said she was on shift, Mike said he'd pay her double to come help him. He said Frank had busted his butt for taking so much time on repairs and now the hay was going to get rained on. Rose, seventeen, wanted to protect Mike. His father was too hard on him. Mike was an eighteen year old who barely finished high school because of how much time he spent working on the farm. Rose called in sick and met

Mike at the gas station.

Rose hadn't blamed Mike for hiding her from his parents for so long. Frank, a Mormon bishop, was grizzled and stoic and generally unkind, especially when it came to his son. Annie fell in step behind her husband. Rose was a baptized Catholic who wore a cross around her neck and had a tattoo of a starfish on her ankle. She'd moved from Houston once her dad bolted on her and her mother. That was two years ago; she still felt like a stranger in rural Idaho. She met Mike at a bonfire out in the country, then he started coming by the sandwich shop (Rose later learned Mike didn't even like tuna, he ordered it because it was cheap then threw the sandwiches away, after he'd seen her), then they started going for late-night drives, and now they were going out proper. Mike finally took her to a Mormon Stake Conference. Rose could see, even from her metal folding chair set up on the basketball court overflow, that Frank had big hands and cold eyes. The man gave her an uneasy feeling.

Rose parked her car on the far side of the haystacks and climbed up the ladder to the swather's cabin. Mike swung open the glass door and cleared his jacket off his lunch cooler so Rose had a place to sit. He throttled up and trundled the swather along the dirt tracks at the edge of the field. A speckled red fawn spooked in the hay and surged through the emerald lucerne. Mike stopped the machine and they watched the deer stott out and disappear into the trees.

"My gosh!" Rose said. "It was so fragile. With every jump I thought those little legs might break in two."

"Ten bucks says its ma will be by shortly."

Sure enough, the doe appeared. It pawed and huffed until it caught the fawn's scent spoor and followed it into the woods.

Mike started back up and traveled the swather to the field's bottom and then navigated up the gravel ramp to the road on top of the levee. The levee was ten feet high and bisected the two Trafton fields. The high-riding swather suspended Mike and Rose ten feet higher than that. Sheldon had built the dike to keep the Snake River—which in wet years swelled with mountain runoff—from flooding his crop. Rose imagined she was riding shotgun on a stagecoach.

"If this isn't a perfect day," Rose said, sitting on the lunchbox and hugging her knees, "I don't know what is."

Mike slowed the machine to a crawl and inched down the levee and into the field. He put the machine in park and patted Rose's knee.

"Sit up for a second. I need a sandwich."

Rose got out two cans of soda, a Mason jar of peaches, and two ham-and-cheeses. Rose ate and watched Mike drive the clunking machine with his elbows and take hurried bites of his sandwich. At the end of the pass, Mike stopped the swather and moved the seat's armrest. Rose squeezed next to him in the chair and they pressed together and started kissing. Rose thought Mike's mouth tasted of cheddar and wheat. Beneath that, though, Rose tasted Mike's desire for her. That made it more palatable.

When static crackled from the farm CB—Frank calling for Otto, the mechanic—Mike jumped to attention. As if Frank himself was banging at the door. He took his arms from around her neck and put his hands back on the steering wheel.

"Better get back to work," Mike said. Mike lowered the header and engaged the machine and nudged the swather into the hay. It chewed a wide path and behind it left the hay piled to dry in a windrow.

Rose moved back to the cooler. Her mood went from electric to dead. This was the story of their relationship: once Frank showed up, even in static forms through the airwaves, Mike's fire blew out. Rose had hoped, early on, that this might change. But it hadn't. Rose fixated on the space between the swather header and the big drive tires. In that open swatch, she saw black flitting mice, running for their lives.

"What happens to all of those?" Rose said. The rodents flitted and zigzagged over the exposed earth.

"Well, first, they die. Then what the hawks don't pick up gets baled. I've seen just about everything in bales. Pop cans. Twine. Bird bones. Badgers. Bunnies."

"Gross."

"It's fight or flight. Running would save them most of the time. But there's that idea to dig down, hunker in, and see it through."

"Stop! Now I'm thinking about cows eating mice and me drinking their milk and then all that garbage floating around inside me."

"It gets pasteurized. All the germs boil out."

"Please, stop."

"They don't feel any pain. I promise. It happens so fast..."

"Everything hurts, Mike. Don't be dense."

"I'm dense, huh? What do you know about all of this? Zero. Zilch. Nada."

Rose hugged her knees and scooted around on the cooler. "This is really comfortable, Mike. Thanks for bringing me along. To sit on your floor and be berated by you."

"All of the sudden I get the feeling this ain't about mice at all."

The swather hummed and rocked. Mike made two passes along the outside and started working back and forth across the field. When Mike raised the header to turn, sunlight glinted off the row of wet knives and sparkled the reel's steel fingers.

"Does anyone live back at the house?" Rose asked. "I left my CDs on the seat."

"Just an old lady. Nothing to worry about. She spent her whole life in the milk barn working with her husband. He died last year."

"And she's still here by herself? That's so sad."

"It's something."

Rose looked up at Mike. He had one hand on the steering wheel and the other on the throttle lever. His eyes were on the edge of the header so he could keep his line. She liked it when he concentrated.

He pursed his lips and squinted and looked very serious. She regretted what she said. Mike didn't know any better. And it wasn't too bad on the cooler.

"That would be a good life," Rose said. "Waking up together, working side by side."

"Trust me, it ain't peachy. Frank and Annie have their days."

"What other way would you want it?"

Mike started to speak but stopped himself. He turned the tractor and grimaced out the window and leaned his head to listen.

"I can't be pinned down forever," he said.

Rose grew quiet, then sad, then mad. Was Mike saying something about her?

"How could you leave a place like this?"

"I'm not so sure I have a choice. Frank has a way of keeping me around. But if I could, I'd buy my own tractor-trailer. A Peterbilt. Base out of Rigby, which would keep Pops and Ma happy, and still see the world."

"I've been on too many highways. No way. Huh-uh."

"If you were with me, we'd have a good time. Promise."

Rose thought about the trip that brought her and her mother from Texas to Idaho. The wind had blown so hard that the police closed off the interstate. They waited half a day in Pocatello. When they started again, they passed a semi tipped over in the borrowpit.

"Truckers call a Peterbilt 'The Celestial Body' because they ride like a piece of heaven. Pops only has the Kenworth—it's about as smooth as a bumper car."

Rose scraped beneath her fingernails with her thumbnail. That truck looked like a turtle on its back, unable to right itself. She imagined herself trapped inside the cabin, belted into the seat, hanging upside down until someone showed up to save her.

"It wouldn't be like this piece of crap," Mike said, and knocked the swather's steering wheel with his knuckles. "Two chairs, both air-ride. I'd get a good mattress for the sleeper and put in a TV and a mini-fridge. We could get white-line fever and go on forever."

The header bounced, a hard thump interrupted the whirr of the machine. Mike jerked back the throttle and raised the header and shut off the motor. He went down the ladder backwards and jumped the last two rungs to the ground and swished through the hay to the front.

Rose was embarrassed for second-guessing Mike. If he wanted to truck, why shouldn't he? She felt bad for making him explain himself. Rose imagined that he felt like she had felt when she told her mother she was going to church with Mike. Her mother cried about how her only daughter was going to depart from the only thing that had been the only constant in her lonely life. Honesty, a tricky business, hurt people.

Mike came back up the ladder.

"Slide me that toolbox. And come down. I want to show you

something."

Rose did. Mike took her by the hand and they ducked under the reel to the intake. Thousands of ladybugs teemed inside the machine and made the metal look alive and shifting.

"They eat aphids," Mike said. "Nature's own pest control. Pretty crazy, right?"

"So those are in my milk too? Gross. Do you have to kill them or something?"

"See this? I hit a rock and it broke the knives. Looks like someone punched out the swather's two front teeth. But it's better than what I thought. I figured that little fawn had come back and I'd hit it. Wouldn't be the first time. Won't be the last."

Rose went back up the ladder and sat in the chair behind the steering column. She looked out the front window and saw Mike's feet sticking out of the swather's mouth. She considered how many years of this she'd have to endure if she stayed with Mike. She loved him, sure, and he was her only real friend in this place. But what if she wanted something different? How could she go to college here? And no matter how perfect her relationship was with Mike, Rose had to consider the drama his parents and the church could cause for them.

Mike climbed up, carrying the two halves of the rock and his toolbox. He dropped them on the outside step. Rose noticed the sweat beaded on his brow, and his pale gray countenance.

"What's the matter?" Rose asked. She got out of the captain chair and they orbited around each other in that cramped space. Mike plopped down on his seat. Rose crouched on the cooler. "You look like you saw the devil himself."

"I...I don't know. Something happened to me down there. Look, I know you're mad at me. Look, I know I talk too much, and I push things. I was thinking about that, turning the wrenches, and I knew you were up here at the controls. And I thought, 'What if Rose turns the key?' I'd be stabbed by the tines and diced by the knives and squeezed through the conditioner and shot out the back end."

"Oh, Mikey. I wouldn't ever hurt you," Rose stood now, pulled Mike's clammy head against her neck. "Calm down, everything's okay."

Mike pulled back. "I thought, 'My life is in her hands. What is she going to do?'"

"Nothing happened. We're both okay. I'll protect you, I promise."

Mike wiped his forehead on his t-shirts sleeve. "Cripes, I'm sorry. For everything. I know things are weird right now. I'll make them better. Swear it."

Rose hushed him and took her seat and they went back to work. They cut hay for hours. They talked and laughed and argued playfully. For twenty minutes, Rose laid her head on Mike's leg and napped. Later, in the gloaming, when it was dusty and dusky and the lights didn't make a difference but Mike turned them on anyways, they stopped for a break. Outside, it smelled of pepper. They got out and stretched and grinned at the parallel harvest rows behind them. Windrows, though everyone around here called them Win Rows. Rose followed Mike through the poplar trees to the bank of the Snake. They sat in the sedge and watched the dirty rushing water and listened to the red-winged blackbirds.

Soon, they started kissing, and did that for quite a while, until they couldn't anymore and were agitated enough to progress. Mike pulled off his shirt and spread it behind Rose, and flattened down the weeds. All the while Rose could hear Mike's father lecturing from the pulpit about the sin second only to murder, fornication. Fornication meant damnation, it was an all-important life-or-death choice every time. Rose had been warned by the bishop himself, and and yet she could not stop her passion, nor could she stop Mike's, and there in the weeds like beasts they again succumbed to the flesh. It was only when they were walking back to the tractor that Mike became incensed with himself for his based and fallen behavior, and he began to blame Rose, saying it was her fault, that her jeans made him do it, and that's why he'd forgotten to use any protection, he'd been distracted by her beauty and allure, and had forgotten it once again.

Rose did not panic outright. This wasn't the first time something like this had happened to her, or them. Mike had promised it wouldn't happen again. Like the times before, Rose thought of her own mother, pregnant at seventeen, now living in a trailer behind Rigby's lone museum—a place full of taxidermied moose and deer and elk and stuffed bears and mountain lion rugs and rusted plows and black-and-white photos. She did not want to be trophied in Jay County. She did not need a cub. What she needed was for Mike to do what he said he'd do. And he didn't. He hadn't. He'd lied.

Rose diverted from Mike in the dark and went deeper into the woods saying she needed a private moment. She considered walking on, all the way to town and then some, she was so mortified. Or hiding until Mike left. She could not face her mother—or heaven forbid, Frank and Annie—with a taut belly. She could thumb back to Texas and stay with her cousin. There were clinics there, too. But it was night-dark now. She knew ten more steps and she'd be lost until morning. Rose called out for Mike, and followed his voice back to him.

"Rosy," Mike said, and took her hand. "I didn't mean to. You looked so good, I couldn't stop myself. Let's just wait and see."

Rose shook loose and marched in a direction she thought led back to the swather.

"If this goes worst-case scenario, I'll tell my parents and I'll ask your mom for your hand and my dad can marry us and we'll live on the farm and, seriously, I'll take care of you, you'll never have to worry about a thing."

Rose stopped. "Worst-case scenario? What are you saying, worst-case scenario?"

"I mean. Oh, Rosy, you know what I mean."

Rose walked right past the swather when they got to it. Mike climbed up and started it; he'd have to park it back at the house. Rose started to run. She climbed the levee and made it halfway back to the Vega before Mike caught up to her in the swather. The bright halogen lights enveloped her and made ghosts of the dust she kicked up. So bright and otherworldly that Rose thought of the women on TV from the shows her mother watched while she drank herself to sleep. The women who were first blinded by the alien's UFOs, abducted and whisked away to a life of experimentation and, afterwards, confusion, and eternal damnation, of course, and outer darkness after that.

FALL

Frank and Mike trashed the Trafton place. They knocked off fence poles until the strikes from the sledges shook their forearms to a throbbing numb, and wound handfuls of baling twine into oversized skeins, and gathered maverick soda cups, lengths of lead pipe, gunny sacks, and felled tree boughs. They piled everything inside the milk barn, where buzzing flies rose from calf skeletons and bounced against the walls.

The operation was in that few-week September limbo between grain and potato harvest. The leaves from the trees were brown and wisped, the grass a dry dead gold. Other men had started turning their soil for fall work. The moon smoldered orange from stubble burns. Frank thought of all that needed to happen in the next few weeks, but also of what the Trafton place lacked for next year. He had plans, like always, two steps ahead of everyone else.

But lately, Frank waxed nostalgic for the past. Hard to believe that when he was a kid in Poplar, there was a movie theater, a two-story log hotel, a hardwood rollerskating rink, Sappington's Drug Store, and a New Year's Eve Dance that brought folks from three counties. A pool hall suitable for ladies, four grain elevators, and two lumberyards. Even though Poplar got a late start as far as frontier towns went—1914, officially—it boomed when world wheat hit records during the Great War. The railroad sent a crew to lay a spur to the nameless town, and the chief dubbed it after the trees along the river.

The winds of change, Frank thought, blow in quick and sure. Now, without the gas station and the sandwich shop, Poplar wouldn't have food to buy. And though Beto reminisced of calmer days on the farm, Frank only knew go, go, go. Tractors ran from April until they were stopped by snow. Starting with the first crop of hay, seconding and thirding into August; itchy weeks of cutting and trucking barley; then grain; then a half-month of spuds. Plus cows to feed and calve and keep healthy all seasons in between. Back in the day, the schools let out for Spud Harvest and all the kids got jobs on farms. Now, all of

Frank's farmer friends worked alone, their children off to college to be lawyers or accountants or entrepreneurs with their parents' money.

That morning, Frank brought Mike to Trafton's and pointed out what he wanted demolished. Mike hadn't said a word in response, whereas usually he asked for further detail, wanting to know what Frank had in mind. Mikey seemed to be miles away, in his own head. So Frank didn't tell his son that he'd build up new aluminum corrals for calving and install a shipping chute. A nice winter calving facility protected by trees. Maybe even buy fifty extra off-colored beefs, or some pigs, just to finish-feed and truck to auction.

What a boy, Frank thought. Looks about as happy as a knot.

Frank and Mike emptied the tools—two shovels, a pry-bar, hammers, and sledges—from the back of the pickup and started in. There were two sets of pole corrals with cracked concrete mangers. A massive mound of manure climbed the pens. Old crap pushed against the bottom rung. The milk barn with bars over the windows. A horse trailer faded to a lackluster pink and missing one of its four tires, its hitch resting on a piece of cinderblock, parked in weeds. Next to it was a pea-green Dodge, one headlight, rusty rims, no tailgate. An open-cab tractor near an orange pipe trailer, and a broken fertilizer cart.

An hour into the destruction, Frank discovered a bunch of cracked, mismatched, unusable tires. He called for Mike and asked him what they should do with them.

"We could save them," Mike said. "For the vine roller or something."

"No," Frank said. "Let's burn them. Roll them over to the barn pile."

"Let's put them in your pickup and haul them," Mike suggested.

"I just cleaned it," Frank said. "Go see if that Dodge'll run."

Mike popped the hood and checked the oil and hooked up the battery. It started. They loaded the tires into the back of the truck and drove to the barn door and stacked them there.

Beto showed up in the haying John Deere, four long spears sticking off the farmhand. He revved up the tractor and plowed into the bad fence. He picked up what he could with the forks and dumped it on top the milk barn, and brought down the implement's heel against the main joist and caved in the roof. The pile grew into a mangled pyramid.

This is the work I need, Frank thought as he pitched on more garbage. Not a tractor jockey. Not a chauffeur. Not three-hour bank meetings. Sweat and ache, like my younger days. Even now, old as I am, I can outwork Mike or Beto or anyone else. That's power.

But Frank found himself caught off guard when Mildred appeared after noon. By then nearly everything was in shambles. Frank stopped and watched her pull past her former house, vacant now a month, in her powder blue Oldsmobile and, for a split second, he thought to hide himself behind the barn. That old bird was the last person he wanted to see. Frank felt as exposed as that one time Mike came around the shop and caught him pissing in the bushes. Mildred parked and bonked on the horn.

"Mike," Frank said, "go see what she needs."

Mike leaned his pry-bar against the truck and jogged over then came right back. "She wants to talk to you."

All the while, Mildred kept on that horn, blaring it Frank's way. She didn't let up until Frank started in her direction. When Frank was close enough to talk, instead of rolling down the window, Mildred threw open the door and stuck out a leg. Tan slacks reached up mid-calf and exposed pasty ankles, sagging socks, worn-out sneakers. Her hard-bitten fingers hooked like claws and rested on the handle. Respirator tubes, connected to a tank on the floor, traced her chin and ended with a fixture that metronomed oxygen into her nostrils.

"I lived a good life here," Mildred said, her voice a broken green bottle.

Frank shoved his hands into his pockets and scanned across the wreckage. He was exhausted. From being the big bad boss, from being bishop, from trying to show Mike how to be a man. Dang, Mildred. It's not my fault Sheldon didn't buy more land, or get his crops to make grade, or finance your daughters. It's not my fault you two didn't expand or adapt. I'm not building my mansion overtop your lot or hooking my pickup to your trailer or subdividing this rocky parcel. I'm just doing what I know how, what I judge best. Nothing more, nothing less.

But Frank didn't speak. He stood there, gruff and quiet. Mildred looked over her bowdlerized plot, a place where she'd clocked thousands of hours, tended to her garden, ate picnic meals spread across the hood of a pickup with her one and only.

"Don't burn all them tires," Mildred said. "Someone's always needing a spare."

"Mildred, those tires are older than both of us."

"Set them aside. I'll get a guy to come get them."

Frank stared at the slicks. With such thin walls and cracked rubber, they'd blow and put a truck into a tailspin and kill everyone involved. But then, this argument was destined for a dead-end. The goal for Frank now was to frost this deal up, be done with this woman, and move on.

"Sure, Mildred, we can do that."

Mildred sat with her door open and nodded. Frank hollered instructions at Mike. Mike started to roll the tires one by one and stack them beneath the cottonwoods.

"Tell him to get your pickup there, Frank," Mildred said. "He'll be all day doing that. Throw them in back. Work smarter, not harder. Sheldon's words, not mine."

Again, Frank hollered instructions. Mike did as told, driving Frank's spotless pickup through the dust and garbage, and backed up to the garbage pile.

Frank and Mildred watched Mike struggle to rip the tires from beneath the posts and wire. Mildred started honking the horn until Mike jogged back over.

"What? Frank never buys you any tools?" Mildred asked Mike.

Frank felt his face burn.

Mildred popped her trunk. "Dig around back there. Find something useful."

Frank went with Mike to the back of the Olds and lifted the trunk lid. Tools were scattered across the floor, piled in milk crates, in the seam near the spare tire. Mike and Frank began to sift: pipe wrenches, crescent wrenches, monkey wrenches, hammers; a hatchet, files, zip ties, duct tape; sockets of three-eighths, five-eighths, seven-eighths... and then Mike discovered a pair of shiny, red-handled, slip-jointed pliers. They were stainless steel, long and heavy, and held together by a smooth rivet.

"Those won't work," Frank said. "Better get some dikes."

"They're fine," Mike said. He showed them to Mildred for her acknowledgment and went back to the tangled tires.

"Anything else, Sister Trafton?" Frank asked.

"You can tell a man by how he works a pair of pliers. Sheldon taught me that."

"I got to get back to work myself. Take care now, Mildred."

Frank waited for the woman to get her leg inside the car. He shut the door for her and waited until she fired up the Olds and chuffed and sputtered past the house. Frank grumbled while walking back to Mike. He stood a few feet away, thinking to himself, as he watched his son. Mike gripped the pliers and tried to wrench loose a knobby rim from the wire. But he fumbled the tool. He dropped the pliers more than once and finally resorted to operating it with both hands.

"No, no," Frank said, talking the pliers from Mike. "One-handed. You know better."

Frank tried to give them back to Mike but he wouldn't take them. He kept his arms stuck in his pockets. Frank dropped the pliers in the dirt at Mike's feet.

"Do I have to do everything around here?" Frank asked.

"You know what, Pops. You do. Because I quit."

"Oh, you do, huh?"

"This is bullcrap."

Frank picked up the pliers. "Just like you were done when you didn't move your pipe and I caught you? Or like when you stopped feeding the cows and I found you asleep on the stack?"

"I ain't spending my life feeling like I'm the runny crap on the ugly boots of my rude dad."

"Watch your mouth."

"Whatever." Mike slung his pry-bar deep into the trash pile and started for the road.

"How you going to get home?" Frank yelled. "Whose food are you going to eat tonight?"

Mike never even turned around.

Frank went to his pickup and set out a box of matches and jugs of diesel. He waved Beto out of the tractor and sent him in his pickup with instructions to stop and get Mike and take him to the house. Give a kid an inch and he'll take it a mile. He'll sort it out tonight.

Frank spent the rest of the afternoon digging a firebreak. A few hours before dark, Frank set the debris pile on fire. He threw the pliers in for good measure. Frank looked through the smoke and wondered if Mildred had returned. Or Mike. Of course, neither of them did, and this made Frank feel worse.

Where had he gone wrong with his boy? This boy, who had exited Frank's life in phases. Out of diapers, out of the house, out of the Church, and now right off the farm?

In the last hour of the dim gray day, Frank leaned on his shovel and listened to the canal's purling, and the pops and hisses of the posts and planks. Frank smelled the smoldering tar, the manure, and his own mephitic reek. He looked to the road and exhaled and watched the smoke dissipate into the dark. Annie would know to come pick him up sometime tonight, he was sure. Mike can leave. Let him. So can Mildred. Both deserve what they get. But one thing's for certain, Frank thought. I earned this place. All of it—every acre, each machine—is mine. I've done it all from start to finish. Lest they forget: It was me who scaled that rotten mess. I sloshed out the fuel and watched it pool onto the boards and soak into the poles. I struck the matches. I set the flame. And while Mike told his sob story to what's-her-name, and Annie fixed supper, and Mildred wheeled her tank through the rest home doors, I scrambled down the pile and saw the fire lick the sky. I stood alone against the fire and, when the heat grew too strong, I used my hands to hide my face.

WINTER

Mike brushed sheaves off the haying flatbed and backed it inside his parent's garage. Otto, the mechanic, helped him carry his bed and dressers and boxes of clothing up the stairs. They lashed it all in place on the truck with motorcycle tie-downs. Mike took the backroads to the Trafton house. Otto, in Mike's Jeep, beat him there. Mike backed to the front door. He and Otto shuffled the items across the threshold and inside the house. Mike kept watching the road for Rose's Vega. They'd agreed to meet at the house at ten. It was eleven now; she was nowhere to be found.

"You know, life ain't easy," Otto said. "It takes a big man to own up to his mistakes."

Mike nodded and said thank you and watched Otto leave in

the flatbed. Mike felt a twinge of shame. Otto had been honest—why couldn't Mike be honest in return? Mike's sense of honest had changed; it no longer meant speaking every thought that came into his mind. Silence was honest. Maybe the only honorable thing he could do. So he hadn't told Otto to mind his own business, that he had no right judging Mike's life as a mistake.

And, in the same way, Mike hadn't told Rose about his fears. He was not sure that he loved her. He wasn't even sure he knew what love meant. But when Rose started to talk about returning to Texas and giving the baby up, or giving up on the baby, Mike panicked. He never discussed with Rose about what exactly this meant—if she was talking Texas because she wanted out, or giving Mike an ultimatum to move ahead—and instead went to a pawn shop in Idaho Falls and bought a two-hundred-dollar ring and proposed. They married at the Jefferson County courthouse the following week, Rose's mother there to sign for her seventeen-year-old daughter. They found an off-duty cop who agreed to serve as second witness. The four of them stood before the judge. Mike and Rose Fisher, man and wife.

That was two months ago, before Rose really started showing. She continued to live with her mother; Mike with his parents. Mike didn't tell Frank and Annie. He'd taken a job working for one of the grain elevators in Poplar, unloading trucks and sweeping bins. Everything seemed fine until Annie ran into Rose at Wal-Mart and saw the secret. That night, Mike came home to Frank and Annie waiting in ambush at the kitchen table. There was yelling, then tears, then Frank—the ever-present planner—out with his notebook penciling Mike's budget.

Frank offered Mike a job that very night, salary with a company truck and phone and housing included.

Mike, seeing the string of numbers he'd have to service—hospital bills and medicines and diapers and electricity and food costs—accepted.

When he told Rose the next day, she flipped out, saying how it was Frank's way of controlling them. Just another instance of Mike rolling over for his father. Mike slammed an open hand on the table and left steaming. Mike was bent over one way and humped the other. No winning for him.

Now, in this matchbox of a house, Mike lined the cabinets with a few jars of peaches and raspberries pilfered from his mother's cold storage, waiting for a wife that might not even show, having to wake up for a job he did not want, working for a man he did not understand. Outside, early December, the first snow still not having arrived but chilly as bull teats.

Mike was searching the walls for the thermostat when he heard a car. He was excited to see Rose, but he knew he'd ask her what took her so long and pout until she apologized. But it wasn't Rose; instead, Frank and Annie in Annie's SUV. A surprise visit. Mike watched them park, open up the back, and unload brown bags full of food.

Annie started to fill the fridge with milk and bread and cheese and stacked meat in the freezer while Mike and Frank set up the bed in the back.

"You didn't have to do this," Mike said. "I can get by on my own."

"A guy would never guess there once was a dairy back here. We did ourselves a favor by cleaning up that mess. Looks real nice."

Mike nodded. Just like Frank, to disregard him. In the month following the demolition, men hauled away the Dodge and the trailers but never took the stack of tires. Mike's job one Saturday had been to take them to town and get stuck with a recycling fee.

"Where's Rose?" Frank asked.

"She got hung up in town."

"It'll be good to have a lady's touch around here. She'll doll it up nice."

Mike and Frank assembled the bed-frame. Mike spun the bolts finger-tight.

"Wish I had those pliers Mildred gave me. They'd be nice right about now."

Frank moved off his knees and hunkered on the balls of his feet and rested elbows to knees. He took a pair of pinchers from his belt holster and passed them to Mike. "For cripe's sake. Drop it. You got bigger fish to fry now."

"You don't understand..."

"I'll buy you as many pliers as you want. But move on. What you once had is now gone."

They finished the frame and lifted the mattresses into place and went to the kitchen. Annie fussed and explained her food ordering, but after a minute threw up her hands.

"Oh, Mikey, what am I saying? You're big! You can figure it out!"

Mike followed his parents out. He waved to them as they left. He could see his mother crying. As if she had so much to be upset about. As if her pain meant more than Mike's. He'd given up everything. Now, here he was, alone. Where was Rose? Had she gone in to work? Or was she on the Interstate, headed south? Mike opened a can of soup and drank it like a pop.

Mike felt suffocated in the house. He put on his jacket and his rancher hat and walked outside. Across the dead grass, through the dead weeds, into the naked trees. He kept his hands in his coat pockets and listened for fowl. He found the canal, a feeder that was twenty feet wide and straight as a fence line, and walked down into its empty bottom. The canal company cut the water a week ago. Large puddles were left. Mike moved upstream and eyed the stagnant water looking for whitefish that might still be breathing.

He walked and wondered. What if Rose didn't come home tonight? He'd drive to her mother's house. But then what—make her come home? If she didn't want to be with him, then fine. But what if she did show up? How mean would he be to her? The poor girl was pregnant, so not too harsh. But it wasn't fair he was left alone to do all the chores. He'd have to let her know that. Then Mike's thoughts got away from him. What if Rose miscarried and they were left married and without child and stuck on the farm? What if Rose died in childbirth? What if Rose's mom got sick and had to come live with them? What if the ham fell out of the tree and killed the baby?

Mike was so worked up he didn't hear the boy until he was nigh upon him. A young kid, maybe ten, standing along a large puddle with a big forked stick. The boy dipped into the shallow pool and flipped a suckerfish onto the rocks. A golden dog latched onto it and shook it dead.

"What are you doing?" Mike asked.

"Fishing," the boy said. He had a speech impediment, said his Ss like THs. He was freckled with dirty blonde hair and wore an old tattered ski coat two sizes too big.

"No, I mean, what are you doing out here by yourself?"

"Fishing. And looking for my cat, Whiskers. Seen her?"

Mike shook his head.

The kid flung out another fish. The dog ate it, threw it up, lapped up the puke.

"Where do you live?"

"Mom said not to talk to strangers."

"Does she know you're out here?"

"She's at work."

"What about your dad?"

"He went to Hell."

"It's almost dark. You want some help getting home?"

The kid stopped fishing and looked Mike up and down.

"You look sad, mister."

"I am sad."

"Me too. I haven't seen Whiskers since last Christmas. She used to hunt mice with Buster. That's my dog. Buster's sad too. Look at him."

The dog had moved into the grass on the bank and was laying his head on his crossed paws, content and asleep.

"Come on," Mike said. "We better get home. Our moms will worry about us."

"Help me look for Whiskers."

"Only for a bit," Mike said. "But then we have to go."

"What you got to do," the kid said, "is put your hands like this and say, 'Whiskers! Whiskers!' then make kissy noises."

Mike did it.

"You're saying it wrong. 'Whiskers!' Whiskers!'"

Mike said it like the kid, with a lisp, and the kid's face lit up. They walked around the river bottom saying the cat's name over and over, smacking their lips, for ten minutes.

Nothing doing. The kid whistled for his dog and, without saying goodbye, disappeared into the trees.

Dusk came. Mike walked back up the canal toward the Trafton house. He was calmed some by the kid, even though he knew that cat was long gone. Nevertheless, Mike kept calling for that cat, even after dark all the way back. He walked into the house alone, and called for the cat, and got no response. Mike stood alone in the kitchen. He had everything, a new house, a new wife, a new life, and he'd never felt more alone.

THE FOURTH ELEMENT

2011

"If it'll grow sage brush," says Kent, "it'll grow grain." A staid man with a shadow of a red stubble beard who has farmed for my father for thirteen years, he clears his throat. "That was my grandpa's rule when he bought land."

Kent's family land—dry farm fields in the hilly country forty miles north of our farm—would have been irrigated had the Teton Dam not suffered its catastrophic failure in 1976. The dam collapse killed eleven people, over thirteen thousand cattle, and the dream of irrigating acreage that before had only been watered by rain.

My father directs his pickup across the washboard gravel roads and adds, "The taller the sage, the better the drink. That's the way I learned it."

Outside, the season showcases dry Idaho July, and the three of us drive through country high above the basin that holds many of Idaho's fertile farms. The prairie grass and thistle paints the horizon in parched amber waves; the blue-gray outline of northern mountains stand like afterthoughts. We roll up and down the hills in search of a clearing where we can spy on the Californians who have been stealing our water.

Eventually, my father stops the pickup on a bald knoll. Our lookout rims the southern edge of a horseshoe-shaped valley. A newly cut road switch-backs down the basin around the far hill's face. It's drastic, this carving out, a scar tearing through the grass. Down one swale and into the valley's bottom is a winding stretch of quaking asps and cottonwoods and willows: the trees' bright green a stark offset to the surrounding toasted flora. The green denotes water, that slippery commodity that controls this land.

"That stream must feed the lake," my father says. He reaches behind the driver's seat, extracts binoculars, and glasses the streambed as if hunting for elk.

Every Monday morning from May until September, my father and Kent calculate how many square inches of water to put across their fields of potatoes and grain. Their pumps pull from Birch Creek and pipe the water over three miles of fields. But for the past two weeks, their irrigation system has been running with insufficient water pressure. Their estimates have been undercut; subsequently, their crops suffer. At first, they were mystified. But then, just last week, my father figured it out.

Earlier this year, California investors had purchased a ranch above Birch Creek and subdivided it into twenty-five lots. My father and Kent had watched the investors as they built roads and stretched power lines to their land, not paying them much mind. But one day last week my father was driving up and down Birch Creek Road and discovered an industrial-sized tanker pumping water from the creek.

"He was just leaving," my father says, "so I blocked him with my truck and walked up to his window. Just a worker guy, no say in anything, but I lit into him and got his boss' phone number. At first, the boss denied that he'd told his crew to take water from the creek, but eventually he admitted to it. They were using the water up on their roads to keep the dust down and to mix their cement. Once he admitted to it, he even had the nerve to tell me the investors had the legitimate water rights."

Water rights—the legal permission to use water from wells, springs, rivers, canals, and aquifers—are paramount in this country. When property is bought and sold in Idaho; mature water rights can often double and triple the land value. Water rights don't prove ownership of water, but rather deed a possession of usage. The use of public waters without a water right is illegal, the sole exception being domestic-use water, as a homeowner deserves water for his or her home as well as enough to irrigate up to half an acre. Idaho law provides civil penalties for appropriating water without a valid right.

"But that's a bold-faced lie," my father says, handing me the binoculars. "They don't have water rights up here—I own them all."

I know my father means business. When I recall memories of family prayer (a rite my father and mother and sisters and I practiced together every morning) I cannot remember one invocation that didn't contain a plea concerning water. We prayed for snowpack in the winter, rainfall in the spring, and celestial restraint during planting and harvest. My father watched the Weather Channel like it was prophetic alarm, carrying his muddy boots into the living room and dressing in front of the television. He'd edge out on the couch and strain to hear everything. I've been hushed innumerable times during the five-day forecast.

A discussion of western water rights—a topic so convoluted and complicated on its own—is difficult to have today without including ecology. Salmon, trout, river otters, and myriad other fauna enter the conversation. But one species that perhaps I never before considered is the beaver. Our vernacular today provides varying connotations that involve the fury dam-builder: the eager office worker, a person with incisors like Chiclets, even an anatomical reference to the polestar of feminine sexuality. But often overlooked is what scientists have dubbed the water-dwelling rodents: Little People. Beavers mate for life, protect their family, build hovels and lodges, congregate amongst cousins and grandparents and aunts, and fight other beavers that don't share their bloodlines. Studies show that humans and beavers share survival mechanisms. Like humans, beavers are incredibly adept at altering their habitat to their suit needs, even diverting streams so that the water runs closer to more favorable stands of trees. It would be much easier for the beavers to burrow for shelter in the riparian muck, but instead they stop the water and build dams. One scientist employs that beavers always have to be moving, working. Hence the busyness. Another posits that beavers disdain the sound of running water and construct dams in the narrowest, noisiest point of streams to quell the riffle. In one study, a man put out speakers near mature beaver dams and amplified the sound of running water. He returned to discover them buried under sticks and stones until silenced.

In 1889, a New York Times writer visited the Gem state and published an article entitled "Idaho Has a Great Future." He wrote: "When this territory was named 'the Gem of the Mountains' it could not have been for anything that was seen in Pocatello; or if it was, then it must have been named just for its hardness." He later noted, "The only crop secured from the soil is one of dust."

I imagine the writer alone in his slat-board hotel room, plunking out his article while the wind whistles through the wall cracks and railroad cars thunder past his window. The man coughs and coughs again, the ever-present dirt clouding his lungs.

Technically, most of Idaho is a high desert with its annual rainfall of eight to twelve inches, though I recall years mostly between four and six. Once the mining petered, all that remained was dry, unusable land. Irrigation had been attempted a number of times. First up north in Spalding, the year 1837, at the Whitman missionary farm. In the 1850s, homesteaders dug crude ditches in the Boise Valley to irrigate small vegetable plots for harvests to be sold to the influx of prospectors. Near modern-day Preston, Mormons migrated from Utah and claimed water from Maple Creek. Idaho's population hardly grew in the 1850s and 60s, and then was restricted to areas close to rivers and streams. Farmers tried water-wheels and other primitive transports but none could be used large-scale. The 1880s brought private-venture canal companies to establish an intricate irrigation diversion that would take water from the Snake and other rivers, but money soon ran out. By 1889—the year the Times writer visited— private investors and farmers had dug nearly forty canals. But none had ever carried water; before that occurred, the banks had sent foreclosure notices.

The rub was that the Snake River plain—a broad tectonic depression on top of rhyolitic ash-flow tuff—held immense agricultural potential. With nitrates and residual ash compressed for millions of years (Idaho's whole southern section is pocked with volcanic remnants), the dirt could grow a wide variety of crops. But by 1890 momentum for growth had waned considerably; without water, life out west proved impossible. A series of government acts saved the land, at least for human habitation. The 1877 Desert Land Act morphed into the 1894 Carey Act, which finalized in 1902 with the Newlands Reclamation Act—all of these plans centering on the sale of public land to private investors. The federal government would sell tracts and with the money, "plan, construct, and manage irrigation projects for the purpose of reclaiming marginal lands." Farmers and ranchers supported the ongoing costs by paying agreed-upon fees and taxes.

Once canals were established, Idaho blossomed, but more problems followed after the surface water ran out too quickly. In the early 1900s, the Snake—the Columbia's largest tributary and the US's twelfth-largest river—ran dry for nearly a month along a ten-mile stretch: all the water had been diverted. To catch and manage the massive amounts of runoff that came from snowmelt (and better regulate water volume), nearly twenty-five large-scale dams and reservoirs were built along the Snake and other Idahoan waterways for irrigation storage and delivery. This dam-building era lasted nearly sixty years, totaled 472 U.S. Bureau of Reclamation built dams, and ended with the Teton Dam failure.

But still, this surface water didn't suffice. With so much fertile ground, farmers needed more drink. They finally found it beneath them. In the 1940s, locals discovered the Snake River Aquifer. At an estimated 10,800 square miles, the aquifer boasts an area larger than the state of Massachusetts. High-lift pumping that bored four- to seven-hundred feet below ground level made valley bottoms fecund; in turn, the aquifer limited the amount taken from rivers and canals.

Combining surface- and groundwater-pumping makes Idaho's current water usage staggering. Four western states (California, Idaho, Colorado, and Nebraska) make up half of the U.S.'s surface and groundwater withdrawals. But Idaho and California stand in a category of their own; as is, they are the only two states that pump between 15,000 and 31,000 million gallons per day. Considering that California houses approximately 36 million inhabitants compared to Idaho's population of just under a million and a half, and the fact that Idaho's irrigation season lasts only six to seven months, and that mining and commercial and domestic usage of Idaho water accounts for less than three percent total, an outsider can gain a sense of how vital the fourth element is for farmers. Annually, irrigation draws approximately six trillion gallons of water for Idaho's crops.

The water altercation that brings my father, Kent, and me to the hills is timid compared to most. If water decides a crop's success or failure, landowners are willing to fight over it. Here's a true story from the annals of the western ditch bank:

Two boys grew up as friends on neighboring farms. It was the 1970s when flood irrigating still pervaded, and farmers used the ditch water according to a schedule put forth by the local watermaster. Sometimes the water came in the day, sometimes at midnight. Regardless, one had to take the liquid as it came. The boys both inherited their family farms. As adults, their friendship waned, as both accused the other of using too much water, or water out of turn. One summer, words aggressed to threats, and one July day, threats climaxed to fists. In the brawl, fists wielded shovels. Mid-scuffle, one man brought his spade down on the other's face, knocking his right eye to blank blind nothing.

Years passed, and the men never apologized. Almost a decade after the melee, in an eerily identical summer, the one-eyed man rode out to the ditch bank with his rifle. He wasn't scheduled for water, but had closed his neighbor's headgate, diverted the stream, and then slipped into the brush, knowing his neighbor would come to find out why his river ran dry. Once the neighbor showed, the man put a slug in his chest, killed him dead, then returned home and called the sheriff. With a life-sentence in prison, the one-eyed man never again needed to water-worry.

Icy, youthful memories come from the irrigation canals. I loved opening my eyes in the frigid water, watching green and blue rocks skitter along the river bottom. A number of days, the canal babysat my friends and me—we'd float the six miles into town on inner tubes. When moving pipe as a kid, I'd overheat such that I'd bury my head in the canal and drink the murky water in great gulps. Not once did I suffer a case of giardia (or Beaver Fever, as my father called it), even after we found a dead pig upriver, bloated and stuck in the cattails. During the slow summer days, Kent and the other workers and I would steal away to the reservoir for a few hours of waterskiing.

Like most farms, our land pulled from both surface and groundwater sources. The desert farms out in the flats used deep aquifer wells, the farms near my home used canals, and the hill farms relied mostly on mountain creeks filled with winter run-off. Because I was small and liked to swim, cleaning the canal pumps became my responsibility. For a long while, it was something my father and I did together, but one summer I decided to work on my own. The initial dives went fine; the pumps sat above a concrete intake filled with canal water, the mainline stretching ten feet deep. I had to shut down the pumps, dive, and bring up handfuls of debris. No problem. But at this particular pump, sitting solitary at the edge of a hay field, my trunks caught on a broken edge of the metal screen and held me deep enough to just break the surface with my fingertips. I started to drown. Panicking, I wedged myself upwards, pulling on the concrete and mainline, and tore free, the metal ripping off my shorts and opening up skin from my lower back to butt cheek. I drove home naked and wincing, in search of Neosporin and clothing.

One summer, the water ran out on the Antelope Creek farm, so a few workers and I climbed into the mountains to find out why. On that farm, an earthen dam had been built to stop the creek and collect the run-off. At an elevation of six thousand feet, most of the neighbors dry-farmed hard grains, but here we'd planted seed potatoes. Due to the weak winter and dehydrated summer, we'd run out of water in early August, six weeks before harvest. The crop was thirsty.

That day in the pickup, we climbed the road along trickling Antelope Creek. I could see the bottom rocks; there was not even enough water to cover the three-foot bed. We crossed the boundary of the farm and traveled the road until the fields disappeared, replaced by stretches of sage and quakies, then pockets of pine. The road butted against a thick stand of timber. I took two shovels, one worker carried the axe, and another slung the five-foot iron bar over his shoulder. We climbed into dark, unknown territory. Blistering August, even in the shade. By noon we were lost in blotches of tree shadows.

We hiked and climbed for a while. In a moment of near bitching, as I plotted my next dry words to encourage a trek back to the pickup and a drive straight to the gas station for cold Mountain Dews purchased on my dime, we came to the first beaver dam.

The soupy pool stretched across the clearing, creeping out in the gullies and filling the draws. The creek sounded a sporadic and minimal weeping of water, an underpinning to our heavy breathing. Not large or impressive, the dam stood four feet high and equally as long, a rats' nest of sticks and pokes and points. We gathered our tools and then went out on the dam and attempted to wreck it. We chopped and pried and hacked with all we had, but were thwarted by an impenetrable crisscrossing of branches and logs. We worked an hour to remove an inch, and even then didn't free any of the water. We removed one stick only to find ten—damp and solid—in its place.

The trick came not in pulverizing, but circumventing, the construction. We dug a canal into the swampy ground next to the dam and watched the water drain out in liquid rush. We left the first dam and continued upstream to find more ponds, a chain of ten escalating up the creek like stepping stones. We made quick work and gouged out the trenches in thick shovelfuls. The entire afternoon, we spotted only one beaver, massive and graceful in the water, before it disappeared below the murky surface.

At dusk, we shouldered our tools and slogged downhill, exhausted but pleased with our success. With air conditioning full-blast we traveled back to our dam and, to our surprise, saw that the water level had not risen at all. Later, Kent said that all-told we gained less than a foot of water. We talked about going up again, perhaps taking more men and more shovels, but then came a better idea: dynamite. I wasn't in the hills the day the workers exploded the dams, but a dark part of me admits to having wanted to see how the beaver's construction measured up against gunpowder and blasting caps.

A neighbor turned us in to Idaho Fish and Game, and the agency ordered us to cease beaver dam destruction. We were fined, as that sort of destruction was unsightly and wrong. We knew it, too, but what else could be done? Our crops were dying of thirst. Regardless, our work was all for naught: the potato crop stunted and valued nothing. Eventually, my father sold the farm for its lack of production. The new owner trenched out the canals and added three feet to the dam, erected irrigation pivots and replaced the pump. But even that seemed meaningless: if I had learned anything, it was that sweat alone could not water a crop.

Through the binoculars, I follow the green line of creek flora and find the lake. It is tiny, maybe fifty feet by a hundred, relatively a drop in the bucket. The way Kent and my father jawed, I figured the lake would at least be sizeable enough for a motorboat. A man would be hard struck to take out a canoe on that pond.

"Doesn't look like much of a water feature," Kent says. "According to the real estate agent, the lake was going to make or break this place."

"Come on," my father says. "Let's go down and see what this creek does." The two tromp into the brush and disappear.

I stay near the pickup and ruminate over the jaundiced land. I can't understand why anyone would want to live up here. All this dust and heat. These California investors must have different eyes than me. When I see dirt, my considerations turn to farming scenarios. Try as I might, it's impossible for me to envision these hills dotted with mini-mansions and manicured lawns.

This proves my mistake. According to a recent Associated Press story, our government is considering a resurgence of western dam building in response to the nearly twenty percent increase in the population of western states during the 1990s, which now totals upwards of sixty-four million people.

John Redding, regional spokesman for the U.S. Bureau of Reclamation in Boise, says, "The West and the Northwest are increasing in population growth like never before. How do you quench the thirst of the hungry masses?"

Unlike the first era of dam building that hinged around irrigation and power production, our next will focus on providing freshwater for western residents. Doing so creates an obvious conundrum: without our first dams, the west would be unlivable; now that it's inhabitable, what end result will come from too many people? Although other ideas are in the mix—including conservation, storing water in natural underground aquifers, constructing water pipelines from the mountains, further metering water usage, and desalination plants— dam construction is once again in the forefront. Major water storage talks concern Colorado's Yampa River, California's San Joaquin River, Nevada's Colorado River, and even hint at rebuilding Idaho's Teton Dam.

I think that, like the beavers, the only reason investors are building here is because they have the ability to divert the water. Perhaps they develop from the need to move and shake. Or maybe that echo of empty land—the eminent silence that reigns here—is just too much for them to bear, and they have to cover it completely. Full of wonderment, I sit on the tailgate and wait for the men to return.

"Three beaver dams," my father says when he arrives at the rig, panting from his hike. "Nothing else blocks the creek."

We load into the pickup.

"I don't have a problem with their lake," my father continues. "They can boat and fish it. They just can't use it up. I need it."

We look out over the development one last time. My father says, "Guess I'll call my water lawyer. He'll know what to do. He's the best in the State."

Kent says, "Imagine they'd at least file for aesthetic right."

"Well," my father replies as he shifts the pickup into drive, "I'll probably fight that too, just out of principle."

We take off on the gravel road and disappear in a cloud of grit, headed down into the valley in search of something cold to drink.

CLOSE CALL:
A FEVER DREAM

2011

In a worn out western town, I make friends with a policeman. He is enamored with a married woman. I am enamored with the married woman's daughter. We spend time commiserating and talking about what it would be like to be with each of our crushes. Later that night, the cop comes to me with three five-gallon paint buckets, the tops sealed. He loads them into the back of my car and asks me to drive them away, along with the grief-stricken woman and daughter. I get in the cop's car with the buckets and the women and head south. Along the drive I realize that the husband has not come home that night and that is why they are so upset. I have a hunch that my cop friend has dispatched the man, and that I am transporting the body parts. I drive to the Clark Church, where it is morning, and where there is some giant trade-in/disposal of trinkets and junk. The women disappear, and I'm relieved. I take the buckets and get in line to get rid of the evidence, not sure what else to do. I begin a conversation with the people ahead of me in line, and when I look down, the buckets are gone. I panic, knowing I will now be implicated in the crime if the evidence ends up with the wrong party. I walk around the church building and see my cop friend sitting in an office with 2 other cops, the buckets in their custody. I go in with my hands up, surrendering.

We end up in a ratty hotel. There are two king sized beds, on each bed 2 of us lie. There are jezebels in the room with us. As well, there are 2 hulking dumb men as bodyguards for the women. All of these people work for some kingpin. I sense we are in a boomtown of sorts, a North Dakota town fueled by the fracking business. The ladies rotate around me; I don't interact with them. I watch the bodyguards and my policeman friend. They are enjoying the attention from the women. Soon enough, the kingpin arrives wearing a dingy gray suit. He is bald but for the sides of his head, five o'clock shadow, nostril hairs, and a neck as thick as an 80-year-old pine tree. Huge shoulders. Straight lines, top to bottom. He removes his jacket and requests that everyone take down their pants for a safety check. Everyone pulls down their pants, the cops' service revolvers sliding down with them, those knuckle-heads. The 2 bodyguards draw guns on the cops. The kingpin gets out a revolver and loads it with four bullets and snaps the drum back into place. He is more concerned with the cops than with me. I look across the bed and see my paramour, my crush, the daughter of the married woman, in pink sweat pants. She mouths something to me. She is one spot away from me, but we will never be together, as the kingpin orders all the women to leave. They are all herded into the bathroom and locked away. The cops get up out of the bed at once to rush the others and are quickly shot dead. The kingpin draws his gun on me, and I see the bullet is at the bottom of the drum. He has two empty chambers before he has a bullet. I rush to the alcove near the door and grab for anything to protect myself. I find a livestock syringe and engage the man. The quarters are close and there is no way for the henchmen to get off a shot without shooting their boss. We lock into a struggle, he with his gun and me with the oversized syringe. I force it into the crown of his head and inject whatever is inside the vial. He loosens his grip on me, starts speaking a language I don't recognize. I run outside and around the corner of the motel, in full flight. There is a wide shallow river running alongside the road, and a bridge crosses the road to the motel parking lot. I get into the river—it's 3 feet deep—and I drift and swim with the current, feeling the river rock with my hand and feet. I am just like John Colter, Porter Rockwell. I am predestined to escape. I will find overhang and brush in which to hide and live to tell the tale because I know the secrets of this river.

PARTIAL MEMORIES

2010

*As I later lay in bed going over the call I remember
thinking that things just did not add up. The patient
in my opinion had what I would call selective memory.*

— Responding Firefighter, Madison County
Emergency Services, "Letter to Rigby Police
Department," February 2, 2004

On February 1, 2004, at 3:36 AM—a frigid seventeen degrees with wind gusts nearly twenty miles an hour—a barefoot woman in blood-soaked sweatpants parked her 1989 Pontiac Grand Am at the Fastop gas station three miles south of Rexburg, a town in the heart of the rural farmland swath of southeastern Idaho. The woman staggered through ice and snow and dialed 911 from the payphone on the north side of the concrete building.

"Hi...uh...my name's...uh....I need some help..."

The emergency dispatcher asked for details.

"I have blood on me and I don't know where it came from. But... I...I'm bleeding and I, I, I don't know where I've been, where this came from."

"Okay. What is your name?"

The woman grappled for words.

"What is it?"

"It's...it's...Shana."

"Okay. And you don't know where you're bleeding from?"

"I don't. I have, I have blood. There's blood in my car. There's blood on me. I don't know where it came from."

"I'm going to put you on hold for just a minute and get my officer on the way. Do you know what happened at all?"

"I don't. I don't. I don't even know why I'm here."

The dispatcher established Shana's age, 38, and asked where she was coming from.

"I don't know. I just saw the Fastop sign. I was coming down off...I don't even have shoes or a coat. I need to really get in my car. I'm freezing. I'll just..."

"Okay. Just hang tight with me on the phone, is that okay?"

"I'm freezing. I don't have any shoes or coat. I'll stay here, I just, I'm freezing."

The dispatcher called for an ambulance.

"Well, it's just, my hand, I just, my hand."

The dispatcher allowed Shana to return to her car. She broadcasted for police and ambulance. Eight minutes passed while the dispatcher communicated with local authorities and then, surprisingly, was patched in with dispatch from neighboring Jefferson County.

An officer reported the scene: hardened blood smeared along the driver's side of the car. Fresh blood on the steering wheel, the gear shifter, droplets of blood on the right of the driver seat, bits of blood-soaked tissue, blood smeared on a bottle of Lime Coke, a bloody handprint on a pack of Marlboro Lights, a blood-soaked cigarette and a red butt in the ashtray, a blood-caked Bic lighter. The officer collected three empty Bud Light cans, a roll of disinfectant wipes, an empty knife scabbard. There was a drawing on the back of a legal pad: two hearts floating above a home, a knife piercing one and blood dripping from it onto the other. In the ambulance, Shana asked if her children were okay. She claimed her ex-husband had broken in.

Madison Dispatch conferred with her Jefferson counterpart. Then Madison addressed her officer at the scene with Shana: "Just for information, this is unknown if she is the suspect or victim in this case."

Jefferson County has an estimated 24,802 residents over 1,095 square miles of land, equating to about 22 people per square mile. Settled in 1893 by Mormon farmers, Rigby, the county seat, is the largest city with an estimated 3,312 inhabitants. In the early 1900s, Rigby postured to be the commercial hub of southeastern Idaho. Its slogan: "All Roads Lead to Rigby." Today, take US-20 or Highway 48 or the Lewisville Road and head for the smell. Rigby is bordered with potato processing factories whose open wastewater sump pools exude steamy rot. Most of the county belongs to, or did belong to, or at one time had family in, the Mormon Church. Here, people share meals and tools. From 1995 to 2004, the county had two murders, both those crimes involved drugs and gangs. I grew up riding the school bus with the criminal from one case. He drove the getaway car after he and two friends shot and killed a convenience store clerk. I had basketball class with the victim of the second, executed in the desert for an unpaid meth debt.

My people have inhabited Jefferson County for more than half a century. My grandfather graduated from Rigby High in 1946; my father and mother in 1976; I finished in 2000. The trunk of my family tree roots deeply into Jefferson ground and its branches seem defined by its geographical borders. With us, there isn't distinction between generations: I have cousins that I call cousins that are technically seconds or thirds; I refer to my great-uncle as Grandpa. I've worked with myriad distant-but-close relatives on my father's farm and called them all family.

Large families make nothing easy; if anything, it just means more funerals. As my uncle once said, "We've had enough hard, hard things in our life that we've learned to hide, tuck emotions away and never bring them up again."

Ours is a history of hardship, starting with my great grandfather, a failed farmer turned railroad worker who lost four fingers to the boxcars. My grandfather had a shot at grain ground and did well but it wasn't long before his kidneys failed. His youngest sister Sharon donated an organ that didn't take. My grandfather died in 1972, 44 years old, when my father was 14. Sharon made it to 45 before cancer took her. She gave up the ghost while in her recliner. My father, then 29, on one side of her; Sharon's son Gregg Whitmore, 21, on the other. After, my father and Gregg went outside. Darkness fell. From the house they saw the high school football field floodlights illuminating a game. My father could think of nothing to say to Gregg. Gregg, too, stood silently. My father was gripped with anger. A woman had died, and these fans across the lot cheered a first down, a lucky catch. Did they not understand that this match meant nothing? That someone's mother had just gone on? That a boy was left afloat?

After his mother's death, Gregg mechanicked for his stepfather at the diesel repair shop. Gregg hunted elk on our ranch and fished the Snake River near our irrigation pumps. He transferred to our farm shop and drove truck through grain and potato harvest. In 1990, he joined up, and the Army sent him to the Gulf War. Gregg was assigned to the 82nd Airborne as a paratrooper. In the Army, Gregg mastered darts, made stalwart friends, and served his country. Before he departed for Kuwait, Gregg gifted my father his five-drawer tool chest along with all his wrenches and ratchets. He swore to never do shop work again.

Upon Gregg's return, many others and I greeted him at the Idaho Falls airport. The Jefferson Star had encouraged the citizens to support the local serviceman with letters. A high school student randomly chose Gregg and wrote often to him. The boy, by his own admission, had low self-esteem and few friends. He and his mother were at the airport too. Gregg hefted me on his hip while I held his celebration balloons. Gregg was a fit, strong man with a contagious smile. Three days after Gregg's return, he went to the high school and found his pen pal, thanking him for his correspondence and giving him his army beret.

Not long after his return, Gregg met Shana. Shana was petite, freckled, and pretty, and, in those inexplicable attractive coincidences, shared Gregg's exact birthday and year: May 11, 1965. They were both 26. Shana, though, had come into the family problem early and had born daughters when she was just 16 and 18 years old. She supported them through minimum wage jobs, as the fathers were deadbeats. But here was Gregg, an able and attractive man who shared some of her own loves: gardening, canning, genealogy. They married in 1992 in the backyard of Gregg's stepfather. A son followed in 1993, and four years later, a daughter.

After the wedding, Gregg disappeared from our family's orbit. His younger sister kept us updated on his status. Gregg became foreman for a cement company. A skin disease discolored Shana's face and arms. This disfigurement affected her so profoundly that she quit her job at a Rexburg stationary factory to work from home. In 2001, my grandmother died and Gregg showed up at the funeral. Gregg cried and cried, for reasons more than just her death. He confided in my father that his marriage was falling apart. Not one to fail, Gregg stayed with Shana in their house on 2nd South near the Jefferson County Rodeo Grounds to work things out. But in August 2003, he moved in with his stepfather and started divorce proceedings. Shana could stay at the house with the kids until after the holidays but then Gregg would return and Shana would have to find someplace new to live.

Everything she tried to do in life seemed to work against her.

— Carma Harris, "A Tough Life That Was Turning Around," Post Register, February 8, 2004

In November 2003, Gregg met Karen Cummings on a blind date. Karen had her share of hardships: nine years younger than Gregg, she'd dropped out of high school, married poorly, had a child, and divorced. Karen didn't have custody of her seven-year-old daughter because of her extensive health issues. She lived with her mother in Sugar City, a town twenty miles north of Rigby. The two fell hard for each other, and Gregg was ecstatic. He called my aunt and came for a surprise visit to explain his blossoming relationship and how he planned to buy a promise ring.

Little did we know what else was happening in Gregg's life. Shana called his cell phone dozens of times a day to keep him from work. Gregg always answered, fearing it had something to do with his children. Since the final separation, Shana's behavior had grown erratic. She'd taken Gregg's most cherished items he'd left at the house—family photos with him and his mother and sister, his military records and pictures of his tour of duty, even his uniforms and patches—and incinerated them in the backyard firepit. On November 25, 2003, Shana came to Gregg's worksite with custody papers. An argument ensued and Gregg shoved Shana. Madison County Police were called but no charges were filed. The following day, Gregg went to the Rigby house to see his kids. Shana was drunk when he arrived, and she smacked Gregg in the head with a beer bottle and crashed additional empties against the wall. Gregg talked to Karen's mother about filing charges but nothing was done. On Thanksgiving, November 27, the back tire of Gregg's Suburban was slashed. The police came and filed a report. Gregg fixed the Suburban and went to Walmart on November 28. He came out to find his driver's side door kicked in.

Throughout December, no police reports were filed between the two. Shana kept calling; Gregg kept answering. Karen's mom remembered going Christmas shopping with Karen to buy Gregg a new tackle box and filet knife, as Shana had disposed of his. Gregg brought Karen to my family's Christmas dinner and she showed off her promise ring. They wanted a spring wedding. Gregg told us, "I finally found someone I can love. I'm finally free."

In January 2004, Shana left the Rigby house and moved to Rexburg to live with her 22-year-old daughter and her grandchildren. Gregg returned to the Rigby house, astounded but not surprised: Shana had taken the furniture, the dishwasher, screws from the bathroom towel holders, even the garbage disposal from the sink. But most disturbing were the kitchen cabinets and the empty bed frame. The wood had been sufficiently knifed in bizarre patterns, gouged and hacked and maimed.

On January 5, 2004, Shana filed a report with the Madison County Police that strange footprints encircled her daughter's house, and that her ex-husband had recently been abusive and forced her from her home. An officer followed up and marked the situation as a low priority. On January 23, a witness who had previously worked with Shana saw her in a Rigby gas station. She described Shana as distracted and upset. Shana explained that she and Gregg had split, that Gregg had kicked her out on Christmas Eve and two days later moved in his new girl. The clerk—buoying her friend—said that all exes were a-holes, and that the worst was that now a strange woman lived in Shana's old home. Shana said she wished Gregg were dead. The clerk said she'd considered burning down her ex-husband's house during their split.

The woman ended her statement to police with this: "I was saddened I didn't tell her that things would eventually, no matter how bad they seemed, get better. She seemed to be at such a low point, like her world had fallen completely apart. I wish I could have helped her instead of adding to her anger."

PARTIAL MEMORIES

Discussion of partial memories. These are scary for her.

— Clinical Progress Note from State Social Worker, Narrative of Session, Shana, July 16, 2003

One of the paramedics asked Shana her last memory before arriving at the gas station. She recalled watching TV with her children and grandchildren at the Rexburg house.

Much happened before that Sunday morning. On January 24, Karen was at Gregg's house watching Gregg's children when Shana unexpectedly stopped by. Karen didn't dare open the door. She called Gregg, who came to resolve the problem. Gregg wanted Karen to meet Shana, as Shana wanted to meet the woman who would be watching her children. Karen refused. Shana called Karen's mother at work, wanting to talk about Karen. Karen's mom dodged the calls.

The problem with exes didn't just reside with Shana. On Friday, January 30, Karen's ex's new wife called to say that her husband had left in a drunken rage with Karen's daughter. Karen and her mother drove to Utah to resolve the matter. On Saturday morning, Karen gained custody of her seven-year-old for the weekend while her ex sorted out his personal issues. Saturday afternoon, the three traveled back to Idaho. Karen decided to stay at Gregg's with her daughter. Karen's mother tried to persuade her not to numerous times, even calling Gregg while Karen and her daughter were inside a store. She invited Gregg to stay the night at her place, but Gregg said he planned to work late refinishing the cabinets and that everything would be fine. Later that night at home, Karen's mom saw that she'd missed another call from Shana. This time, she called her back. They had a long talk about Gregg and Karen.

In Rexburg, Shana's daughter reported that she and Shana and the kids stayed up until about 1:30 AM watching the movie Freaky Friday. Other than a watch alarm going off around 2:00 AM, which woke her, Shana's daughter remembers nothing out of the ordinary. As she later reported: "[Shana] was not sad, but not happy. She was just okay."

At 2:58 AM, a seven-year-old girl in Rigby called Jefferson County 911. An intruder named Ken had injured her mother and her mother's boyfriend. By the time police arrived, both Gregg and Karen were dead. 38 minutes later, Shana called from Fastop. After she was treated for cuts on her hands, Shana was placed into custody while Rigby City Police, Jefferson County Sheriffs, and Idaho State Police examined the crime scene on 2nd South. A house with walls and linoleum painted in blood. Bare, bloody footprints in the garage and down the back alley. A blood-covered boot dropped in the snow.

A week later, an amateur photographer found suspicious items at Twin Bridges, a popular riverside camping spot eight miles east of

Rigby on the same road as Fastop. As the snow melted, police collected torn rubber gloves matching the cuts on Shana's hands, the second boot, and a Fiskar's fillet knife with a seven-and-a-half inch blade that paired with the scabbard found under the seat of Shana's car. Shana was charged with two counts of first-degree murder and a count of burglary. During the trial, timetables were calculated; 911 calls, reevaluated; Karen's daughter's police interview, played. Perhaps it's conjecture, but the hypothesis follows.

Around 2:30 AM, Shana parked at the end of the alley in Rigby. She made her way behind Gregg's house, squeezed between the Suburban and the garage door, and let herself in. There was no forced entry, as this was the one lock Gregg had failed to replace. Shana removed her boots near Karen's garaged car, entered the kitchen, and crossed the linoleum in her socks. She passed the empty spare bedroom and bathroom in the hallway. Gregg's bedroom was the last on the left. Shana entered, circled to Gregg's side of the bed, and stabbed him three times in the ribcage. He was on his side, naked, and curled toward Karen. Gregg awoke and got out of bed, steadying himself at the post. Shana went to Karen and stabbed her in the chest, puncturing her heart. Karen stood and took a hammer and stumbled across the hallway toward the bedroom where her daughter slept. Shana followed with the knife. Karen fell into her daughter's room. Gregg gathered his strength and went after Shana. They battled down the hallway—the walls mopped with blood transfers and splatters, the carpet soaked, slipped footprints of failed traction on the linoleum— and eventually Gregg, facedown, bled out on the kitchen floor. Karen's daughter stayed in the bedroom. Shana came back. The seven-year-old yelled "Please! Don't!" and Shana disappeared down the hallway, over the body of Gregg, and out the garage. Her bloody footprints paced up and down the cement stairs, perhaps in debate over what to do with the girl. Shana had stabbed Gregg 33 times and Karen 12, in doing so severing the webbing between her left index and middle finger. She picked up her boots and moved down the alley to her car in her socks, leaving a blood trail and dropping one of her shoes. The girl ran into the kitchen, grabbed the phone, and called 911 from the bedroom closet. Police were on scene within minutes, even though the girl did not know the address of the house or the name of the town. By then, Shana was headed east toward the Archer Highway, crossing through the country in which most of Gregg's family, myself included, lived. At Twin Bridges, Shana disposed of the evidence—the knife, one boot, a distinctly colored towel, her bloody socks, and the gloves—into the icy Snake River.

Shana claimed innocence throughout the trial, though she never took the stand. The defense and prosecution called psychiatrists to testify. Both agreed she had several mental disorders: depression, borderline personality disorder, generalized anxiety, and post-traumatic stress disorder. The defense argued, too, that she suffered from dissociative amnesia.

Many oddities crept into the collective memory of the murder details. The defense argued that Karen's daughter reported the murderer as a man Gregg called Ken, but as my cousin argued, "'Ken' is just 'Karen' said with a punctured lung." In Gregg's autopsy, it was discovered he had only one kidney. One of the officers who rescued Karen's daughter had her drawing pictures at the station: the girl herself in bed with, "Twenty or thirty angels floating above her to protect her." Another officer, a friend of Gregg's, went into a deep depression: that morning he'd been on a routine patrol on the road that led to Twin Bridges. He figured he probably passed the Grand Am, and blamed himself for not somehow inherently knowing about Gregg's death. The girl wore white socks and there wasn't a drop of blood on them after traversing the murder scene. One account had Karen crawling into her daughter's bedroom with the hammer— "breathing in blood"— to protect her. They held hands until Karen finally expired.

On February 5, police released the house. My uncle and Gregg's father went to collect Gregg's personal belongings. They found a tape recorder in the nightstand on which Gregg had recorded Shana's phone calls.

"Gregg was doomed to die," my uncle said. "He knew her better than anybody else. I think he was literally scared to death when he was out of her grips."

On February 7, my cousin, my father's uncle, and I went to clean more from the house. We walked across the places where the CSI units had pulled up carpet and cut out pieces of linoleum to send to the lab for examination. We passed the carved-up cabinet doors and carried out the lacerated bed frame.

In the end, Gregg proved his killer in his autopsy; he held strands of Shana's hair in his rigor-mortised hand. On October 8, 2005, Shana was convicted on all counts and sentenced to twenty-seven years. "Drunk drivers get more!" one of my relatives exclaimed. But Judge Anderson said that coming up with the sentence was difficult because he believed that the killings were premeditated, but he also believed that Shana suffered from serious mental disorders and a lifetime of physical and mental abuse.

When Karen's father made his statement in court, he turned to Shana and said he would be impressed if she "could be honorable and admit her culpability."

Shana replied that she was still trying to figure out the events in her head but she couldn't admit to something she was unaware of. Instead, she said, "I'm sorry I can't give you what you want. If my life would take away your pain, you can have it."

That Sunday, none of us attended church. We gathered that afternoon more to support each other than watch the Panthers play the Patriots in Super Bowl XXXVIII. It was a morose and gloomy day. At halftime, Justin Timberlake and Janet Jackson committed the infamous wardrobe malfunction. Maybe it was the only thing that diverted our attention. Hollow conversations dominated discussion. Was the stunt accidental or planned? CNN published that TiVo reported the event as "the most replayed moment not only of the Super Bowl but of all TV moments that the young company had ever measured."

About Gregg, Uncle Brad said, "This was one of those things that was so sad to me that I put it aside in my mind. I just tucked it away and I haven't brought it back up for a long time."

My father questioned my motives for revisiting "this evil that fell upon our family."

I cannot answer why I've exhausted valuable hours scouring news reports, speaking with lawyers, examining autopsy photos, revisiting police reports, and piecing together timelines. The crime was solved as soon as Madison County had Shana in custody at Fastop. When the police arrived Sunday morning at Gregg's father's house to report the murder, his first response was, "What has Shana done now?"

After the halftime debacle, FCC chairman Michael Powell launched an investigation. He praised TiVo's capabilities, calling it "God's machine." To me, the implication of Powell's statement is unclear. Perhaps he means there is nothing more omniscient than the power to pause and replay. However, examining an isolated occurrence forward and back doesn't guarantee comprehension. Most often, the unknowable stays clouded in mystery. The power of slow motion fails to answer the vexing question of design.

PLIERS

2010

I spoke with Ralph only once, on that June day when Uncle Brad called the police to guide cars through the black smoke of Ralph's smoldering livelihood. I saw him more than that, cruising the narrow streets of Ririe in that whale of a car, slunk way down in the seat, rheumy eyes dimly focused on the dashes bisecting the pavement, hands twisting the wheel in unsteady bursts. Ririe's citizens, all 497 at the eastern edge of the county, proved more familiar to me than the west laying county seat, Rigby (the municipality home to my high school, Dairy Queen, and Rigby Chevrolet). Boyd and Brad's farm was based in the hills near the reservoir, just a few miles outside of Ririe's railroad track borders, where Dewain had started with a few hundred acres. Since then, the brothers had roped and cultivated more and more land, waiting for the right time to gobble up the fields of failing neighbors. Because of that I spent more time in Ririe—at the Pillsbury grain elevator, Pronto Auto Parts, Gumercindo's apartment—than I ever did on Rigby's crumbling main street.

Gumercindo and I trashed Ralph's farm. We knocked off fence poles till the strikes from the sledges reverberated our forearms to a throbbing numb, and wound handfuls of baling twine into oversized skeins, and gathered maverick soda cups, beer cans, pieces of lead pipe, gunny sacks. We piled everything inside the weather sheds. Inside one small building, flies left calves' skeletons and swarmed me. It had a low ceiling, maybe once a pigpen. The only thing to pick up was a rubber feeder. At the back of the corrals, rolls of chicken wire and jugs of pesticide littered the pens. A woebegone water line connected to a bullet-riddled trough had formed a stagnant puddle on top of the manure. One end of a red gate sunk into the mud. That's where Gumercindo and I started. Tied together with wire and twine, the panels formed a tight pen within the corral. I cut the strings, and all the pieces leaned together and sunk deeper.

Out in the middle of the farm, I saw the outline of ancient machinery—the farm's equipment boneyard. Later that summer, I'd cut the hay here and stop to examine the rusting potato combines, hay balers, scythes, wondering how long it must take to harvest eighty acres with a machine only four feet wide. In December, we'd bring the heifers here, and I would feed all five hundred cows in less than twenty minutes from the back of a converted Army convoy truck able to run on diesel, gas, ethanol, or airplane fuel. It must have been different for Ralph, some ancient nativity celebration, milking twenty head and spending the rest of the day collecting eggs, breaking through iced-over troughs, exchanging lassos and tinsel-wrapped wrenches as Christmas gifts with a handshake and a nod. Nowadays, things worked differently.

Fifty years ago, Ririe prospered, supporting a movie theater, a two-story log hotel, a hardwood roller-skating rink, Sappington's Drug Store, and hosted a New Year's Eve Dance in the community center. Now the town's social scene revolves around Sweet Surrender—a bakery and hamburger joint housed in the old drug store—two gas stations, and Ririe Auto Parts. Surrounded by fertile plots fed from with irrigation canals, the family farmers turned profits on white wheat and spuds. When potato harvest arrived in late September, schools let out for two weeks to supply the farms with sons and clod pickers, hired help and line cooks.

Enrique—called Henry by gringos who couldn't pronounce his given name; an ashen-bearded immigrant from Hermosillo—toiled for Boyd and Brad for thirty years. Enrique left the farm because of the work; he needed time for his family, and now owns a taco stand in Tucson. Enrique complained of a harvest without end. Starting in June with the first crop of hay, seconding and thirding into August; itchy weeks of cutting and trucking barley; a half-month of spuds: "Before, when your grandma here, tú papa just a little chamaco, they used to bring a table out to the field and we all stop—the trucks, the tractors, everything—your grandma bring food, we eat chickens, watermelons, bread, punch, cake—now just hasta la chingadera, eat un pinche sandwich, nada mas."

I've learned this rolling, eternal harvest was uncommon until the days of my upcoming. When the farms were smaller, more than a few enjoyed riches. But now the land jellos into huge family swaths. Boyd and Brad's land coupled with the other big timers, stretching miles from the highway to the lake, picking up again on the far side of the reservoir, a ranch near the crest of Swan Valley. But I was kept in the shadows on my father's success. Had he been born in the right time and place, Pops could have worked two bits to a million bucks at card tables with his elusive responses in regards to his success.

"How much you worth?" I'd ask.

"Not nearly enough," he'd say and laugh, "What makes you think I'd tell you?"

This caused confusing confrontations for me—Boyd's only son amongst five daughters and since Brad sired four girls, the sole progenitor of the Foster name. At school, teachers nodded when they connected me to my stocky, smiling, slightly balding father, assuming I would inherit the operation. But when they asked how many acres I owned, I responded with a blank stare. Nothing belonged to me—I just swept the shop.

As I grew older, this disapprobation didn't wane. I was fed lies about the successful brothers by random community members. "I didn't want to tell you this," they'd say, "but did you know both your dad and uncle have hair plugs?" Since both were active in Mormon church leadership, many lines stemmed from deep-harbored sins: "I heard your old man has racing horses at the Santa Anita—I thought a good Mormon didn't gamble?" At nineteen, in Indiana as a missionary, I met a transplanted Ririe-ite who noticed my appellation and asked if I was an Idaho Foster. When I affirmed it, his nod seemed to tap out acreages and crop returns in a slim thin smirk as if to say, Oh, you're one of those.

And another time, much more embarrassing, at my first Sunday dinner with a high school girlfriend. Her father and I small-talked into a hunting discussion. An avid golfer, pyramid-scheme aficionado, and a father of two grown boys, I had no idea of his outdoor orientation. When I asked him if he enjoyed hunting, he shot, "Not everyone owns a private reserve like your people." I choked down dry chicken until the meal ended.

I let these digs go by without much more than an ignorant laugh— my situation was not lump-summed into my father's money or land. As quiet as the two were about their business, who knows what they did with their money? The truth: I considered myself, and was treated like, nothing more than an employee, one to work alongside the Mexicans, drive truck or tractor, shovel trenches, grind angle-iron. Boyd and Brad confirmed this with my job allotments, aptly proving that a boss's son deserved no special treatment. Among the twenty or so of us that were full time, we joked that we didn't work for the farm; rather, we lived and died for the farm. A common deflection from the head cowboy Drue, when detailed for the day's advances, was, "I'm about ready to slap my balls up on that anvil and pound them flat, that's how good it's going."

The B Foster Brothers hit the market at the right time, gathering up land as technology advanced and commercial contractors like Idahoan and Anheuser Busch arrived, nudging out the uncompetitive farms. Of course, the stubborn valley men taloned into their farms and worked into their late eighties, combing over their rocky fields and waiting impatiently for someone to strike oil, or at least something more valuable than sugar beets.

So the day that Ralph's farm went sunder was the first time I crossed the bridge into his place. It sat on the county line road that enters Ririe on the west side, a right angle from the Rigby-Ririe Highway. The road mouthed into the valley where the small farms began, barns and shops alongside the roads, open-cabbed tractors pulling miniature hay rakes, aluminum handlines paralleling down the fields.

Before, the run-of-the-mill farmhouse sat on eighty acres surrounded by bending weeping willows and white plank fences, and just down would be an identical house with a rogue dog crouching along the shoulder to stalk station wagons. Today the scene morphs. Hay fields that once stretched from backyards to tree lines are now crisscrossed with heaped up gravel roads, orange flags, pavers, scrapers, plows, back-hoes; fields once outlined with electric fence and used for fall fallow are now checker-boarded in half acre lots, three-quarter acre lots, 1.2679 acre lots, beginner home lots, residential lots, lots for mansions. Lots too rocky for shrubs or grass. Lots too close for goats and horses. Lots financed and refinanced. Waterfront lots and secluded lots. Lots in developments with blue-sky names like Elk Meadows and Spring Grove and Cedar Park Estates.

In months, new houses appear: a hole, then naked foundations, ribbed walls, trusses, shingles, siding, and realtor sign. Just add family, just add memories: the Model Ts of the Idaho valleys. When I ran the sod farm, I plodded afternoons through such housing developments shilling discounted sod. Mechanics and bus drivers, grocery store clerks and math teachers all facing their first mortgages leaned up on beat up cars and questioned, "Grass? Shoot, can't even afford dishes."

The plight of progress—the snake eats its tail. Just the same, the farmers who proceeded my family, Ralph and a myriad others, slowly go the way of the buffalo, driving their squeaking pickups and boat-cars into blood red sunsets.

The bridge, made from railroad ties, rattled when Brad drove across it. We pulled into Ralph's farm yard. Gumercindo—a five-foot-three arrival from Oaxaca, head full of black, wire-brush hair—peeked over the seat and swore. The weeds had overtaken everything.

Later, when I ask Brad what he recalls of the day, he says, "All I remember was all that crap, just piles of it everywhere—I bet it was fifty years old." There were two sets of pole corrals. The concrete mangers along the outside were cracked and broken. A massive mound of cow crap climbed up in the middle. Manure pushed against the bottom rung. A three-sided weather pen—two slat walls and a tin roof—were built inside one of the corrals, room for cows to escape the sun and snow.

A road separated the corrals. There were two additional wooden outbuildings on the property, one tall and skinny, and one smaller with windows and a door. In front of the tall one squatted a horse trailer missing one of its four tires, the other three flat, its hitch resting on a broken piece of concrete, devoid of paint on its roof and tongue, the rest having faded to a lackluster peach. Along it was a pea-green Dodge, one headlight, rusty rims, no tailgate, and a bed full of rods and wooden blocks. An open-cab tractor, bronzed, backed against the tree line alongside an orange pipe trailer and a fertilizer cart. A bleached cinderblock milking barn with bars on the windows filled up the corner.

"There are a million farms like that one," Brad says. "A guy would get himself a few hundred acres, have seven, eight, nine kids—just like Ralph—a couple milk cows and live a whole life right on that plot."

In size and business, there are major distinctions between my father and uncle. Brad, ten years older, is a thin, busy man constantly working deals, bouncing around in his pickup from farm to farm, doling out instructions and speeding off to the next big thing. Pops, thick-shouldered, has the same businessman's intuition but works into deals such that, years later, former partners call with complimentary tickets to a Utah Jazz game or the like.

Brad worked into the middle of the Ralph deal by bartering with both Ralph and the owner of an outdoor archery range and ended up buying the old farm. I didn't know any more details than that. When I questioned Brad about ending up with this weird plot, he said, "Can you imagine what a house would sell for along this canal? You have to think for the future."

Brad showed us what to do and promised to return that afternoon. Gumercindo and I emptied the tools from the back—two shovels, a pry bar, hammers, a sledge. Brad bounced back across the bridge and left. Gumercindo shook a fence pole that was tied up with orange baling twine, and the pole fell into the dried manure.

An hour into the destruction, Gumercindo yelled and waved me over to the Dodge. There were keys in the ignition. We started the truck and it banged to life with a shot of black exhaust. Near the pipe trailer were a bunch of cracked, mismatched, unusable tires. We threw them all in the back of the truck. Enrique appeared in the haying John Deere, four long spikes sticking off the farmhand. I guided Enrique across the bridge, the tractor so large there were only inches to spare. Smiling, he revved it up, waved, and plowed into the weather shed. The roof dropped like a boxer, caving in the walls and crashing onto the garbage we had stuffed inside.

Enrique moved to the gates and ripped them out of the puddles, stacking them away from the wood. Everything else went into the pile. It grew ten feet, then fifteen, and at twenty began to spill into the yard. Gumercindo and I unloaded the tires from the truck into a divot between a wall and some posts, waiting for Enrique to cover the rubber with more debris.

Brad had told us the wooden grain bin was off-limits. One of Ralph's sons wanted the lumber. As Gumercindo and Enrique worked to remove the cement anchored corral posts, I jigged the door and let myself in. The obsolete silo reached double my height with a trapdoor in the top large enough for an auger. The walls were thin, constructed of two-by-fours on end that lapped one over the other like a giant Jenga tower, creating a water-tight seal. The only light that entered came from the door. I ran my fingers over the walls, completely smooth, sheened from the hundreds of bushels of grain that had filled it in years past and financed Ralph's operation. Dust kicked up as I shuffled around, wafting in thin wisps. A pair of hay hooks lay in the dirt. Shaped like wire-hangers but crafted from hefty iron, the hooks were taken, one in each hand, by the farmer, who would grapple them into a hundred-pound hunk of hay, and then buck the hay onto the truck bed. "Grueling," Pops says. "Paid a nickel a bale."

Now it's work for the John Deere, not me.

Just before noon, Ralph pulled up. By then, we'd destroyed nearly everything. Ralph's baby blue Oldsmobile sat alongside the trash pile. When I walked over to Ralph, instead of rolling down the window, he threw open the door and stuck a large leg out onto the dirt. Pants that reached up mid calf exposed pasty ankles, sagging socks, and loafers. A gut that rolled up over his waistband and bunched on his lap. Pudgy arms and hard-bitten fingers thick as quarter rolls rested on the steering wheel. Respirator tubes traced a lapping chin and ended with a fixture that metronomed oxygen into his nostrils. Tank in the passenger seat. Oblong, murky eyes. I introduced myself as Boyd's son, something I often did. Josh was superfluous in times like these.

"I been here most my life," Ralph said, his voice as rough as a broken green bottle.

Finally, at twenty-two—after years of harassing PE teachers, ex's fathers, the imported Hoosier, and unrelenting friends—the dissention got to me. Hands in my pockets, scanning across the parsed wreckage, I was tired of being the boss's son, the big bad capitalists ruining everything. I wanted to say, Look Ralph, I'm not doing this. It's not my fault you didn't buy more land, or finance your sons, or get your crops to make grade. And I'm sure you're getting paid way more than this bottomland ground is worth. You know how much I'm making here? Six bucks an hour. That's right, and I'm Boyd's son. It's not like I'm building overtop this joint, or hooking up my brand new truck to your horse trailer, is it? I'm just doing as I'm told, taking my lumps, trying to get ahead. You as well as anyone can understand that, right?

But I just stood, gruff. Ralph didn't say anything, but looked over his bowdlerized plot, a place where he's clocked thousands of hours, taught life-lessons to sons and daughters, ate meals leaned up against pickups and tractors. A place that was disappearing right before him.

When I moved to return to work, he said, "You ain't going to burn all them tires are you? Got to be something a guy could use them for. Seems like a man always needs a spare tire."

"Brad told me to burn everything."

"Those are still good. I know a hundred guys who'll need tires come harvest. I have a guy or two stopping by a week, asking for tires."

I stared at the mismatched slicks, knowing companies didn't manufacture tires with such thin walls and weak rubber anymore. Tires like those were liable to kill a man.

"You mind setting them aside?" Ralph said. "I'll get a guy or two to come get them."

"Don't know," I said.

Ralph's stare carried to the fields he had worked for decades, glazing out to the creaking, rusted boneyard. I imagine his mind filled with memories of a wife having brought a lunch of fried chicken, a green apple, thick bread, cold water in mason jars and riding along with him for a pass on the wheel well; of a son who jumped the clutch as Ralph hucked up a bale onto the truck, only to have it tumble off and break, wasted; of late moonlit nights changing water accompanied only by the purling and breathing of the siphon tubes and thirsty dirt.

I said, "Yeah, we'll save them, why not?"

Ralph nodded. He sat with his door open and watched me roll the tires one by one toward the canal bank, where I stacked them. Gumercindo and Enrique continued to pummel the gray fencing with the chains and tractor hydraulics.

"Get that old pickup there. That'll run. Throw them in back."

I fired up the Dodge and loaded it a second time. Fragments of the farm had covered some of the tires, and I struggled to rip them from the intertwined posts and wire. Ralph saw me struggling with one knobby, rimless shell. He bonked the horn and called me over.

"Dig around back there and find yourself something useful."

I opened the back door and found tools everywhere, on the floor, the seat, in the cracks towards the trunk, the thin sill below the rectangular window. I began to sift: pipe wrenches, crescent wrenches, monkey wrenches, hammers; hatchets, metrics, sockets, files; three-eighths, five-eighths, seven-eighths—and then a pair of shiny, red-handled, slip-jointed pliers. On the farm, a pair of pliers is invaluable. A large majority of farmers, rather than burdening their belts with pagers and cell phones (like so many of the entrepreneurs and narcissists populating the valley) strapped a pair of pliers to their waist in a leather holster. Just like the irons that were used to settle disputes at high noon, the quality of the tool and the skill of the operator precipitated their worth. Cheap pliers valued nothing, as their teeth would strip when biting a rusty bolt, or the pivot pin would work loose. In a month, they'd be worthless.

Watching an amateur work a pair of pliers—no matter how well crafted the tool—was as uncomfortable as turning the corner to face a coworker peeing in the bushes. But Ralph's pliers were large and heavy, the handles nine-inches long, constructed of glistening metal, with a thick rivet holding everything together. When I picked them out and showed them to Ralph, he grunted in approval. Using a tool correctly in this world means a lot. I once spent an afternoon laying brick with a friend, a self-employed mason named Braden. We worked on a new home in the hills of boomtown Rexburg, the house on ground recently bought and divided from a third-generation farmer. Up on the scaffolding, I handed my friends tapes and crimps, cuts of red block and buckets of mortar. I envied his skill as he eyeballed the lengths and lines, the grooves of gray, his pride as he tapped and tested with his trowel. When we climbed down to use the mixer he held a bucket while I scraped out globs with a spade. He said, "You can tell a man by how he works a shovel." I was pleased with my simple ability.

I gripped the pliers and tried to pry the wire loose from the tire, but with Ralph's eyes on me, the tool fumbled in my fingers. I dropped the pliers more than once and finally resorted to operating the tool two-handed, chomping away as if I had reverted to an inexperienced adolescent under the knowing gaze of a grandfather. The tire came free, and the rest were easy to detach. I finished and returned to Ralph. He opened his door and I offered him the pliers.

"No, no. You'll need them again."

I lied and said I had tools of my own.

"Just keep them for the day. I ain't going to use them."

I stuck the tool in my back pocket, the heft pulling my pants down that much further, and walked off to help the others. A few minutes later, I saw the exhaust cough out of the Olds and watched Ralph chuff across the bridge and coast down the road.

Brad came back with diesel and matches and chuckled when I told him of the tires. Sometimes people just can't let go, we reasoned. Since Brad had been in enough trouble with the police for burning without proper warning, he called into Rigby. A cruiser parked a little way up the road to warn truckers to slow down or they'd miss the stop sign altogether.

Enrique left in the tractor, and Brad took Gumercindo and everything but a shovel to the shop. Ralph's place burned fast. I spent the rest of the afternoon bashing out flames that licked the weeds along the ditch bank and digging a fire line around the silo. Halfheartedly, I'd look out to the road when I heard a vehicle, wondering if Ralph had the brass to see his place go down in flames. I stayed until dark and in the dim-day gray heard the canal lapping along, the pops and hisses of coals of posts and planks; I smelled the smoldering tar, the manure, and my own mephitic reek.

❙❙The thing to remember," Brad says when recollecting that day. "We did a favor. We cleaned that mess up. Old Ralph just couldn't bring himself to let the new take over without a few words of his own."

Ralph's son came and pieced out the silo, hauled away the Dodge and the horse trailer, but never took the stack of tires. Again, I had to haul them off, this time to tire store in Rigby, which stuck me with a disposal fee.

Boyd and Brad weren't able to zone the lot for housing developments and now it sits solitary but for the hayfields. Brad hired an excavation team of three locals to smooth out the crap piles, extract the old plumbing, and bury the ashes. Now the Ralph plot is an oddly shaped piece of bare land connected with that ratty old bridge.

156

Ironically, the land around the Ralph, in another county, is pocked with developments, instant communities every mile or so.

I used the pliers the rest of that summer. On the farm, holding onto one's tools was difficult; Poncho and Freddy, tractor operators, were known to squirrel away ratchets and sockets and scurry them off to their own farms in Mexico; Garland automatically assumed everything belonged to him. But with those glossy red handles and brawny metal, they were branded mine. Secretly, I hoped to cross paths with Ralph at the gas station and return them once and for all, but I never saw the old man again.

Soon enough, the pliers were stolen and lost. I left them in the shop while I ran out to the blue room (the plastic outhouse next to the diesel tank) and that was that. Garland later told me that Drue had pilfered them. When confronted, Drue confessed: "I had to go up on Heise and fix the water. They must be somewhere on that dang hill. How was I supposed to know they were yours?" But he knew good and well, just as everyone did.

The fact the pliers were gone rubbed me wrong. I demanded Drue buy me another set, and not a piece-of-garbage cheapees but a big heavy pair like the ones he had lost. A few weeks later, Drue delivered a green-handled pair from the ranch store. Those lasted two weeks before breaking. They cost eight dollars—I saw it on the package— charged to my father's account. Drue hadn't even paid his dues.

Still, I think about Ralph's pliers with remorse and anxiety. The summer, I pocketed them proudly every morning, brandishing them like a remnant gift from long lost kin. And when Pops or Garland would bitch about not having three hands, I whipped them out and gripped down on whatever needed reparation. I imagined the pliers left on top of a leaning fence post, or laying open on a porous piece of lava, the handles bleaching to pink, the heavy neck and mouth rusting in the weather. Perhaps years from now, some bush-league anthropologist hiking through the sagebrush might find my tool and wonder how they came to be before launching them farther into the grass.

But my thoughts go back further still to the June day by the canal when the Ralph melded into Foster land. Because what Ralph and Drue don't know is how the fire started: I scaled up the leaning garbage pile with two jugs of diesel and my pocketed pliers. I sloshed out the fuel and watched it pool on the boards and soak into the poles. And about the time that Brad and Gumercindo were loading up the shovels and pry bars—about the time that Ralph stumbled into his cramped house and fell into a worn recliner trying to steady his breath—I struck the match, then the second, the third, until the flames whipped close, and the heat made me stumble back from the pyre and shield my face.

HUNTERS

2010

My father taught me to shoot a gun in the city park across from my grandmother's house during the few months we lived there. I was ten that spring, the only time I lived in town before college. We'd take the bb gun from his pickup, cross the street to the park, and take aim at the aluminum garbage cans chained to the picnic tables. The gratifying shuck of the lever-action that chambered the next shot only rivaled the plunk of copper bb on aluminum lid. When I tired, my father would take the gun and swing-cock it, hold it out one-handed, and tag the cans. Once, a police cruiser drove past and slowed. My father shadowed the gun along his leg and waved. The cop returned the salutation and kept driving. Pops slapped me on the back, somehow telling me that was how things were supposed to be done.

Irrigation canals crisscrossed the land around our house like intricate stitching. The cover brought Canadian geese and sand-hill cranes but, more than anything, ducks. We shot the quackers like we swatted flies; daily and without remorse.

We cleaned them near the well pit. One of my father's favorite gags was to cut off a leg and pull back the orange skin and find the tendons. He'd coax one of us youngsters near to examine the foot—otherworldly with its scaly webs and bumpy nails—and pull the tendons, flexing and constricting the toes. The first few times we shrieked and shied away, but once the shock wore off we took turns pulling on the flossy string that ran parallel to the bone.

Once, I took a duck foot to show and tell. I can't recall the class's reaction but remember it made my backpack smell like wet and living leather.

My father is a hunter. For many years I could not figure out why. He hunts all his game on his own property. If he itches for ducks and geese, he walks to the canals behind his house. If he's antsy for deer and elk, he drives twenty miles to his ranch and stakes out runs and paths. I cannot remember a year he hasn't shot a big game animal.

Before I could carry a rifle, I'd push brush for my father on the annual elk hunt. The hunt ushered in transition, marking the end of the farming season. We met at the farm shop, sometimes in snow, sometimes rain, usually a stout wind. In the black anticipation of the eerie sunless morning all of us milled about as serious as wolves. My father divvied out assignments to the group: one pickup here, another there, fan out along the hills, plant near the cliffs. Then we left, a cavalcade of headlights humming toward the crags.

I carried a pellet gun. My father dropped me in the thick draws and then took station farther up the mountain. I crept through the forest barrel-first, my hands sweating through my gloves. Morning came, and the sun shot down in kaleidoscope spirals through the tall conifers. At that point of complete vanishment and panic—me not knowing north from south, or where the big guns were, or if the hunters would mistake me for game—that echoes of gunshots sounded. Fool hens boomed out from the grass and scared me so bad I thought I'd been shot.

Here's a story for you, Pops. I shot a cat near the granary at the old house. I heard you complaining about how many strays were around so I took my pump twenty-two—the one you gave me for my twelfth birthday, the only gun I'll ever love—and waited in the driveway until a cat came wandering. It hunched down in the gravel about twenty feet out. I put a bead right on the thick of its chest and paused. I watched that mangy orange tom breathing on the other side of the barrel and something stirred in me. I couldn't do it. I put down the rifle. But then I didn't want you to be bothered by this cat, so I brought the gun up and shot behind it in warning.

The lead ricocheted, drilled the cat in the hip. The red painted its hind legs. Mewling and caterwauling like I'd never heard, the cat came to me wanting help, crying as it dragged itself through the gravel. I rose up to put it out of its misery, now it was on the driveway pavement, but again I balked. I ran for the garage. The cat followed and crawled under the suburban and pulled itself into the undercarriage and knelled. I shut and locked the back door. The cat must have died up there, fallen out somewhere on the road. I never found its body.

You probably didn't see the blood on the driveway. I washed it off with the hose.

One epic year elk hunting at the ranch we harvested four bulls and four cows in one morning. My cousins and I added three fool hens. We dragged the animals back to the house and laid them out for a photo, their chest cavities propped open with branches of pine, their blood running rivulets down the hill toward the dirt road. I stood in the photo with my bird and pellet gun, my orange safety hat, my bloody jeans; one among a dozen other identical men.

THE GOSPEL OF
WILD DOGS

2010

He that hath ears to hear, let him hear.

Nearly two decades ago, a hard-luck pioneer named Bob settled near Lava Hot Springs in southeastern Idaho. Bob and his girlfriend Dot came from Oregon with enough cash to buy five acres of sage-covered hills. Bob and Dot purchased a camp trailer and moved onto the land, where they collected a mismatched pride of lions, tigers, and wolves. Bob dreamt of opening an exotic zoo, but many forces worked against his big-cat utopia. City water ran through the property, but Bob had no funds to dig a sewer. The couple planted a power pole, but didn't have scratch to purchase electricity. He constructed the barrier to his ranch—dubbed Ligertown once the lions and tigers interbred—with poached poles and fencing. The animals lived in a dilapidated school bus that Bob stationed at the crest of a hill, in a few rusted-out sedans, and in pens made of discarded pallets.

Bob fed his brood road-killed deer and rabbits. Soon the ranchers complained that the animals had breached the fences and were watering at Fish Creek. Some cattleman even argued that their livestock were being tracked and targeted. Twice, Bannock County brought charges. Both times the couple defended themselves, claiming private property rights, and won.

The situation culminated on September 20, 1995. The cats and wolves grew uneasy outside the trailer. That night a lioness attacked Bob, the resulting injury minor but warranting medical attention. Hospital officials notified police, and Bob and Dot were arrested on counts of cruelty to animals and creating public nuisance. At dawn, the cops moved on Ligertown.

In three days time, nineteen cats were killed. Reputedly, one was shot five-hundred yards from the town's elementary school. Two were taken by area ranchers protecting their livestock. And one straggler, as reported in the New York Times on October 1, 1995, was shot by Woney Roberts, a forty-year-old railroad worker, from the balcony of his home. Woney had recently returned from town with his wife and daughter. He spied the lion sprawled beneath a tree not far from the horses. Woney said, "It was about the scariest shot I ever shot."

From the eighty-four animal cruelty charges and sixteen counts concerning public nuisance, Bob was fined nearly $10,000 and sentenced to a year in jail. Dot received a six-month sentence. Twenty-seven big cats—twenty-four African lions and three ligers—were sent to a Californian animal rescue. But the three-dozen wolves, coyotes, and wolf-dog hybrids remained homeless. The state wanted the canines for evidence but had no place to store them. A deal was struck with my father who had recently rented a one-of-a-kind cattle feedlot that also had once been a private zoo. Included among the stockyards were monkey hutches, giraffe barns, rhino pens, aviaries, and kennels. Plenty of room for the wild dogs. The evidence came transported in semi-trucks, and the state paid my family $60 a day to provide basic care.

The dogs' plight broke national news for a week, and animal rights groups from across the country responded by donating feed and funds. Inside the door of both barns sat stacks of fifty-pound sacks of dog food and bales of straw for bedding. Supplies were replenished weekly. New metal bowls graced every kennel.

The canines were a thin, mangy bunch. Some were deformed from growing in the cramped quarters of Ligertown, stooped in their back loins, tails permanently tucked between their legs. Some of the dogs were ghosts, leaving only fecal deposits to prove their existence, while others lapped near the barn barrier, waiting for food.

The novelty of the wolves soon wore off, and the work became mundane and tiresome. Winter brought severe conditions. Adopters waned and donations expired. My family contacted local stores asking for broken bags of feed. Nature took its course—litters of pups were born.

My last memory of the wolves came on a spring day when I went to muck out the pens. And there was a kennel-full of curious pups, with perked ears and a youthful ignorance that perhaps I mirrored. While my family washed-down, I crawled through the small kennel door to the exterior run. I hunkered by the door and stared at them. We stayed deadlocked. I stretched forth a hand, and soon enough, the pack crept towards me, shuddering close to the ground. One broke free and ran within inches of my fingertips. We nearly touched when, inside the barn, someone dropped a shovel. The pups bolted back to the corner, again a mass of shivers and fur.

Later, I read a story about Bob. He was so close to his pets, he gave the animals free reign inside his camp trailer. The cats lounged beside him on the couch, fascinated by the powerless television, and Bob raked their backs with both hands.

By summer, the state ran out of money and, compelled by the fact that no animal rescue would adopt deformed and inbred dogs, the government asked my father to dispatch the pack and bury the carcasses in the feedlot's dead pit. My father recalls this incident with much trepidation. This problem was not his fault. He hunts; he does not off, nor rub out. But my father had his guns, and this pack was abandoned on his property. So he did what had to be done.

I imagine him out there on that summer morning, his two-twenty-three—a caliber that fires fast and kills clean—shadowed along his right leg. He wiggles into a pen and strands straight, brushes crap from his knees. Come unto me, my father mumbles as he raises the gun to his shoulder, levels the barrel on the closest animal, come unto me all ye malformed and mistreated, all ye that have starved and survived, ye limpers and ye with broken backs, ye stooped and one-eye blind, and I will give ye rest.

162

INSIDE OUT

2009

One Sunday morning in January, I overslept and my family left for church without me. Granted, the rest of those Fosters all had reasons to be at the chapel before service started—mom and my three little sisters practicing with the choir, my fourteen-year-old brother Joshua off to prepare the sacrament, my father Claxton gone since first light. Dad would be furious if I was late, so I stood in front of the bathroom mirror, trying for a suitable tie knot, hurrying towards perfection, when I heard someone knocking at the porch door. This was a year before I got married, or better, a year before I had to get married, and ended up leaving the ranch after my eighteenth birthday, just before grain harvest.

By the time I got to the door, the knocking had become pounding, and I opened to find Jarrett Buckett—rubber overshoes unbuckled and manure-caked, coat unzipped, a cock-eyed fowler cap brushed with snow and hay sitting slanted on his head—waiting for me. Claxton had hired Jarrett to calve out the heifers on the weekends. Before this, though, I'd only seen Jarrett in town sitting on the tailgate of his jacked-up Dodge, smoking cigarettes and scamming on the trailer park girls. He was a few years older than me, a burnout from Sunnydell, in the foothills out by Herbert.

"Hi-ya Jeremiah," Jarrett said. "Hoping to catch Claxton before he ran off to the big house." Then, my father was serving as bishop of our Mormon ward, and he spent most of every Sunday at the chapel.

"He's not around," I said. "Won't be until four or five."

Jarrett stepped back and leaned against the porch banister. He slipped off his hat, showing red hair askew and sweaty, and rubbed his head with the back of his hand.

"You know if he's got his cell?" Jarrett asked.

"Not in church," I said. "Maybe it's in his truck."

Jarrett slapped the hat against his knee and replaced it. "You wouldn't know if the Mexicans were done feeding?"

"I saw them leave," I said. "They usually go to town on Sundays."

"That's what I figured. Just thought I'd ask." Jarrett looked at me and stood up straight. "What about you? Off to church?"

"Planning to."

"What if I could talk you out of that?" he said.

"Something wrong?"

Jarrett hum-hawed around. I figured he probably wanted the morning off to go drink coffee in St. Basil or ride snowmachines in Kilgore. Maybe he'd fake sick, I thought, and half-expected a weak cough.

"Well, sort of." Jarrett said. "Yeah, you could say something's wrong. I got a little gal at Heise that don't want to go in the calving pen. Needing an extra hand for a bit."

"You call Drue?" I said. Drue was our head cowboy.

"He's in church too," Jarrett said. "Least I'm assuming. He didn't answer." Jarrett put his hands in his pockets.

Everyone was gone, unavailable, leaving me alone. I debated what would cause more trouble: missing church or letting Jarrett sweat it out on his own.

"Hold on," I said. "I'll meet you in the truck."

Jarrett nodded and walked across the backyard through his own snow tracks.

I pulled off my church slacks and white shirt and tossed them onto the bed and put on jeans and a hoodie. In the garage, I found my insulated boots, and grabbed a pair of feeding gloves and a stocking cap. Outside, Jarrett leaned against one of the white farm flatbeds and smoked. When he saw me, he flicked the cigarette into the snow and got into the truck.

I jumped in the passenger side, the door grinding shut on uneven hinges. The truck's transmission whirred beneath us and we reversed out of the driveway.

"You owe me a smoke," Jarrett said, arm propped on the seatback. He squinted out the back window. "I only had two puffs before you came running out."

The seat springs squeaked beneath me. I leaned over and adjusted the fan, changing the heat to the dash. Pieces of alfalfa flew out and smacked against the back window like dead flies, and stale air warmed my face. Jarrett turned the truck onto the highway and we accelerated. Between us, inside the truck, sat a small cooler full of cattle medicine. Jarrett fished out a serrated steak knife from under the cooler and stabbed it into the crack between the dash gauges and the air vents.

"Wouldn't wanna lose good Foster cutlery," Jarrett said.

I didn't respond. Outside, ice crept across the road in irregular formations. The morning air seemed brittle but invading, and we drove along in a pocket of our own lonely visibility.

Jarrett reached across the cooler and punched my shoulder. "Shiz," he said. "You don't owe me no cigarette. I was just messing."

"You shouldn't smoke," I said.

"Correction," Jarrett said. "You shouldn't smoke. I do whatever I dag please."

"It'll kill you."

"So'll ranching," Jarrett said. "So'll pop. So'll TV. So'll driving this jalopy truck. Criminy, the u-joints are thin as wire."

"Fix them then. It's your truck too. I mean, jeez, I don't want to die in here."

"We all gotta die somewhere. We all gotta die of something."

"Deep," I said, halfway quietly. This was not how I expected our first conversation to go.

"What was that?" Jarrett asked.

"Nothing," I said. The ranch hands had told me all this before. Pickup truck philosophers, horse-bound sages. Give a man a coffee thermos and he becomes a modern day Moses.

"If you got a problem with me, speak up."

"Forget it," I said, louder.

"Well, I don't care who you are, boss's son or not, I don't like my ideals being drug through the mud." Jarrett looked at me over the cooler.

"I didn't say anything," I said.

Jarrett punched me again. "Lighten up, man." He grinned and propped himself tall in the seat. "You seriously gotta ease up. You think I got anything figured out? Look at me. I'm just a harelip. I don't know no better. In fact, you're probably right. I ought to quit smoking. But I guarantee if everyone had a smoke a day, this world would be five degrees calmer."

We passed houses huddled among cottonwood trees, the smoke inching out from chimneys and hanging above the homesteads like shawls, and took the old state highway that split the snow-covered fields. Drifts had blown up near the road, rock-hard and tinged dirty, and bare spots of frozen field soil showed through. Jarrett searched around the seat of the pickup and found his pack of cigarettes and shook one out of the box. He held the cigarettes out to me, I waved him a no, and he cracked the window and lit up.

"Figured," Jarrett said, blowing a stream of smoke out the open window. "Just being cordial."

"Thanks."

"Let's get down to serious business here, Jeremiah," Jarrett said. "Tell me what it feels like knowing you're gonna be a prince of mostly eastern Jefferson County, Idaho someday."

"What?" I said.

Jarrett chuckled. "It's gotta feel good, I imagine, knowing one day all these trucks, all this land, all of it will be yours." He patted the pickup's dashboard emphatically.

"None of it's mine," I said.

"You're Claxton's kid, aren't you?"

"Yes."

"Parents give presents to their kids, right?"

"Right."

"Then you stand to get all of this. You're the oldest."

"Never thought of it that way."

"Sassafras-and-kiss-my-crack you've never thought it. Cheese, I figure you're jerking off to the thought on a nightly basis."

"Seriously," I said, lying, since I'd considered owning it all many, many times. "I'll go on a mission, then probably college. Maybe I'll be a dentist or something."

Jarrett snorted. "Listen, buddy, I like you. But you're not fooling no one. It's nothing to be ashamed of. If I had this spread, I'd give the mission double-birds, say humparoo to all that, and take over right outta high school. You seem like a smart kid."

We traveled in silence. Outside: ice blue, blanket white.

Jarrett turned up the country music and tapped on the steering wheel, glancing my direction. We crossed the Snake River and wound around the hot springs, passed the empty camper park, turned down the gravel road. Another slow mile across ruts and snow, and we arrived at the Heise ranch and drove to the yard. Jarrett parked the truck along the bunkhouse and got out. I followed him across the yard to a pole fence.

In the day lot, out beyond the pens, the pregnant cows lulled around the feeders. Trails traced the fence line. The government-leased land where we summered the cattle was white but splotched with the muted green of junipers and sage.

"There's that ornery snot," Jarrett said. "In the corner." A lone cow paced along a jog in the fence.

Jarrett switched in the four-wheel drive on the pickup hubs, and we got back in and drove out into the day lot. Cows followed us for a time then broke back to the manger. We reached the cow, a small red and white heifer wet with sweat, and Jarrett stopped at a distance.

"I'm gonna go open up the corrals," Jarrett said. "You push her up the fence."

I thought about pulling rank, telling Jarrett I'd do the driving and he'd do the walking, but instead I bailed out and jogged through the snow. That cow, full of skitters and venom, bucked when she saw me and bolted down the fence line. Jarrett rodded the truck and cut her off from doubling back. The cow ran dead-force into the barn pen. Jarrett left the truck driving and jumped out for the gate. The truck puttered into a high drift and died trying to push itself through. We dug the truck out with a pitchfork and a board, sweating great clouds of steam, while the cow thrashed around inside the pen.

Once back in the yard, Jarrett and I leaned against the fence and watched the heifer, high-tailed and panicked, move from one corner of the pen to the next, sniffing for a way out.

"Guess you can take me back down now," I said. I figured I could still make most of the church meetings.

"Horse hay," Jarrett said. "You're here to help. Gotta figure out what's going on. She's been acting like this all morning."

I shivered, compelled by cold. I had calved plenty, or should say, had been with many others who knew what they were doing. I had grown up on the farm assisting, running back and forth fetching tools and medicine, shoveling holes and pulling rye from wheat. It would be a stretch to say that I could diagnose, repair, or manage without help. I couldn't. I watched the cow bolt around the pen, eyeballing through the cracks in the panel fence. She held her tail high, and she was gelled-up and cat-backed. She was trapped, and she moved from corner to corner as if driven by some inexplicable tornado force.

"You want my coat or what?" Jarrett said.

"I'm fine." It was my mentality to never take something on the first offer, to let a person bargain and beg me into it. Truth was, that coat looked inviting.

"Suit yourself," Jarrett said, and left me. I heard the truck start, and turned to see Jarrett backing it up. I walked over to him.

"Where do you think you're going?" I asked.

"Get in and see," he said.

I walked around and got in. Jarrett maneuvered the pickup around and nosed it up to the fence, facing the cow. He shifted into park and turned the heater on high.

"May as well be warm," Jarrett said.

"Won't we waste a bunch of gas?" I said. The truck idled faster then dropped down to a normal rumble.

"Claxton would want you warm right now," Jarrett said. "Gallon of gas ain't nothing compared to no help at all."

We watched the cow through the window. She calmed some, which was good, and for a time stayed in the straw. Jarrett laughed, a sound like a hard hiccup.

"I ever tell you about the time I whupped on that St. Basil boy for calling my sister a hooker?" he asked. "Best part, I ain't even got a sister."

"Jarrett," I said, "this is the first time we've ever hung out."

Jarrett said, "I know. Just wanted to see if you were asleep over there."

Jarrett told me his yarns: dirt bike rides, bar fights, and the Great Montana Bush Company, a strip club in Missoula, only pausing to light another smoke. The cab filled up with blue gray haze. I felt warm within this cloud, dizzy, talking of things that would make my mother blush, topics that my father condemned in all his meetings.

Finally, I egged Jarrett on, saying, "You talk big, but I bet you're still a virgin."

Jarrett laughed so hard I thought he'd puke. "You waxing me? You just wanna get your rocks off, hear about some real hot stuff. Well, it's your lucky day, Jeremiah Foster, because I'm just the guy to indulge your dark side."

"I bet," I said.

"You're proving me right by the minute, Jeremiah. We're all just a bunch of animals."

"Thou sayest. But you still aren't talking."

"So here it is: my cousin and me, right, we got these girls from Archer who tell us—straight to our faces—that they're ready and willing, all's we gotta do is find a private place. So we had an idea in that my cuz's old man has a tree stand on the river bottoms he uses for deer hunting. We just have to class the joint up a bit. So we get some plywood for a roof and some walls, some camp mattresses and what not, and we call those girls and take them up there and—"

Mid-sentence, Jarrett plopped out of the truck and went over the fence, not bothering to shut the truck door. I saw the cow down on her side, her back legs rigid. Jarrett leaned down to her, the cigarette caught in the corner of his mouth. I shut the truck off, jumped out, and scaled the fence.

"Get that barn open," Jarrett yelled.

I ran across the pen and swung open the aluminum gate to the loading alley, unlatched the plywood door to the barn, and went inside and shut the newborn pens. I came back out and Jarrett was pushing against the red heifer, trying to make her stand.

"Get her on her feet," Jarrett said. We both pushed against the cow's haunches. She groaned. Jarrett knelt on her, wrapped her tail around his fist, and pried it over her tailbone. At the pressure, the cow stood quickly and bucked. The movement sent Jarrett off the cow's back in an arc, and Jarrett flew and thudded a few feet away. But he was up like a hare, and we chased the cow down the alley and inside the barn.

The cow thrashed through the moldy straw and crashed against the walls. She seemed gigantic and desperate in that small space, panicked and ready to eat us whole. At the head catch, I pulled the rope and snapped the gate shut behind the cow's ears. She yanked back hard, stressing the wooden joists, and then stepped forward to take the pressure from her throat.

Jarrett had his coat off. He'd sweated through his checkered shirt.

"Get her tail," Jarrett said. He rolled up his sleeve.

I grabbed the tail and pulled it out of the way. When Jarrett buried his hand inside the cow, her tail went rigid as a tree branch.

"What the frick?" Jarrett mumbled, then slid in further. "Can't feel nothing." He closed his eyes, I imagined him visualizing what should be where. "Not sure she's got anything," Jarrett said. He pulled out his arm and shucked off slime. "No face, no front hooves. Nothing." He picked up some straw and used it to clean his arm. "She ain't dry. She's got a bag full of milk."

"We should call someone," I said, growing worried.

"Fetch no," Jarrett said. "This is our bad. We should have been paying better attention. Crap. Let me try one more time." He went bicep-deep again, eyes closed, talking to himself. His face lit. He propped his free arm against the barn wall and strained backwards. The cow contracted, and a tiny hoof emerged. Jarrett pulled again and this time the hoof came free and Jarrett fell back into the straw. Pale, Jarrett stood, holding the calf leg like a club, and looked down at it, perplexed and angry.

"That can't be good," I said, pointing to the leg. I'd seen calves come breech. I'd seen calves stillborn. But I'd never seen a calf in pieces.

"What in the fetching … " Jarrett trailed off, patting the front of his jeans and his shirt pocket. "Where's that phone?"

"That's just a leg," I said. Jarrett dropped the appendage and searched pockets with both hands. "That's not normal."

"Mother. Effing. Shizballs." Jarrett shuffled around the barn kicking wet straw. "Where's that cell? Go out and look in the truck."

I ran out and went through the jockey box and the door panel pockets and the crack of the bench seat and even looked inside the medicine cooler. I paused,

I searched around the yard and re-walked our path to the barn. Finally, out in the pen where Jarrett had been bucked off, I found the cell, squashed in the snow, a crack down the screen. I took it to Jarrett, and he shook the phone a few times as if trying to revive it. We walked back to the pickup, Jarrett swearing all the way.

"You want I should go back down to church and get my dad?" I asked.

Jarrett took a small spiral notebook and half a pencil from the cooler. "No," Jarrett said. "I'm gonna get my nalgas canned over this. I know I am. Eff. It's closer to go to my house. I'm gonna draw you a map and you're gonna drive down and get my personal cell. Soon as you get it, call everybody you can think of and get us some help."

Jarrett moved so I could get into the truck. He shut the door and walked off towards the barn. He climbed the fence but waved me down before I could leave.

"And bring my calf puller. It's in the garage."

"Isn't there one in the barn?" I said.

"Yours," Jarrett said, "is a piece of crap. I got us one that works."

Twenty minutes later, I pulled into the driveway at Jarrett's. Crystalline flakes fell from the gray sky. I went inside the kitchen and found the cell and flipped it open and dialed the house number. As the phone rang, although a twinge of nervousness invaded me, perhaps warned me, I walked down the narrow hallway of Jarrett's trailer. I examined the bathroom, the guest bedroom, Jarrett's own room. This invasion filled me with excitement.

What did I expect to find? A tattooed woman asleep in his bed? Fleshy magazines of carnal positions? But all in all, it was clean and private but for a poster above Jarrett's bed of the Budweiser girls in red, high-cut bikinis. No one answered at my house. I walked out to the truck and called Claxton and Drue on their cells, but both went straight to voicemail. I called the house again as I walked to the garage for the calf puller. This time mom answered, home to put some water on the roast before church let out. I explained the situation. She said she'd go find dad. I left the garage, puller in hand, and went back out into the bleak day.

A minivan sat behind the pickup, blocking its exit. An overweight man and woman took up the front seats. The woman in the passenger seat rolled down her window and I walked to her.

"Jarre..." the woman started. "You're not my son!"

Inside the van sat the whole family: Jarrett's father in slacks and white shirt and tie, his mother with her purple flower dress and ski coat, two young carrot-topped boys—miniatures of Jarrett himself—in the backseat, and a skeletal woman, a grandmother, sitting straight-backed beside them.

The father leaned over his wife and grinned goofily. "Cold enough for you?"

"Pretty cold," I said.

"I was hoping," the mother said, "that Jarrett was home early so he could come for Sunday dinner. He's been working so much we never get to see him."

"You need a coat?" the father said before I could answer. "Got one in here somewhere." He turned to the backseat, huffing and shifting his weight, the van rocking with his movements.

"No, I'm fine," I said. I spoke to both of them. "Jarrett sent me down for his phone. We have a, uh, situation. On my way back now."

"Are you hungry?" the woman said. Before I could answer, she said, "There's a ham in the oven that I started before sacrament meeting. Should be perfect."

"No, no. I have to get back."

"Let me make you a few sandwiches. Done in a jiff." She nodded to her husband, who turned the van. They drove slowly down the road and pulled into the neighboring driveway, not two hundred feet from Jarrett's trailer. Jarrett's mother bustled up the steps and into the house, Jarrett's father helped the elderly woman across the snow, and the two brothers packing their bibles paused long enough to plaster one another with snowballs. Two heeler dogs rounded the corner and eyed me warily and disappeared under the porch.

Soon came the heavy woman with a plastic grocery sack. "Tell Jarrett we missed him again," she said. "At church and at supper."

Back at the corrals, the barn was filled with a mish-mash of urgency and anger and overexertion and the hot foul smell of things gone wrong. Claxton had arrived and was standing behind the cow. He wore the mechanic coveralls that he carried in his pickup—a gray jumpsuit that had seen every job created by his farm and ranch. I could see my father still had on his white button-down shirt and tie and black slacks beneath his coveralls. His shiny dress-up church boots were splotched with excretion and blood.

"Let loose her head," my father was saying to Jarrett. "She's got to lay down."

Jarrett ran to the head catch and flipped free the catch pin and opened the beams. The cow stumbled back and flopped onto her side. I tried to give Jarrett his phone. He shooed me away, shaking his head, saying flip and hell alternately.

"Jeremiah, where's that puller?" Claxton snapped.

"In the truck," I said.

"What good is it to out there?" he said. "Go fetch it."

I went to the truck for it and when I returned, Jarrett had the cow by the tail and Claxton stood waiting for me. He took the puller and knelt in the straw.

"Calf's been rotting inside," my father said. "The vet'll be here soon but for now we're going to take out the pieces. She's pushing like she wants it out." Claxton sunk into the cow, chains in hand. "Think I got another hoof. Jeremiah, come work this." He motioned for me to take the calf puller.

I took the chains and hooked them to the sliding handle and then began to crank, hesitantly. The chains pulled taut. The cow moaned. I felt tearing on the other end, inside her, bone from socket, muscle from bone. I had pulled a calf once or twice before. Work with the cow. Pull the calf through the narrows. Then, in a release, in a wave of pink and gush, there comes the baby, alive. Break the sack, stick some straw in its nose. Make it sneeze, breath. There is the mother, warming its child, licking it clean.

"Faster," Claxton said. "Hurry. Work those contractions."

"Dad," I said. "Hold on." This was not the normal sensation. I cranked and—nothing. Nothing resisting, nothing waiting. I reeled in an empty line. The chains floated inside the cow, connected to void. And then I rocked backwards, past my balance point.

"You got to go faster," my father said.

I sat down in the straw and stopped cranking. "Give me a second," I said, dropping the puller. I propped my elbows on my knees, made fists, and rested my head on my knuckles.

"Are you kidding me?" Claxton said. "Jarrett, come run this thing."

Jarrett rushed over and took the puller. My father and Jarrett ignored me, focusing their attention on the metal and the flesh. I went outside, breathing in the freezing air, and leaned against the pole fence to watch the bovine movements out in the lot. So calm and predictable. Colored blobs chewing cuds in the great white cold.

A bright red diesel pickup arrived. It was the veterinarian, a big man with a gray moustache and knee-high boots that lived a few miles from our place.

"Hello Jerry-boy," he said. "Where's the action?"

I nodded to the plywood door, even though he was already headed that way, swinging his med box like a brown paper bag. I followed him inside, hoping my father wouldn't say anything to me in front of a stranger. Claxton conferred with the cow doctor.

The vet injected the heifer with painkillers. He made an incision, coated the innards with anesthesia, and reapplied the chains.

The vet held up his hands, which were coated in slick lubey goop, and said, "Jarrett, you need a vat of this for all that tail you're getting on the weekends?"

Jarrett smiled weakly, and my father knelt down and pinched open the heifer's eyelid and gazed at her eyeball for a time.

"Slicker than snot," the vet said, pulling out the dead calf in chunks and appendages. He flushed out the residual gunk, zipped her back together, and dosed her with steroids and antibiotics. The mother cow, near death, lay in the straw.

"Good as new," the vet said, as he wiped his instruments clean on his pant leg.

Finally, the four of us left the barn. Jarrett, the veterinarian, and I all climbed over the fence, but my father, thin as he was, went horizontally between the poles, and then cleaned his hands in the snow. I carried the calf puller to the flatbed.

"Claxton," the vet said, "why don't you follow me down to the clinic and I'll get you the doses you'll need for next week."

My father got in his truck and rolled down the window. "You coming with me?"

I looked back at Jarrett, who leaned against the wall of the barn with one boot pressing against it, staring off into the hills.

"What are you doing?" I asked Jarrett.

"Push the herd to the night lot, then go home," Jarrett said.

"Mind if I stay?" I asked him.

"Why not?" Jarrett said. "Can't screw anything else up."

My father, who'd been listening, rolled up his window and followed the vet down the road before I could answer him. I walked over to Jarrett and gave him his phone.

"Sorry it took so long," I said, "but your mom and dad stopped me."

"Where'd you see them?" he asked, slipping the cell into his front pocket.

"They just got home from church," I said. "They sent up some food."

"Let me guess. Ham."

"Yep," I said.

"Fricking ham. You'd think that woman would throw in a roast every now and again."

We walked back to the truck. Jarrett took a soda and drank. I fished out a sandwich and handed it to him.

"I can't eat that today," Jarrett said. "You want it?"

"Not hungry," I said.

Jarrett took the sandwich and did some terrible looking baseball wind up, kicking his lead leg high and pumping the sandwich behind his head, then hurled the dinner roll and meat as far as he could into the snow.

"Your old man," Jarrett said. "He can be a hatchet, can't he?"

"Your dad treat you like that?" I asked.

"Used to," Jarrett said. "But he's not too keen on it anymore."

"You know," I said, "I met your family, saw your place. Seemed nice. You and me, we aren't so different."

Jarrett tried to blow a ring into the shapeless sky, then flicked the spent butt into the snow. "You know what else? My forearms are so tired feels like I spent all day wrestling a flipping elephant."

We waited until dusk and then went out to the day lot with a broken bale of hay on the flatbed and drove around until the cows followed us into the night pen.

Jarrett turned on the floodlights while I double-checked the gates, then together we went into the barn and made sure the heifer still lived. She breathed shallowly in the shadows.

"She ain't three feet from death's doorstep," Jarrett said, nudging a hoof with his boot. "Come on, let's clean up this mess."

Jarrett took the ribs and leg and the hips, I gathered the backbone and ill-formed head, and we took it all to the burn barrel near the bunkhouse. Jarrett dumped in fuel from a gas jug, and then lit a handful of straw off his cigarette and dropped it in the barrel. Flames jumped out.

"I don't think it's going to burn," I said. "It's all wet."

"Well, what else is there to do with it?" Jarrett said as we walked back to the truck, "leave it for Drue or the Mexican boys? Forget that."

Jarrett drove the truck slowly back to the valley. We traveled mostly in silence. I thought about that cigarette, and even considered asking Jarrett to finish his tree stand story. But Jarrett looked tired and unhappy, annoyed, and I didn't push the subject. About a mile from my house, Jarrett spoke up.

"I think it's time I uprooted," Jarrett announced. "I heard a guy can make a grip of cash roughnecking out in Wyoming."

"What about your family?" I said. "They seemed nice."

"They're all right," Jarrett said. "Just too close."

"You got to go someplace to eat Sunday dinner," I said. "That's what my dad always says."

"Your dad ever hear of ramen noodles?" Jarrett said. "Or Taco Bell?"

"That's not the point."

"Then what is?" Jarrett asked. We pulled into my driveway and

Jarrett parked. "Listen, my family ain't going nowhere. I know where to find them if I need them."

"Do they feel the same way?"

"Look at me. I'm just a harelip. What would they miss if I hit the road?"

I nodded, then looked behind me to my house, making sure no one was outside. "Hey. Don't say anything to the other guys about me smoking, okay? Or my dad?"

Jarrett got into his own pickup and started it. "Jeremiah, I'm like a bear trap. Skull and crossbones and daggers and all that. I won't tell a soul." He grunted goodbye and left.

I walked towards the house. Below zero, for sure, by now. I bent down and took snow in my hands and scrubbed them together. Jarrett hit the highway, the exhaust pipes of his truck popping like gunshots.

In the garage, I stripped off my boots and jeans, caked with barn straw and manure and afterbirth, hung my sweatshirt on the pegs by the back door, and went inside. In the laundry room, I pulled on an old blue robe, then went into the kitchen. I heard mom somewhere in the back of the house, the other kids downstairs. Dad stood at the sink, a plate of food in his hands. He ate and looked out the window.

"Your mother saved you some dinner," my father said, nodding down to a plate covered with tin foil. Mom usually did this every Sunday for dad, who rarely made it home from his church meetings to eat with us. She'd dish up a plate and mark the foil with a CLAX. The foil from dad's plate lay crumpled on the counter.

"How's she doing up there?" Claxton asked.

"She's breathing," I said.

"Cows go in okay?"

"Yes sir."

My father scraped clean his plate. "What do you think of that Jarrett Buckett?"

"I don't know," I said. "What do you?"

Dad set his plate in the empty sink. "I wish he had a head on his shoulders. Plight of the cowboy, I guess."

"You're not going to fire him, are you?"

My father said. "The truth about people like Jarrett is that they don't last, wherever they go. You never get the chance to fire them. They run too fast." He said no more and left the kitchen.

I unrolled the crinkled foil left from my father's plate and found that my mother had written JERRY-BOY across the top. Dad had eaten my food. I opened up his plate—CLAX as prominent and evident as a banner—and held it up to my face and sniffed. Mashed potatoes, corn, roast beef, all of it soaked in gravy. In fact, the beef was from our herd, a decent young steer that broke a leg. Our typical Sunday ranch meal. But as I breathed, I smelled my hands, still covered with that wet dead stench from the calf, and a faint hint of blue tobacco smoke laced beneath.

I couldn't eat this meat-and-potatoes, not today, maybe not ever again. I scraped the food into the garbage can, washed and dried the plate, and went to the basement to shower.

In the stall, I turned on water as hot as I could stand. Why had Dad eaten my food? Because of him, a fierce emptiness ached in my gut. I took the pumice stone and scrubbed my hands and forearms and ankles and thighs and the goop beneath my fingernails and the tops of my feet and my ashen fingers until my body glowed pink and tender, until my skin looked like it belonged to someone else.

LONG IN THE TOOTH

2008

The Idaho winters are dying. The winds blow less and less each year, and the snow seems to come later, once it has wandered and lost itself on the Canadian prairie or to volatile Midwestern ice storms, and only reaches my mountain valley a few days before Christmas. The mountainous, nine-foot-high plowed piles of ice from my childhood are now three-foot gravel-filled humps cornering the driveways. The piles stand as misshapen, bleached sentinels guarding the breezeways and bridges of my dead-end country road.

But before the snow falls, after the potatoes are dug and the barley is stored up in silos that are capped and sealed with caulk, the cold creeps across the hills and settles in for a six-month stretch. The ground, chisel-plowed and duck-footed, is barren and brown. The stubble fields are spotty with golden straw stalks sticking up through swaths of blackened ash, left from the ritualistic fall burnings that recycle nitrogen to the soil. As I return from Tucson, the sagging barbed-wire fences and huddled houses along the highway, the shelves of snow-capped peaks on the horizon, remind me that nothing—not even dying—really ever changes. Sometimes there's snow on the ground, and other times there's just yellowing grass.

The night my wife Renae and I arrive, I pull our luggage into my parent's garage. Heads of animals killed by my father line the unfinished walls—glassy eyes of three trophy elk and a white-tailed buck stare down at me, the racks nailed to bare two-by-sixes that form the carport. Pepper, our four-year old border collie, stands quickly from her pillow with an irreverent tail wag that shakes her entire body. I can't say that I'm as happy, but scratch her hard between the ears. Pepper lays back down, satisfied. She's much fatter than when I left, so I make a mental note to discuss it with Abby, my youngest sister. The rest—my four other sisters and me—do much better dictating the rules rather than complying, and often delegate the nitty-gritties down to the more responsible, blondish seventh-grader.

The next morning, I leave for a jog down to the local chapel and find Pepper in the garage, growling at another black mutt whose hair is clumpy and stringy like a musk ox's. Later, my mother tells me its name—Cubby—and its owners, a new family that lives in the cottonwoods. Charging at the larger, less-fierce dog, Pepper's teeth glisten like rain-gutter icicles. Cubby prances, occasionally breaking for the interior, but Pepper cuts him off and lunges for his muzzle. She's no guard dog, rather a high-strung cow dog that suffers from ADD, opting to roam underneath the apple trees and catch horseflies instead of participating in shepherding or pickup-truck riding. Unless Abby, who enjoys that familiar caretaker's bond, was injured, the dog would not defend the family. If someone were to invade, Pepper would greet the intruder with her familiar sideways wag.

What distresses the dogs so much is plopped on Pepper's pillow—a red fox squirrel, frozen solid. I jump, but once I realize the creature is dead, try to pick it up. Pepper flashes a toothy snarl, so I sidestep and jog off into the clear, cold morning, leaving it to them to battle out.

The Mormon chapel, a red brick, two-story country church house with a simple white steeple, sits a mile and a half away. Our little rural community was founded around 1884, when Wilford Woodruff, a prophet, dictated the Wagon Box Prophecy, claiming that the cruel climate would be tempered if Latter-day Saints relocated from Salt Lake to farm the Idaho foothills. The first Mormon bishop in the area was named Clark; the chapel carries his name.

In my youth, it was a strange occurrence to meet someone who wasn't Mormon, who you didn't see at Sacrament Meeting or Boy Scouts. In those flat valley hinterlands, the church is society's mechanism. I remember knowing the specific families that lived in the various slat-board manufactured homes and squatty brick houses that stood so woefully at the edges of the bare fields. Part of my knowledge came from a hand-crafted pole that stood on the corner of the highway, nailed with peeling planks of wood to direct travelers up or down the roads, names like SCHOLES or BARNES branded into the pieces with arrows pointing in the appropriate direction. Sadly, the sign is no longer; a Jefferson County snow plow must have clipped and ended its helpful, yet tacky, existence.

As I run, I think of my friends, the Martinez family, and how I should call them. They live a half-mile east of the church in a faded tan trailer. It sits back behind an irrigation canal and has an elevated, narrow bridge that I've nearly backed off of twice. Old, irregular corrals shaped from throw-away lumber, corrugated tin, and pallets make a shifty feedlot on most of their small property, and shaggy, mismatched cows lull in ankle-deep, soupy mess. Two of my best friends, Victor and Hector, live there. They've been fatherless since last November.

The next day, I sit down with Abby at the kitchen table before she and Malorie, my fifteen-year-old sister, drive into town for school. They're both eating toast smeared with sloppy raspberry jam.

"You know, there's this thing humans do," I tell Abby. "We'll eat as much as is in front of us."

Abby continues to chew, rolls her eyes.

"Certain dogs can't stop eating, either. Dad told me you just tear a hole in the dog food and let Pepper eat all she wants? You gotta knock that off, she's getting way too fat."

Malorie interjects, spitting jam onto the table. "Oh! My! Gosh! I thought you were talking about Abby!" and laughs sophomorically, as if cheerleaders surround her. Abby nods quietly and bites off more toast. They aren't quite sure what to make of their college-educated brother who insists they ration out the Kibble-n-Bits with the acuity of a Weight Watcher, so they leave.

My mother—a short, kind-hearted woman attracted to homeopathic medicine and prone to tear up during Lifetime made-for-TV movies—enters the kitchen.

"It's not Pepper's fault she's fat," my mother says. "It's the hysterectomy."

This catches me off guard, and I imagine Pepper and Cubby lounging on the ditch bank, Pepper explaining that while she'd love to mother Cubby's pups, it just wasn't going to happen. I wonder if other surgeries as well, maybe a breast reduction, would be reasonably priced at the South Fork Vet Clinic to lift Pepper's saggy, indecent mammary glands.

"And it doesn't help that Jack died," she adds. It's never been confirmed, but openly believed, that Jack, our now-deceased Golden Retriever, had sired the summer litter of Pepper's puppies. Jack was a sort of Don Juan on the dead-end street, and many of his bastard pups still roam there. Along with his natural tendency to impregnate every bitch on the block, Jack had an unhealthy fetish for porcupines—he tried to eat them. He finally died when undetected quills sunk deep into his nose and throat, lodging in his stomach, infecting him to the point he couldn't stand. My father had him euthanized.

"We all deal with it differently," I say to my mother. Out the kitchen window, we watch Pepper and Cubby racing in and out of pine trees at breakneck speeds. One catches the other, and they tumble together across the frozen grass.

My friendship with Victor Martinez began the day my mother convinced me to invite him to Boy Scouts. The invitation was frightening enough, since Victor, at six-foot-four and three-hundred plus pounds, is the largest Mexican I've ever seen. The second largest is his younger brother, Hector, who became a friend when I started bumming rides with Victor after football practice. Hector is six inches shorter, but brawny as a bull-calf.

Victor and Hector's massive shapes were a true anomaly since their father, Lauriano, weighed one-hundred and forty pounds. Both he and his wife worked at Idahoan Foods processing hash browns, and ran their eighty-acre hay farm on the side. When I stopped in, Lauriano was usually in their shop repairing a rusty tractor or feed truck—the only man I knew who kept a fifth of honey-colored liquor in the toolbox to pull from as he worked. Mrs. Martinez offered me heaping plates of rice and beans. Victor's younger brothers, Omar and Amador, hovered close enough to laugh at my stories, but hid when I looked their way. I finally won them over by eating a habañero pepper in one bite, a feat that nearly hospitalized me.

Back then, Lauriano had an interesting way of arranging the chicken-pecked, gravely yard. It seemed as though parking the farm machinery in an orderly fashion, or arranging the one-ton, four by four by eight-foot bales of hay in straight, high stacks were out of the question. It wasn't uncommon to see two or three bales stacked lop-sided and tipping in random corners of the yard. Sometimes the maroon Dodge would be pulled in front of the house for an oil change. While the neighbors burned garbage in fifty-gallon oil drums, making sure to keep them out of sight, Lauriano displayed his at the corner of the bridge, sending the acidic fumes of charred corn cobs and chicken bones across the canal, where they settled in gray clouds on the road.

And it seemed that no matter how bad I had it, working after school or weekends, the Martinez boys had it ten times worse. Victor nearly wasn't able to play football because Lauriano needed him on the farm, but ultimately his size and skill for the game won out. After practice, however, he jogged to his pickup in his sweaty football pants and drove straight home while the rest of us took our time showering and flipping each other with towels.

The one time I spoke with Lauriano was after my doctor's appointment where I learned that a back surgery could salvage the nerves in my right leg. I went in search of Victor to tell him my last season of high school football—and subsequent dreams of playing for the New York Jets—were crushed. He wasn't home. Hector and Lauriano were fixing fence along the road, so I spilled my sob story to them. Hector said nothing and stretched the barbed-wire tight with the rusty fencer. Lauriano, on the other hand, engaged me for the first time.

I had always assumed he didn't know English. I stepped closer and elevated my voice, making a ring with my fingers and trying to say that my lumbar disks had bulged like jelly donuts. At a loss, I gave up.

Curt, direct, he said, "Just tell me. I understand. I American too."

The Martinez family was Roman Catholic, but from junior high on, Victor attended Boy Scouts, played on church basketball teams, and even attended a Sacrament meeting every now and again. During potato harvest, he and I worked eighteen-hour days for Foster Agro, our only time off was driving to the valley for football practice.

The summer before my senior year, I quit the farm. It was a sunny Friday, and, tired of minimum wage and back-breaking hours, I just didn't go. My father pulled up in his big white Chevy and we yelled at each other until his tires squelched out of the drive. Victor, working at George and Jessee's OK Tire and cutting cabin logs on the weekends, gave me a job. I spent Saturday and Sunday with him, sleeping among tall sage brush and felling lodge pole pines. He did all the work—hefting the thirty-footers onto a hodge-podge trailer—but paid me more than my dad ever would.

After high school, Victor was recruited to play defensive line at Ricks, an extinct Mormon Junior College that required church attendance, regardless of the student's denomination. Victor, and I shared our first dorm with four others—Victor was one of only eight non-Mormons on campus. One day after practice, Kendall, another friend from our hometown, reported that a Lutheran kid invited Victor to attend church with him a few towns away. Victor looked around the locker room—massive Mormons, in towels and sweaty, soaked shirts, slowed to listen—and he replied, "Why don't you just come to mine?" He meant his Mormon one.

So even though my friends and I had spent our high school years vandalizing and cursing, we hadn't pushed Victor away from the church. As is customary, the missionaries came to our apartment and taught Victor the lessons. We pulled our mattresses into the front room and sat cross-legged, scriptures balanced in the oversized crotches of our pajamas, toothpaste ringing our slackened mouths, while Victor learned about Joseph Smith and the Book of Mormon.

On September 18th, 2000, Victor was baptized by Greg Price, our nine-fingered half-back. Although the typical baptism consisted of an audience of a dozen or so, Victor's crowd filled the chapel—an entire college football squad, coaches, cheerleaders, Rigby High students. But absent were Hector and Lauriano, Omar and Amador.

Freshman year forged us into something different. Victor lost his grandmother, and I sat on his bed as his giant shoulders heaved. Months later, Grandma Melba passed, and Victor watched my own silent shivering. At the end of term, Victor decided to spend the summer as a door-to-door salesman. The rest of us were called to preach the word to heathens in distant lands—I prepared to leave for Indiana that July.

Sesty, a Jersey kid next door, one of our cohort, knew he wouldn't be back for two years, so he chained his barely used Diamondback BMX bike underneath the stairwell, hoping it would stay put until he returned. As soon as we dropped him off at the bus, Victor and I threw out the seventh commandment and Rexburg laws and bylaws; with a Leatherman, a screwdriver, and a large rock, we broke the lock and took the bike to Omar and Amador for an early birthday present.

A year into my mission, in a sweaty town named Shelbyville, I received a letter and a photo from Abby, who turned eight, the typical age at which children born into the church are baptized. It explained that since I was so far away, Victor had performed her baptism. The photo was stunning—Victor, dressed neck to ankle in white, roughly the size of a mattress, with one massive arm reaching down to the shoulder of my fragile young sister, who, also in white, barely crested his knees.

It finally snows a few days before Christmas, and the squirrel disappears. I rise early to clean off the driveway and sidewalks, and Pepper stands watch, following every movement of the plastic shovel and prancing on the cold, naked pavement. She greets me every morning.

But three days before our trip ends, she's not there. The thought doesn't really strike me until I return from my jog to wake up my wife. My mother meets me at the door with the phone in her hand—her eyes are filled with tears: "Dave found Pepper on his lawn—she's been hit."

I think to find a gun—first instinct—but they're all locked up. Instead, my mother drives me to Dave's, a cousin-in-law, who has wrapped Pepper in a blue bathroom towel. When the dog sees the familiar SUV, she rises and coughs red foam.

Dave shows me speckled spots of snow painted with blood and saliva. My mother, late for work, asks that I load Pepper into the backseat of my aunt's Chevy Avalanche and take her to the vet. When I do, Pepper lays her head down on the seat without a whimper.

"Don't let her suffer," my mother says, holding my elbow. "Put her down if you have to."

"She's not mine—don't put that on me."

My mother leaves without an answer.

At speeds reckless for the icy roads, I rush into town, passing dilapidated farms, chapels, and the Rigby-Pioneer cemetery. A young, calm veterinarian at South Fork checks Pepper's reflexes, tests her strength, X-rays her chest. Surprisingly, the dog has no broken ribs, ruptured diaphragm, or deflated lungs. As the vet pumps Pepper full of dexamethasone, he explains that she probably just got bonked on the head. He warns the risk, however, is prevalent—if her brain swells, she's as good as gone. He prescribes food and water, a warm place, close monitoring.

The thought of choosing life or death lifted, the drive home is much slower, almost pleasant. I speak to Pepper in low, hushed tones, and think that in some countries, Pepper would be an entrée. When I make the left turn into our drive, she lifts up in the backseat, recognizing the yard and garage. Her body begins to wag side to side, and she—in the most innocent, supine way—defecates. I use the towel to clean off the seat and carry her inside.

I had called ahead to Renae asking her to remove the rugs from the back guest bathroom and to lay down Pepper's pillow. I lower the dog and begin to clean off her backside. Renae says, "You're gonna make a great dad."

Whether it's the motion or the feeling that crowds the half-bath, I remember my Uncle Vance, who died several years before from HIV complications. A cocaine addict and homosexual, once he contracted the virus he drastically limited communications with his eleven siblings and widowed mother. But when the family was informed that Vance's tired body was failing, five of the sisters and my grandmother rushed to Salt Lake for his last hours. Days after the funeral, my mother told me how gratifying it was to be in Vance's house and, along with the other familial matrons, wash, dry, and dress him before he closed his eyes for good.

As Pepper buries her muzzle into a dish of water, draining three bowlfuls in minutes, I remember the day that Victor lost his father. I had ditched my weekend farm obligations to watch a college football game with two friends. It was early November, the coldness having settled in a month previous, still snowless and yellow. When my mother rang my cell-phone, I almost didn't answer, assuming it would be some request to assist with the endless cattle vaccinations or welding. But, in her shaky bad-news voice—one I'd heard for my grandmothers, crop disasters,   Vance, and pets—she tells me that a hay bale fell on Lauriano Martinez, and that even though the ambulance made it, I needed to come down to comfort the boys.

Only Hector and Omar were at home—the rest in Idaho Falls at the hospital. In the yard, off to the left, I saw the mound of residual hay from the broken bale, and a loader tractor parked beside it. A fierce wind blew from the south.

Hector explained that his father and Omar had been feeding, and that Lauriano had forgotten something inside and walked back to the house alone. Blustery, bitter, the wind compelled Lauriano to walk next to a three-bale stack. It happened in seconds: the wind blew off the top bale, and it crushed Lauriano. Omar said the thud was almost inaudible due to the wind, and he turned from the fence to see the bale rocking to a lopsided stop on top of his father.

Hector, working a shift at the tire store, beat the ambulance. By then, Omar and his mother had cut the six twine strings holding the bale together and ripped off chunks of prickly hay by hand. But the result was unanticipated; instead of allowing more give, the bale peeled and flattened around Lauriano's body. With the loader tractor, they picked up what they could, and tore Lauriano out from underneath.

Hector related all of this to me in a stoic manner. He shook his head a few times and kicked gravel with the toe of his boot, but other than that he dictated as factually as a police blotter. Unlike Victor, he would not let me see him cry.

That night, three other friends and I visited the hospital. Victor had not yet arrived, so in the waiting room, we watched Omar and Amador squeeze their nose bridges to stanch the tears. Victor's mother cried and cried, and in her strained Spanish explained that intentaron, intentaron, hicieron todo lo possible. They tried, they tried, they did everything they could.

In the hallway, I grabbed Hector and explained that in the

Mormon Church and as Elders, my friends and I could give his father a priesthood blessing, anointing his head with sacred healing oil and blessing his body with peace and comfort. Hector, having lived and worked with Mormons his entire life, having heard us cuss and crack beers, talk about dirty women and skipping Church, declined, saying, "It's okay, man. You know, he was Catholic."

When Victor arrived, he spoke hushed to the nurse and waved us back to the room. Down the hallway, I told him what Hector had said, and, nodding, eyes damp and distant, he rocked my shoulder with his massive hand, and said nothing. In the room, Lauriano, tubes in his nose and mouth, IVs hanging from an aluminum tree, lines snaking into the skin opposite his elbow, was eggplant purple. His gown had fallen down like a toga, exposing his bruised and swollen chest. His shaved head was also swollen, and hot to the touch. The four of us anointed his broken body with the oil, placing our hands—hands with which we had flipped the bird, unclasped bra straps, and used for a number of ungodly acts—on his hand, avoiding his damaged head, to pronounce a healing blessing. Looking back and forth to Victor and his father, I believed we could save the man. Even though Jesus didn't start until thirty, I expected that we, none older than twenty-three, had faith to work miracles.

After the blessing and another round in the waiting room, we walked quietly out to the parking lot and realized it was snowing.

Pepper's vomit coats the tile floor. I open the backdoor to air it out, and the dog stands and hobbles before I catch her. Walking like a newborn fawn, knees unbending, head hanging loosely and waving side to side, she falls down three stairs and finally crawls to her normal corner in the garage.

I shut the doors and plug in a space heater to coax her health back, but it seems that the only thing she wants is water, water, water. Four more bowlfuls lapped up faster than her strength allows. I put on a glove and pet her until she falls asleep.

At three in the afternoon, Abby and Malorie return. When Malorie demands that Abby open the garage door, Pepper stumbles out, vomiting, and lies down in a snow bank. Abby screams and, before I can explain, shoots downstairs and slams her door. Once Pepper has cooled, I carry her back inside.

Abby, calmed, comes out. Awkwardly, I put my arm around her and, mimicking Hector, explain the situation in an even tone. Sniffling, she gets a dishful of food, takes my glove, and sits down beside Pepper, whispering beautiful things.

Renae and I leave to Idaho Falls for last minute purchases, and don't get home until ten. Although the garage door is barracked down, Pepper isn't inside. I ask my father, who's watching The Weather Channel—anticipating a severe cold front—if he's seen her.

"She got out—looked pretty hot," he says.

"I wonder if she was hit," I tell him. "Nothing wrong inside, didn't even bark when I picked her up."

"She was walking good earlier."

"Could someone just have whacked her on the head with a shovel? I mean, she's too smart to get hit by a car."

He sits back. "I haven't seen Henry's dog either, or that black one. Maybe someone poisoned them."

Sadly, this is not uncommon. Since all the neighbors own livestock, packs of dogs cause unneeded stress and death. The favorite local remedy is TNT, or Temik 'n Tuna, concocted by hiding Temik pellets— an insecticide dispersed over potato plants—into meat and setting the mixture out for the pests; its ingestion causes an agonizing and drawn- out death. My father's diagnosis makes sense, and my family begins to implicate strange neighbors with motives.

That night, I search the backyard, pasture, and canal bank with a Mag-light, whistling, calling. After twenty minutes or so, I'm too cold to keep looking—it's below zero. She's gone off somewhere to die alone.

The day after the accident, Hector needed help with the herd, so that Sunday three other locals and I ditched church and lined up pickups and horse trailers to load the ratty calves and transport them to working chutes five miles away. We left the mother cows and bulls, broken teeth and short gums, in the corral. It was a misty, depressing, low-hanging day. I joked with George Byram, the owner of the tire store, about high school sports and other meaningless things. Hector, the new patron of the Martinez herd, directed traffic and loaded the bunches, shouting and chasing with sticks.

At the corrals, we medicated, castrated, and dehorned the calves. They wandered down the alleyway confused and jumpy, looking side- to-side for their familiar hay stacks and milk bags. Then we slammed them into the squeeze chute. The injections—two quick shots in the rump. Castration via a thick green rubber band cinched tight around the scrotum, cutting off the circulation. Their shriveled sacks dropped off in weeks. If they were too mature, we'd cut them out with a pocket knife. Dehorning was done with a tool that looked like an oversized pair of toenail clippers. The sickening crunch—done with a fierce outward handle thrust, supposedly painless—severs a vein that supplies the horn with blood. Once clipped, it continues to pump with the calves' heartbeat, and makes them look like undead victims of B-grade horror flicks, crimson fountains spraying and hanging heavy in the mist. When the chute opened, the calves wandered out, shaking their lightened heads, and clumped at the back of the corral.

When we finished, we were covered in blood. Streaks painted the calves' shoulders and foreheads, and it seeped into our tan coats and leather gloves. By the end, we had stopped joking, knowing how the Martinez's must feel to be separated from life with a crack, a thud, a residue that coated everything. We shut our mouths and waved as we pulled the empty trailers home.

After the blessing, Lauriano improved, but three weeks later was transported to Salt Lake. Nothing could be done. The family removed the life support, and Lauriano expired soon after.

His funeral was held in a crumbling Catholic church in Idaho Falls. Unlike the Mormon services to which I'm accustomed, where the families spend hours telling cute and unlikely stories about the deceased, laughing over ham and scalloped potatoes, the Catholic version required us to kneel and pray, everyone wore black, and most of the congregation wept. I was detoured and missed the funeral procession, ending up back at the Rigby-Pioneer cemetery behind the rest.

On that cold, gray day, the empty maple trees seemed to loom up out of the ground like skeletal hands, tarsals and metatarsals, boney knuckles, blackened fingernails. Wet snow coated the ancient headstones, and trails from cars to the grave site wormed through the slush.

Pepper doesn't return and we mourn the fact we can't bury her. Malorie calls Cubby's owners. He's dead, too; a few days earlier, he crawled into his house and never came out. His paws were covered with chemical burns, his mouth and tongue ruined.

The morning we leave for the airport, I haul wrapping paper and gift boxes behind the shop to burn them. It takes one match to ignite. I stand outside, letting warmth wash over me as I take in the expansive, bleak horizon. I hear a sharp whine, and whistle. A strange bark jumps from behind the apple trees. It's Pepper, trapped underneath a pile of rotten fencing boards. She's chewed at the wood, clawed at the earth—too weak to pull her own body from underneath the stack. I jerk her out by the paws. She stumbles ten yards and collapses.

Carrying her into the garage, rushing into the house, calling my father and mother—I'm elated. What a way to leave town, I think. I found her, she'll live! As Renae loads our luggage, I shut down the garage and stuff a white pill coated in peanut butter down Pepper's throat, thinking myself a hero. As we leave, I text my sisters: FOUND PEPPER! GONNA B OK!

Days later, I talk to my mother, who tells me that the dog is surviving, Abby's giving her meds and making sure she's fed and watered. My mother adds, "I think Pepper's heartbroken without Cubby. All she does is wander out to the driveway, look around, and wander back."

My second day in Idaho, Victor and I drove to see his family. He stayed in the car on a phone call—still a door-to-door salesman, but pulling down six-figures. Hector, Omar, and Amador pitched hay with their backs to me. The yard was immaculate: the hay stacked four-high and in one long, straight row; the trucks and tractors lined up. Doors and windows closed tight. The mangers were clean from rotting feed and straw. The shop doors, shut; the fences, tall and taut. No broken bales in sight.

Not used to the cold, I flipped up my hood. Before I left, my hair was long and unkempt; now it was shaved. I wore sunglasses. When they heard me crunching through the straw and turned, they didn't recognize me.

Amador stammered a confused, "Fish?" My high school nickname, Fish, was given by a bully who converted my perfectly shaped earlobes into droopy, detached, nipple-shaped flabs. But when Amador said it, I smiled—instantly I wanted to move back, live in a trailer, throw away my books, and pitch hay.

They were strong and handsome. Amador, seventeen, had a nest of nappy black hair; Omar barely fit in his coveralls. Hector showed me a '73 Mustang, and talked Victor into giving him a ride to the auto body shop to retrieve a project truck. In the car, we joked and cussed, Victor punching me in the thigh when I teased him about slaving for The Man; me feigning and jabbing when he claimed he'd marry one of my sisters.

The project—a 1985 Chevy Short Box pickup—was painted a shining cherry red. Although a skeleton of what it would be—lacking windows, door handles, gauges, a radio, the seat wasn't even bolted down—it was one step closer. Victor paid, and Hector decided to take it to George and Jessie's for rims and tires before the snow arrived.

I climbed in the truck with Hector, and he laughed, telling me I'd freeze my ass off. We rolled down the highway. I'd never driven at high speeds without a windshield. The air rushed into the cab. I cinched my hood up; the bridge of my sunglasses froze and dug into my nose. Hector, hands at Ten and Two, shivered through his thick black work coat. I turned around and screamed an incoherent string of profanity. Behind us, Victor crawled along with his hazard lights flashing. I showed him both my middle fingers.

Hector pushed the truck up to forty-five, and the straining engine combined with the winter air thundered around the cab. Hector looked at me and laughed. I opened my mouth to do the same, but the cold busted through my teeth's enamel, channeling into the nerves of my molars and incisors, grinding into my jawbone, settling in my spinal column like the dull ache of a smashed thumb. Hector closed his mouth and looked away, I did the same.

By the time we passed the cemetery, the cold steadily wrestled tears out of our stubborn eyes, lines streaking across Hector's temples, the wetness flitting out the absence of a back window. We rumbled towards town without hesitation, giving the implication of such emotions no clout, no time, not even a second glance through the red metal frame where something solid used to be.

Ten days later, from sunny Arizona, I call my mother for an update on Pepper.

"She's dead—froze this morning."

I remember sitting on the garage step, watching my black-gloved hand disappear into Pepper's midnight fur.

My mother laughs a strained, forgiving laugh. "It was so strange—it's been so cold here, last night it dropped to twenty-two below." She chokes up. "I thought I'd bring in the heater, because she hasn't been leaving her pillow, but didn't, just shut the doors."

I think, How many times can you watch something revive only to expire, breathe only to choke, warm only to freeze?

"She was on her pillow, just like the squirrel. I bawled for ten minutes," she says.

"Abby?" I ask.

"That's what's funny. I went downstairs to wake her, and," she laughs through her tears, "when I ask her if she's okay, she says, just flat 'Yeah, Mom, don't worry—I'm through the worst.'"

GOD DAMNED THE LAND
BUT LIFTED THE PEOPLE

2007

I

My father's farms sit on hills that don't roll; rather, they pillow and hunker down among the mountains shadows not willing to rise and become mountains themselves but opt to squat along the base of the ranges and grow varieties of potatoes and wheat and beer barley and dairy hay. The hills ascend and escape eastward up the highway towards legions of tourists in Swan Valley and Jackson Hole. The hills never want attention; never strive for anything but to house the crops that feed the world, or at least the rest of the county. If there's ever a road sign that says "Scenic Idaho" it's because we put it there. Those don't grow naturally.

The land wasn't always this way, so motivated, so cultivated. Only four generations ago the Mormons arrived at the tucked away cottonwoods along the banks of the Snake River, big mountain sage and prairie grass then covering the hills. God's Chosen began to clear away the land and dig ditches and diversions, systematically checker-boarding the floodplain with canals ten feet wide, five feet deep. They installed head gates to regulate water flow, dams to direct it to the fields. They herded liquid survival across the high desert to their neighbors and brothers. Before the Mormons arrive, the ground was barren and cursed, but they made it paradisiacal.

But all was not perfect. No matter how righteous, the Mormons couldn't coax water to flow up the Snake's canyon walls and convert the hills. Instead they labored in the lowlands, fighting ancient riverbeds that had filled their land with stone and silt. They knew the lowlands provided survival but to make the hills grow would promise exaltation. The hills remained dusty and dry for years.

My father tells me that the world changed in 1950 when a brave well digger, straddling a bucket, was lowered down a recently dug shaft one hundred and fifty feet deep in the hills above Ririe. When they pulled him out he claimed the shaft opened up into a gigantic cavern and that a river raged underneath them. My father was born in 1957; by then, his father was piping water up the hills from the huge aquifer.

My grandfather started out with three hundred and twenty acres of dry farm land that refused to produce unless enough rain fell, which was rare. The whole operation was sketchy; their machinery repair shop was a retired school bus, his only hired help a Navajo named Woody. Things were tough going until George Lovell struck water. After that everyone knew the dry farm fields, burnt thin and golden year after year, would finally produce.

The discovery brought more well diggers and pump salesmen and power poles. The ground became a fecund soil. Men came with large field equipment. Irrigation stores began to pepper the valley. John Deeres and aluminum pipelines replaced the mules and rubber hoses. And change—conversion, if you will—poured in like a flood.

Tucked away in my mother's library is a tattered shoe box filled with photos of my childhood. We lived in the valley to be closer to town though my father's business had flourished and grown and his land now spread across the county. I'm sure my growing up is common still within the rurality of America; I'm not unique in that sense. The country kid is not yet extinct. We had our fun, my cousins and I, swimming in irrigation canals, and jumping from bridges, barns, and tree limbs.

While fishing through the box of photos, I was startled completely by one shot. Sheathed in neon green sweatpants, a blue sweater featuring a motorcycle, a pair of pink ski gloves, and a neck-warmer the color of a highway caution cone, I'm leaping from our roof into two feet of snow below. My location intrigues me. I've jumped, my mother clicking the shutter right as I stepped off. My form is like Christ on the cross; legs pegged at the ankles, arms outstretched to a T. The difference between Jesus and me, my palms point down. My shaggy brown hair stands on end. The roof's eave is right behind my knees— she caught me mid-fall, and I'm frozen, hovering ten feet above the drift.

I don't know if it's my hands, the way they hang parallel above the backyard, or if it's the stupid open mouthed grin that makes me think. If I was something else—some breed of wintertime grasshopper, an enormous desert jackrabbit—the picture could be me springing instead of falling. But memory solidifies the fact that gravity and my childhood were grounding me without a second's hesitation. Still that look as I peek at the ground from high above seems to say, Going up?

On our dead-end country road we spent endless hours shooting animals. If we weren't jumping our bikes or leaping from bridges or sliding down haystacks, we were hunting. All of us were given pellet guns at eight; twenty-twos at twelve. We took no prisoners. My father had one rule: no red-breasted robins—they ate the hay aphids and for that should be spared. I never told him one day I got seven in ten shots.

We had the whole place staked out: Magpie Heaven, a stand of Cottonwoods in the hay field; an elusive muskrat lived at the kink in the Dry Bed canal; a ball of garter snakes thrived underneath a discarded fridge in the dump. We rode our bicycles to the locations every day and shot whatever moved.

One time, a Salt Lake cousin shot a tree squirrel that I didn't even see. When he came back to the truck, he held it up by its tail and said something about a true woodsman keeps a keen eye. We nodded in agreement—even though he was from the city, his imparted adage would be useful. When the truck fired up and we bumped across the hayfield, we all felt like Daniel Boone.

Jorge Luis Borges argues that the river is time and time the river. As such the farms had flowed away from the flood irrigation and now almost all pumped the water and irrigated with sprinkler pipes. The investments the farmers had to make were incredible. They flattened the dikes, bought and buried foot wide expensive steel mainline pipe to carry the water from the ditch. They purchased hundreds of aluminum connector pipes, three inches in diameter, forty feet long, with a sprinkler stand in the middle to lie out in the crop. With the improvement the farmer didn't have to regulate canals every waking minute. He could attach the connector pipes in a line, turn on an industrial sized pump, and sprinkle his crop in twelve-hour increments. He could sleep the whole night with his wife rather than wake up at three in the morning to change a dam. Generations of Mexicans came to the farms anticipating unlimited work—they weren't disappointed.

The first summer that I had to work, I moved two handlines, each with thirty-two pipe, at six in the morning and six at night, seven days a week. The lines stopped twice to cut the hay. We spent the middays shooting animals and swimming. Moving pipe was a miserable job in that it was tedious and taxing. Unlatch a pipe, pick it up, walk it twenty yards, latch it, return, repeat. Flies swarmed eyes, mosquitoes feasted freely as human hands were occupied with hefting. In the morning, the pipes were ice-cold with canal water; by evening the tin cooked from the summer sun.

Sometimes I would move lines with another cousin together so we could talk as we worked. Once while walking home we chased a mouse out from the hay and it ran under the apple trees in my backyard. Instinctually, we flew after it. It scurried for a small tree along the fence. When we closed in, its random, sporadic movements—the unpredictable flightiness of it—made me nervous. I stayed back. My cousin lunged, got its tail, and lifted it up for me to see. The rodent curled and bit him on the end of his index finger. He dropped it and it scampered away. He held up the finger and squeezed pinpricks of blood from the tip. They weren't supposed to fight back, I was thinking. They never had before.

Historically, rodents have always been a bane to earth's inhabitants. Their first appearance in text, according to Charles Elton, author of Voles, Mice, and Lemmings, appears in the Old Testament. Although the vole passages are omitted from the English Bible, Elton cites the Vulgate and the Septuagint translations as telling how God sent a vole plague to punish the Philistines for carrying off the Arc of the Covenant. Unable to fight off the pests, the Philistines listened to their priests and returned the arc along with five golden mice as a gift to appease the angry god.

Concerning mice, Aristotle remarked that:

The rate of propagation of field mice in country places, and the destruction that they cause, are beyond all telling. In many places their number is so incalculable that but very little of the corn crop is left to the farmer; and so rapid is their mode of proceedings that sometimes a small farmer will one day observe that it is time for reaping, and on the following morning, when he takes his reapers afield, he finds his entire crop devoured.

In 1822, French naturalist and lawyer Charles Gérard said that his town of Alsace was completely ravaged by rodents. "It was a living and hideous scourging of the earth, which appeared perforated all over, like a sieve," he writes. The picture he paints, the devastation breaking like a wave, the "small, swift, flitting forms that infest the ground and devour all living plants," and the inhabitants' vain counterattack of fumigation, poison, plowing, trenching, and prayers is a futile one.

After reading the accounts of rodent infestation, it's no surprise that Hamelin's denizens piled the Pied Piper with praise and gifts when he ridded them of their own plague. I wonder if they ever doubted that their children were worth the trade.

Riding high in a hay swather as a child with my father, I remember watching the small black flashes flee in the seconds that the blades exposed the ground. The mice, out in the open, flitted away from the machine's churning mouth and dodged the huge tires. When one would flatten out and freeze I knew it was a goner. From the air conditioned cab, some seventies band blaring in the background, I saw the world relieved of mice one by one.

As I looked down from the tractor or down the barrel of a rifle, death seemed inconsequential. When I shot a bird, for instance, I usually arrived at the corpse post-trauma. They were done flopping and just lay there, wings folded in like some blemished specimen. Once still and hard, I'd retrieve the bird by its back legs and proudly show it to friends or relatives. But if I arrived on the scene to see it bouncing and flapping on the forest floor or breathing its last half breath, I would spend another shell to end its misery. Only once the creature lay down and died would I dare examine the holes, the warm body, and cover it with a sheet of leaves and grass.

My experience with mice has been limited. The first time on the farm was in a potato cellar. Parker and I were laying out lines of aluminum ventilation tubes. Once set, the potatoes would be piled on top of them. Throughout the winter, fans blew the length of the cellar and into the tubes, circulating air to keep the crop fresh until spring.

Years before, Parker had found a discarded puppy at the corner by the gas station that he named Smoke. The dog grew into a vile animal, some type of spotted-heeler with a humped back and muscled jackal-like front legs. It ran slack jawed and sideways and quixotic, its limp tongue hanging out its snout. Smoke found great pleasure in nipping at my ankles. Smoke became such a presence on the farm that if he wasn't in the back of Parker's pickup, I would ask why, almost as if the dog was a coworker, almost as if we had important canine tasks lined out for the day. When Smoke did show up, however, I avoided him.

But that day in the cellar, Smoke lurched behind us, watching as we rolled the tubes off the stack and down to their places. Parker and I lifted a tube from the floor and a fat mouse scurried out from underneath. I flinched and dropped the tube on the concrete with a clang. The mouse froze at the sound. Parker yelled and pointed at the shivering rodent. In one jowl-cracking snap, Smoke had snagged, chomped, and swallowed the mouse. The dog walked to Parker, working its jaws like some appeased gator, expecting a thorough rubdown in praise.

II

My father's main farm, up in the hills, stretched from a highway back to a reservoir that fed the valley's canals. Once the pumps and wells became available, the previous owner laid more than three miles of mainline pipe from the highway to the lake. The old tar-coated tubes, fifty years old, began to rot and crumble. A constant job for Otto, the farm mechanic, was to load up the welder, drive down the narrow farm roads, and patch the leaks. Watering was so important that even one day without it would stunt the crop's growth. From May to August, irrigation consumed the farmers' lives.

I became a teen and was rewarded with more hard work. Now my middays were spent shoveling grain bins, welding, and servicing equipment. My rifle had been locked away not to be seen again until hunting season in October.

One day in early spring, my father explained the changes that would be happening to his farm. Computerized irrigation pivots were much more efficient than handlines. If placed in the center of a square field, the new pivots spanned a quarter-mile and watered 24/7. The vibrant green hills seemed to grow these long lethargic robots almost overnight. Neighbors bought them and soon pivots were the only way to water. My father had sent Otto out the day before with an acetylene torch to cut off all the risers which connected to the handlines. It was my job to take the backhoe and gather up all of the discarded steel pipes. Otto would then weld shut the holes and we would never have to move pipe again.

The backhoe epitomized my father's concept of economics—unless dead, employed. Not until we had dragged some defunct machine to our farm junkyard would he talk about buying a replacement. For this reason the backhoe lacked vital elements of comfort and safety: front windshield, door, back window, seat cushion, radio, and brakes were all nonexistent. A sparked-out screwdriver served as a key to bridge the solenoid and starter. The kill switch was a wire coat hanger wrapped around the throttle. Both operations, dangerously enough, were performed while standing in front of the driver's side tire.

Spring, and the snow banks had melted almost completely. The rusting backhoe had been winterized and parked, so Otto helped me check the fluids, clean the cab, and start the monstrosity for the first time that year. Red shreds from a paper Coke cup and newspaper covered the floor. Parked machinery made a perfect winter's nest for birds and other such pests.

While the backhoe sputtered and warmed, I went to the shop and dressed for the day. Over my t-shirt I pulled a green hooded sweatshirt, and on top of that wore a thick wool lined denim coat. The jacket's retro collar was wide and corduroy. I wore it open at the throat—an empty hole was left at the top, the remnants of a copper button. For some reason, I had vowed to never buy work gloves, so I stole a pair of leathers from Otto that had holes in the fingertips and palms. A New York Jets winter cap was under the seat of my pickup. I put it on and walked to the backhoe, its black exhaust coughing up into the dirty sky.

Like it always does in spring, the wind roared from the east, down the river canyon and pushing out like a delta over the farm. I wound the backhoe up to 2000 rpms and wandered across the fields towards the scarred section of mainline. Otto had placed a shovel in the cab in case of getting the backhoe stuck. I propped the tool from floor to ceiling along the doorframe.

I turned into the wind and it blasted through the windshield's empty orifice. But the wind blew enough heat from the wrapped-tight engine that I felt sweat gather along my forehead. I threw off my hat and ran a gloved hand through my dirty hair.

My job was more annoying than difficult. Stretched over a mile were the abstracted tubes, thrown out into the field every thirty feet. I would arrive at one, park the backhoe, climb out, load the four-foot pipe into the front loader bucket, climb back in, drive thirty feet, and so on. Once I had a bucketful, I'd drive to the end of the field, stack the tubes, and return.

I loaded the tubes and drove into the wind. Driving back empty, the wind whipped through the lack of a back window. I had to keep the backhoe revved high to push through the loose dirt. All of the noise combined—the wind, the engine, the constant clanging of tubes in the bucket—was deafening. I replaced my hat to cover my ears.

After the third round I had discovered a new system. Instead of stopping when I neared a tube, I'd leave the backhoe in gear and leap from it, snatch the tube, throw it in the bucket of the moving machine, and jump back inside when the tractor ran past. By my fifth jump, I sweated profusely. Running through the dirt, heaving the steel tubes, leaping from soft ground to moving machinery was no easy feat. The wind picked up, and dirt particles blew into my eyes and glazed my sticky face with a gritty lamina. I tromped on, jumping, running, heaving. It was me, my yellow mechanical beast, and the fields, nothing else for miles.

According to Nicholas Collias of the University of California, aggression in vertebrates is most frequently expressed in two forms: defense of territory, and hierarchies of precedence within social groups.

J.P. Scott, in his article "Agonistic Behavior of Mice and Rats," explains one difference between mice and rat young: "Perhaps the most fundamental of these differences is the complete absence of playful fighting in young mice." Rats seventeen days old will begin to romp and box with their peers. Mice will not. For this reason, adult mice hesitate much longer before attacking. While rats have a list of pre-attack behavior, mice have two: "mincing" (prancing about), and tail rattling. In Scott's study, tail rattling, or switching, is seen as a warning and threat to the opponent, similar to growling in carnivores. After switching, a mouse will strike.

I jumped into the backhoe and headed for the next tube. The wind pummeled me; my coat collar snapped and floated against my cheeks. Had I a button, I could have closed the coat and ridded myself of the distraction. Instead, I constantly smoothed down the thick fabric.

I threw in another tube and caught the handrail, letting the tractor's forward motion pull me up. Once I sat, my collar started snapping again. My cheeks stung from being beaten, and now an inconsistent itch warmed my nape. I flipped up the collar, hoping to tame the coat. My hands followed it around the back and found a thin string. I yanked free the string and threw it to the floor.

I caught the mouse's movement as it scurried between my feet. Its brown and white hair bristled, and its leathery tail switched back and forth.

In the milliseconds it took my nervous system to carry the message from eyeballs to brain, then spinal cord to sciatic nerves, I achieved levitation. My knees floated up past the steering wheel and stopped somewhere around my ears. In one graceful but gauche lunge, I flew through the open doorframe feet first. Like D.D. Homes, the 19th century British trickster who in obfuscated dining halls hovered above party guests and royalty, I flew through the backhoe's open door prostrate and, in my case, petrified.

When I landed in the field, I began to strip clothing. Gloves first, then denim jacket, the sweatshirt, the t-shirt, all of which I wildly flung away. Bare-chested and dripping, I rubbed my neck, my hair, slapped my biceps, and cursed in confusing strings of profanity. Had the bastard bored into my neck? Had it nested or laid its eggs?

The adrenaline hit my empty stomach. My fright changed to anger. I ran to the backhoe, which had veered out farther into the field, and from the step shifted it into neutral. With the shovel handle I bludgeoned the fat little fink to death. Then I scraped the mouse's broken body from the floor and flung it as far as I could. The tractors would come to work the ground soon and destroy the corpse completely. Before I replaced my clothing, I shook each piece like a beach towel, ensuring the attacker had left no stragglers.

III

Fakirs are holy men who intentionally live lives of extreme poverty in order to reach a richer asceticism. They employ drastic measures of discomfort and self-mutilation to do so. They lie on beds of nails and immerse themselves for prolonged times in water and hot ash. They keep their fists clenched indefinitely, allowing their own nails to grow straight into their palms. They lie or sit in one place for years and beg for their food. All this, for spirituality.

I'm sure many go home at night after a long day of begging to a loving family and plop down in front of the boob tube to catch the latest Bollywood hack flick. Sadly, charlatans exist in every world. But I'm convinced some have truly renounced worldly wealth, put their trust in something unseen, and pursue greater light and knowledge. These disciples, unlike their fraudulent friends, they'll sleep on coals if they have to.

It has been said that the highest form of levitation is transportation. One example: Jesus walking on water. Post-Biblical texts point out that more than seventy-two Catholic saints have levitated. The power is duplicated throughout the world: wizards, mystics, and hoards of David Blains have achieved this blatant defiance of gravity. Fakirs, too, strive for levitation, and many have been transported to that elevation. Could this be the drive that inspired Icarus and the Wright Brothers? Does the same force make men farm the hills or construct impressive houses in high places?

After I graduated with my bachelor's degree, I returned to the farm to work. My father talked me into it; a new venture, bright futures. The year before he and two other business partners undertook a new cash crop, Kentucky blue grass. A sod farm. My father, functioning as the farmer-in-residence, supplied the machinery and manpower. A plastic surgeon offered his eighty acres. The man who'd landscaped the surgeon's yard became the manager. Within the first year, the landscaper left the venture for different pursuits. Too busy to operate the farm himself, my father talked me into running it before I left for Arizona. At twenty-three, I'd decided to leave the farming life for more scholarly pursuits, perhaps encouraged by the six dollar an hour wage I'd made up until then.

We had rented the ground before the surgeon had bought it, so I was familiar with the watering system. Thinking the sod business would take off without any hang-ups, the trio had purchased top of the line equipment, including a new irrigation pivot. The control panel for it sat right off the highway. The view from the concrete pivot pad was beautiful. The land stayed flat for two hundred yards and then dropped down to a box-valley filled with wheat and hay. The last manager had started harvesting in the back, so the grass butted against the pivot pad. Once summer hit, it was a sea of emerald green back-dropped by ragged cliffs and a mountain road that led northeast to Kelly's Canyon and the Snake.

The sod farm proved to be my first real stake in the family business, and even though I was leaving, I wanted to do well. After graduation, I spent my waking hours on that hill of grass, investigating, planning, and predicting the future. While my father worried in hundredweight scales and worked the ground with forty-foot implements, I employed micro-management. I sold sod by the square foot, and ensured that each foot was as perfect as I could get it. I shepherded the small farm from morning light to sundown.

The winter had caused many problems. Snowfall was higher than usual and melt-off took additional time, which resulted in a drastic spurt of the rodent population. They flourished under the snow pack. Once the snow retreated, the animals were vibrant and healthy. That summer, my father said that when he walked across the potato rows he could feel their tunnels collapse underfoot. The rodents destroyed at least ten percent of the crops. The surplus of mice brought additional hawks and burrowing owls to feed. The birds fought for roosting space on the power poles. During the squabbles, a weak one would fall into the lines and short out the power which would stop the irrigation system. The birds died, the plants died, the mice died.

I faced similar obstacles. The mice had made a chain of tunnels that stretched the length of the sod field. This caused two problems. To harvest, the ground had to be as level as possible. The mice tunnels caved in everything and caused the pieces of grass to break and crumble. The second was dealing with customers. Who wanted a lawn that looked like Swiss cheese?

I remedied the section as best I could with an old pavement roller Pops had bought at a farm auction for fifty bucks. I traversed the farm for two days straight, the wide machine mashing down the ground. From my high view I could see the mice scampering for safety when I roared over top their nests. They were everywhere. The barrel sized pump had holes along the turbine to allow air flow to cool the shaft. After I had oiled and prepped the pump, I pushed the green button to start it. The turbine spun, and a nest of weeds and garbage poofed out and floated to the ground.

After ignition, a baby mouse lay shaking by the pump until life faded out of its body. Perhaps that tiny pink mouse changed something in me. Barehanded, I picked it up by its tail and dropped it into a hole, a burial of sorts.

The grass grew, business prospered, and the hills supported the new crop nicely. I avoided harvesting among the mice's territory—the sod rolls crumbled when we stacked them on the pallets. By the end of summer, I'd sold everything but the strips of mouse grass. We had to harvest that too. It took us hours to take the shoddy stuff but we did it and were done.

An irrigation pivot creates its own tire tracks each year by moving back and forth along its own path, wetting the ground and pushing its tall cleated tires forward. By mid-summer the tracks are three or four feet deep in places, and the pivot will get itself stuck or high-centered. Because overwatering is just as detrimental as not watering at all, making sure the pivot ran smoothly and consistently worried me—the mode of transport for the water had changed since the settlers, but the pressure to keep it running had not.

When we harvested the mouse-infested grass we ended up throwing off more scraps than we actually sold. My last job was to clean off the scraps. I carried them to the pivot tracks and threw them into the deep spots, hoping the additions would keep the pivot's A-beam from dragging the whole contraption to a standstill.

It was one night in the gloaming that I picked up a small piece of sod and touched a field mouse that hid underneath. I jumped back and swore. The mouse hunched up and froze. We stayed deadlocked for what felt like a full minute. I knew Parker or Otto or my father would have no problem stomping the pest. Smoke would snarf it down without a second thought.

But I couldn't do it. Its small form shivered as the day moved to night, and in that retreating light I examined its tan body, its white little feet. I noticed my own dirt-stained knees, the mud that had accumulated in the crooks of my elbows, the soil that glazed my arm-hairs and palms and fingertips. The mouse's coat could not be better colored for its life of digging, scampering, surviving. Its whiskers twitched, the mouse sniffing the air. I smelled the same moisture as the pivot pumped water behind us, fooling me to memories of summer thunderstorms and canal swimming.

But I couldn't let the mouse run away. Goliath-ing above it, I surged out a clumsy kick. In the time that my leg cocked back and then struck, I decided not to kill it but instead scoot the thing through the air and out of sight for good.

The problem, I think, with immature boys is their lack of comprehension. I'd killed hundreds of animals because I failed to acknowledge the strength of molded lead propelled by potassium nitrate and sulfur.

As a maturing man, I blanked on the force that my leg carried and kicked the mouse too hard. Its body flew end over end a few feet and plunked onto the bare dirt. I crouched in front of the injured animal. Blood spotted its yellow teeth and its front paws boxed the air. It breathed labouredly and shallow.

I was too scared to pick it up; I didn't want its blood on my hands. I pulled it onto an oddly shaped piece of sod, its brown body offset drastically by the greenness of the grass. I set the mouse and sod in the bottom of the pivot's muddy path, knowing that in four or five hours the tons of steel that carried the water would churn the mouse back underground. I walked off towards the pickup, leaving for the day.

But I returned—my actions deserved no easy reconciliation—and placed a heavy foot on the upturned sod and lowered my weight onto it. Beneath me, the mouse deflated and expired. When I stepped out of the track, sadness surged through my body so completely that my limbs tingled. Goosebumps appeared and disappeared in places they never had, across my lower abdomen, the backs of my knees. I looked down, imagining what had occurred on the underside of the heart-shaped sod. As darkness overtook the hill, I looked down. Grass licked around my boots and, for a split-second, it felt like I was floating.

CHEDDAR

2007

After hearing about Port's death, I made a rule about not getting in. Instead, I'd sift from the side. But that December night was an exception: I'd found a Miracle Dumpster. In the very first grocery sack was a book-sized brick of cheddar cheese still wrapped in store cellophane. Cheese! I stashed it in my coat's big pocket and then climbed in, reasoning that if someone was to toss out a perfectly good chunk of cheese, God only knew what else they'd dumped.

The dumpster sat in the parking lot of a squatty apartment complex in Rexburg, Idaho. Ten duplexes, tops. I figured a few minutes in the trash, then all the doors, then back to the tracks. Rooting through bags and boxes, I didn't hear the man approach.

"Help you?" he said, kind of scared. Young and pudgy, he stood in the shallow streetlamp light, shuffling in the snow.

"Can't believe what people throw away," I said and offered to shake. "Chuck."

The man came closer and leaned in, scanning through banana peels and diapers and empty cans. "Wouldn't have found some cheese?" he says and looks up.

I covered the pocket. "Haven't found much of anything."

"Forget it." He takes my hand. "Davey."

I helped myself out, brushed off, and fished my laminated magazine subscription card from my front pocket. "Look like a smart guy—you a reader?"

Davey nodded.

"I gotta deal for you. Two magazines, ten bucks the first month, a dollar every month after that."

"Really," Davey said, rocking toe to heel on the icy pavement. He slapped his hands together and blew into them. "Got Sports Illustrated?"

"Buddy," I said. "Got everything from Great Housesweeping to Bustler."

Davey laughed at that. Most everyone did. If I'm anything, it's amiable.

"So what'd ya say, interested?"

"Got to tell you," Davey said. "Things are tight."

"They always are," I said.

"Had much luck selling magazines?" Davey asked.

"Here and there," I said. I was zero for ten on the night. Not that it matters, since they never get the magazines anyways. I'm just too proud to beg and prefer to earn it. I'd found the magazine card in a Sacramento recycling bin.

"How long you been out?"

"A while. Gonna knock these doors and get going."

Davey looked back at the apartments. "It's eleven. Here, people turn in early."

"So I've seen," I said. The whole town had been dead since I'd gotten out of the semi a few hours back. Bummed down from Bozeman with a lumber driver, said he was going out to Mud Lake to scare up an old girlfriend. He let me out on the shoulder of Highway 20 with a cigarette, a worn pair of work gloves, and instructions on how to get to Rexburg.

I had knocked the doors of the houses, framed in blinking strands of red and green lights, on the way in but no one was interested. One man became indignant when I mentioned Playboy, telling me it was wrong for a youth to be spreading such filth through the world. I told him a youth's gotta be spreading something. That's a fault of mine—taking things too far. It makes for awkward doorstep moments. Certain he'd call the cops, I ducked down some back roads and followed the railroad tracks into town. A youth—hell, I'm twenty-six. Haven't been young since the 90s.

All of the stores were closed for the night. Club Strata, a dark and vacant dance hall, was attached to a Jiffy Lube and car wash. In the town center, a lone tinsel-wrapped Christmas tree crackled in the clear cold. A few inches of snow coated the stationary cars, the power lines, the edges of the few two-story buildings. When I breathed my nostril hairs stuck together in bursts. It had been a strange and lonely night until finding the dumpster.

"You sell anything in there?" Davey said, nodding towards the garbage, bunching up his loose neck skin like a deflated balloon.

"Got a few bites," I said. "What can I mark you down for?"

"Chuck, listen, I'd really like to, but I can't."

"It's only ten bucks—that's a meal at Wendy's."

"I know, I know." It looked like he was thinking. Then, "Man, you're skinny. How's this; come in, we'll have a bite and talk it over."

In my eight years of wandering, I've learned to be picky and protective. I've learned truckers aren't strangers—they're normal work-a-day folk, playing the game to make a living. The same with other hitchers. But Davey's kind show up in the papers, lampshades made of stray cats and pickle jars full of human digits.

"What'd you got to eat?" I said.

"I was going to make sandwiches," he said. The yellow light glinted off his wire-framed glasses and illuminated his wispy widow's peak. He looked as dangerous as an oversized eighth grader. "But I have stuff for pancakes too."

"Can't stay long," I said.

"That's okay," Davey said. "I need some shut-eye."

"Ain't gonna call the cops?" I asked.

"Do I need to?" Davey replied, and slapped a good-natured hand on my shoulder. I didn't answer, and followed him to apartment #7, figuring I could take him if things got hairy.

The apartment was small, and nine shades of brown: carpet, couch, TV stand, foot table, picture frames, and closet doors all varying hues from dark chocolate to cardboard. A plank inscribed with Welcome To Our Home hung from the door. A few candles, as thick and tall as coffee cans, colored cashew and nutmeg, stood next to the telephone on the round kitchen table. The only things not brown, it seemed, were a foot-tall plastic Christmas tree near the hallway and a painting of Jesus in red robes that judged down from above the television.

Not that I had a problem with that—I'd grown up with brown. In Guthrie, Oklahoma, it was a staple color, from the hills to Cottonwood Creek. Port would get pissed if you called him black, arguing he was cocoa. Port and I shared some good times as salt-and-pepper Okies until he ran away to Dallas at fifteen. I heard later from a group of bums at Stop Six that Port had liked sleeping in dumpsters. They attributed that to his disappearance, reasoning the garbage truck must have snuck up in the middle of the night, Port's senses dulled by the insulation of black plastic garbage sacks.

Since Davey had demanded that we remove our shoes, warning his wife Deb would kill us for tracking in the parking-lot sludge, I prepared him for my dingy socks. He went back to his bedroom and returned with a pair of gray wool ones, saying to keep them, he hadn't been skiing in years.

"Give me your coat. Relax," he said.

"I got it," I said, taking the hanger and hanging my coat lop-sided, sagging in the closet between crisp sweatshirts and windbreakers. The couch, so soft, pillowed underneath and I sunk down until my chin rested on my chest. Then I pulled on those socks, and it felt as warm as Southern Comfort.

In the kitchen, Davey did the whole shebang: mixing bowls, measuring cups, flour, eggs, milk, sugar. I figured he'd have some premaid box-and-toaster setup.

"Where'd you learn that?" I said.

"I've been on my own a while," he said.

"Tell me about it," I said thickly, "but I can't make pancakes."

"It's a God-given talent," he said.

"Why you cooking, anyways? Thought you were married. Isn't that what she's for?"

Davey pointed to some framed pictures hanging behind the couch. "We've been together eleven months. Deb's a nurse at RMC—that's why she's not here. She works graveyard, except they don't call it that. Too depressing, you know?"

In one photo, they leaned back to back, hands pointed in play guns as if spies, goofing in their wedding getup. In the background stood a fairytale church, all of it—except for the stained glass windows—paper-white, with spires and towers.

"Pretty," I lied. Deb wasn't much in the looks department.

"We met in theatre club," he said.

"Imagine that."

"I know—there were a whole bunch of guys going for her. Guess I got lucky."

"Hope she's funny," I said, taking one last look at her pear shape.

"Oh, she's hilarious." The apartment filled with scents of cinnamon and maple and frying meat. "Go wash up," he said. "It's almost ready."

In the bathroom, I washed my hands and face. On the mirror in erasable marker was a red-stenciled heart and the phrase You're a Cutey Marootey! scrawled underneath in what I imagined was the curly hand of Deb. The mirror opened, a medicine cabinet behind, but I found nothing interesting but Tylenol. I pocketed a palmful.

When I came out, Davey had set the table with paper plates and a stack of steaming flapjacks ten high and a tangle of bacon.

"Look alright?" Davey said.

I sat down and loaded up. The butter slid off my knife and disappeared, the dough sponging up as much syrup as I dared pour. Davey took a few and did the same, but was more interested in watching me eat.

"You look like a kid that lived next door to me growing up," he said.

"Where'd that happen?"

"Rigby. Just down the road."

"Wasn't me," I said. It was quiet, so I loaded up seconds.

"What's your story, Chuck?"

"It's complicated and boring," I said. He asked general questions. People asking my details made me nervous, so I asked him why everything in Rexburg closed at ten.

"Who knows?" he said. "Kind of weird. I just came here for college."

"You gonna be one of those forever students?" I asked.

"Pre-dentistry. I apply in two years."

"Can't imagine sticking my hands in other people's mouths," I said.

He shrugged. "You do what you gotta do."

"Ain't that the truth," I said.

"I sweep the McKay Library from four to six am. Anything'd be better than that."

"How old are you, anyways," I said.

"Twenty-two," he answered.

"And married? Seems like you got life pinned down."

"It's just what we do around here," he said.

"What's that supposed to mean?"

"Well, uh, me—this whole town—we're all pretty much Mormon."

"No kidding," I said. "So where's your other wife?" I licked my fork.

"No." He shook his head. "We don't do that anymore."

"Too bad," I said. "You know, that's a lot of, well," and to not sound crude, I showed him with one finger and my left hand what I meant. Davey quickly smiled and ate a few bites.

"One's plenty," he answered.

My mouth was dry and sticky. I asked for a glass of milk and he obliged.

"But get this—Deb's expecting," he said while he poured.

That was something I'd never considered. Hard enough, trying to keep myself from gnawing off an arm in hunger. Bringing a kid into this crazy world seemed like a one-way ticket to starvation.

"Gee," I said. "Wish I had something to give." I took the two last pancakes and scarfed them down. We moved to the couch and watched TV for an hour. And the food, that soft sofa, the pleasure that comes from being confided in—I could have stayed there forever.

We were both surprised when halfway through the Late Late Show, keys jangled outside the door. In stumbled Deb, wearing pink scrubs and—once she spotted me—a scowl. She looked back and forth between Davey and me and then said, "Who's this?"

"This is Chuck," Davey said. "I found him in the garbage. Why are you home?"

"I threw up at work. They told me to take the night off." She looked back and forth from him to me. "Hon, can I talk to you alone for a minute."

When that happened, I knew it was time to go. I got my coat, the cheese heavier on one side, and slipped it on before Davey came back.

"Hate to do this, but we gotta hit the hay," Davey said.

"Understood." Then I did something I really didn't want to. "I can get you a year of Mother & Child. Just ten bucks."

Davey looked back at Deb.

"No thank you," Deb said. She shot Davey a glance that meant murder. Then she puckered her mouth in a nauseous panic and scampered to the bathroom.

Davey, in a hustle, flipped open his wallet and extracted a twenty. "Good luck."

I crumpled the bill into my front pocket. "You're better than most."

Outside, my boots squeaked in the winter cold. It was a frigid and unfriendly change. I scanned for new garbage while waiting for the apartment lights to click off. Once they did, I tried the cars. Every one was unlocked.

I grabbed handfuls of loose change, a screwdriver, and a wad of bills from the first four vehicles. Then I got into an older Honda Accord and rummaged through the glove box and console. The Accord had an after-market CD player. I tugged it a bit, and then wedged the screwdriver under its lip, busting an air vent or two, but got it hanging halfway out and reached into the car's innards and pulled apart the plugs, sure a trucker would buy it.

The pancakes were a warm, doughy brick in my belly. By the time I had the deck free, my breath had fogged the interior; the old bucket seat was pokey but comfortable enough. With the deck sitting on my lap, I relaxed, shut my eyes for a minute, reasoning it was better than sleeping alongside the tracks.

I panicked and awoke when the car door opened. I jumped out, pushing past the owner into the dark. But I didn't get far, jerked back by the collar of my coat.

"Chuck?" came Davey's nasally wheezing. "Scared the flipping crap out of me."

I wrenched my coat free and faced him. "Get back," I said, and cocked the CD deck behind my head.

"What the heck?" He stepped back a few feet. He had on coveralls and an unzipped coat.

"I'll do it," I said, raising the CD player higher.

He looked to his open door and then back to me, figuring it out. We stalled there in the early morning. A wet mist hung around us, smelling like snow.

He took a step. "Chuck, what do you need?" he said.

I squared my shoulders and inched my arm back. "Don't come closer," I warned.

He took another step.

"Don't—I'm not kidding."

When his foot was midair, I pumped the deck at him. He flinched and lost his footing on the ice. In one lumpy sack-of-bricks crash he flat-assed right there in the parking lot. He sat like a kid, heavy and beat, legs spread, and didn't say a word.

I ran and ran, and things came to me through the fog. Sirens. Naked maples. A deserted playground. The loading docks of a warehouse store. I stumbled upon a riverbank and followed it to a bridge and went underneath and backed myself to the concrete abutment, out of sight.

The morning light crawled in from the east, a thick gray day to beat all. The sirens disappeared, replaced by the awaking city, traffic shaking overhead. Snow fell, wet flakes as big as leaves. The cars slushed through it, sheeting it down both sides of the bridge.

Uneven pieces of black rock jutted up through the frozen river like some small-scale mountain range. The trickle of water creeping through the center seemed to be slow enough that it too would ice solid at any given moment. A gust came every now and again, chilling me like thin wet fingers.

Man, did I feel like a maggot about Davey's smash-up. People helped me out all the time, but the aftertaste of pancakes and my warm toes reminded me that Davey didn't just help me out—it was something bigger. And I had ruined it.

Just like I had with Port. In the dog days of August we'd swim in the floodwaters of the Cottonwood. The creek would raise almost four feet, churning up red silt that colored the water a deep blood burgundy. With a twenty-foot rope and a hardly-missed slab of plywood, courtesy Ace Hardware, we made a boogie-board. We'd tie it off to the bridge and take turns floating out into the current on our stomachs, diving and cutting through the tainted water.

We'd be ten times dirtier from swimming in the canal. We'd dry by lying on the blacktop, each of us faced a different direction to watch for cars. At the end, plastered red from the river debris. One day, we gave each other back tattoos, tracing out messages in the soot. I thought it would be funny to pen out nig. Port wore it through town and was finally told by a yellow-eyed alcoholic named Charley what it said. Port punched me in the mouth and ran home, leaving to Dallas that fall without speaking to me. Turns out, he had drawn a huge pair of tits on my back, but Charley told me they just looked like great big eyes.

Under the bridge in Rexburg that day, I convinced myself that I was low. I started questioning the magazine scam. The CD player seemed to stare with its knobs and screen. It snowed for hours straight; the spot of sun moved from one side of the bridge to the other.

At near-dark, I took out the cheese. It had frozen hard, so I put it under my arm to thaw. When I took a bite, a crooked chomp from my back teeth, it was like a popsicle. I chewed it twice, three times, softening it, and swallowed the gummy mess. It was slow-going down my throat, but then stopped completely near my adam's apple. Coughed, but no air to push. Gulped, but too thick. I stood and pressed against the easement, punching myself in the chest. White flashes blasted behind my eyes. Dizzy, I thought this would be my death— alone and cold, freezing and hungry.

I stumbled towards the creek, hoping water would move the blockage. My boot caught a crag, and I went down hard, taking a rock right to the gut. The cheese dislodged and exploded from my mouth. I wheezed and coughed. Served me right, I figured, for not returning it in the first place.

I waited till midnight, or close to it, before leaving the bridge, figuring to retrace through town and to the highway, make it out a couple miles before flagging down some long-hauler. In one pocket, re-wrapped cheese; the other, the CD player. It had stopped snowing.

I t was no mistake that I ended up behind the dumpster at Davey's waiting for the lights to go out. A few inches of snow blanketed the Accord. The door was locked, a good thing. I didn't try any of the other cars.

I brushed off a spot on the hood of Davey's car and set down the cheese, then put the deck on top, careful not to get it wet. I wanted to leave a message for Davey to show him my sorrow, and thought to write it on the windshield. A fat-lettered Thanks? A sincere and skinny Sorry? The thought of drawing a misshapen penis crossed my mind, and I laughed. Port would have loved it. I ungloved and stretched out my index finger. A door slammed from the apartments.

I fell alongside the car and scooted underneath. Footsteps shuffled towards the parking lot. Staring up at the bending metal—axels and u-joints and oil pan, coated with ice and grit—just millimeters from it, I wondered what it would be like to stick out my tongue and lick, binding my body here until either I was found or dead or both. I sucked in and held my breath.

The steps went out to the dumpster and came back through the lot, stopping near the car. They walked up and paused. Davey's boots were close enough to spit-shine. I heard the cheese and deck lifted from the hood. It seemed like hours, him standing there, I'm sure looking around, confused and innocent.

What would it mean, to reach out and untie a lace, yell "Gotcha!" and tackle him in the snow, roaring like former yard-mates? But Davey trudged back to his home and shut the door hard.

I crawled out and dusted off. Then I jogged into the night, ducking behind shrubbery, reasoning that a southern flight was much needed; Arizona, maybe, or even back to Guthrie.

THE NEWLYWEDS

2006

After our two-day honeymoon in West Yellowstone, we move into this one-bedroom place above the Goodall Plumbing & Heating building. There's a red door right on Main Street of Rigby that opens up to a more-red flight of stairs. Only two places up there—ours is on the right, 1A. The windows are tiny, shiny squares that glare across the street to DJ's Bar & Grill and the parking lot of Washington's. Other than that, there's not much else to look at.

The hallway's narrow, so it's tricky moving stuff upstairs. Luckily, my grandma gave us this table with foldable legs. I sat at it every Thanksgiving growing up—the kiddy table—and since I was the last grandkid to get married she said I could have it. One of the legs is bent due to a post-turkey scuffle with an older cousin. He won, but I got the table, right? Kimberly fixed it by stuffing a folded-up paper plate underneath. It still wobbles if you nudge it the right way.

My dad got me hired as an apprentice plumber at Goodall. He said Patrick owed him. Kimberly got a part-time job at Triple J's Foodtown a few blocks away. She bags groceries and answers phones three nights a week.

So, everything is going okay, I guess, other than we've been watching for our neighbor. Jenn Bliss, Apartment 1B. We keep getting her mail. No one answers when we knock. The old door is warped, and there's no room to slide it underneath. But we know someone lives there because late at night we hear people laughing and moving up and down the stairs.

We don't see her until Saturday. When we walk in from Main with our groceries, she's locking her door. She starts down the stairs. We walk up.

"Hi there," Kimberly says, stopping to talk.

Jenn pushes right between us. "Sorry, hons. Late for work. Come by tomorrow. We'll chat." She leaves without saying more, heels clacking the whole way down.

When we get inside, Kimberly says, "What was that?"

I pile the plastic bags on the table, which wobbles. "Jenn, I guess. She looked nice."

"What kind of nice?" she says.

"Good nice." I open the fridge and put away the eggs.

"How old do you think she is?"

"Maybe thirty."

Kimberly puts things away under the sink and then goes to the living room, which is actually the same room as the kitchen, just where the linoleum stops and the carpet begins. "What do you think she does?" she asks.

"Who knows?" I follow her. "What do you think?"

Kimberly sits down at the table and picks up three letters marked as Jenn's. She puts her feet up on one of the folding chairs and taps the mail on the table. "She looks kind of sleazy."

I take the letters and shuffle through them. Mountain Power. A card from the dentist. Cable bill.

"Maybe she's a dancer," she says and looks up, grinning.

"Maybe she's a dancer," I repeat, and sigh. Sometimes Kimberly is so immature.

On Sunday afternoon—when we're supposed to be in church, Kimberly's mother, Tammy, insists—we make a plate of cookies for Jenn. Really, we just take them out of the wrapping and arrange them on an old St. Patty's Day plate. A shirtless, hairy man answers when we knock. The door stays open a crack when he goes to get her. Faint giggling floats out of the apartment. Jenn comes to the door, no makeup, hair in a ponytail, a pink tank top.

"Hey you two," she says, in this nasally, fake whine. It looks like she's wearing a piece of bailing twine for a necklace.

"Hey," we say at the same time. Then there's that new neighbor awkwardness we've never felt before.

Kimberly says, "Just wanted to introduce ourselves. I'm Kimberly Smithfield. This is my husband, Cal."

I nod. Jenn looks at me and we lock eyes—hers are greener than garden peas.

"You two are married?" she says. "You're just kids! How old are you?" She's obnoxiously chewing gum.

"Eighteen," I say.

"Eighteen," says my wife.

She opens the door a little further and glances back at the man. He watches television and doesn't respond, his stomach rolls lapping over the elastic band of his navy blue sweatpants.

"So did you have to?" Jenn says in a low voice. She smirks, pumps her eyebrows.

"Have to what?" I blurt.

"Get married," Jenn says. "You know, the doc tell you you're in love."

"Well," I start.

Kimberly butts in and shoots me this look. "No. We were high school sweethearts." She says it like it's some trophy to line the walls of Rigby High.

Jeez, I think, staring at Jenn. Kimberly's eyes are this sidewalk gray, not green one fleck. And that stray piece of twine, floating down and towards the creamy crease climbing out of her shirt …

"How long?" Jenn asks.

"A week and a half," Kimberly answers shortly.

She caught me looking, I know it. I glance upwards to the wall jambs and count the flakes of peeling ceiling plaster.

Jenn swears in this long, drawn out way. "Gawd." Sounds from the TV waft to us. "Y'all lived in Idaho forever?" she asks.

"Yeah," I say putting all my weight on one foot, then the other, making the wooden floor creak.

"We made these for you," Kimberly says. She holds out the cookies and nudges me.

I offer the letters. "We keep getting your mail. Sorry."

Jenn takes the things and smiles. "Ain't you two sweet." She holds up the mail and kind of waves it back and forth in the air.

"Let us know if we can do anything," I say, feeling my cheeks rush and redden.

"Actually, I'm leaving town for a week. Pick up my mail?" she says.

"Sure," Kimberly and I say at the same time.

"You might just get it anyway," Jenn says. Kimberly chuckles politely.

When we're back inside number 1A, Kimberly says, "Weird."

"Yeah, she was," I say.

"No, I mean weird because you checked her out."

I try to counter but can't. Instead, I turn on the TV and search for a baseball game. Big fan—I played before getting hitched. Kimberly purposefully avoids me and spends the afternoon on a Tammy call. When she's done, she comes out for a glass of water. Her eyes are puffy and red. I ask her what's wrong and tell her to come and talk, patting the seat cushion beside me, but she opts to drink alone in the bedroom. I'm frustrated. How long can a man live like this? I mean, all I did was look at her, what's so bad about that?

On Tuesday, while Kimberly works late shift, I get the mail. There's another letter for Jenn. I set it in the stack. For dinner I eat a can of chili and a soda, both cold. Cheetos for desert.

There's nothing on TV, so I sit down and thumb through the mail, putting it in two piles. One for Jenn, one for us. Ours has a flyer for the canned food sale at Triple J's and a handwritten note from the postman to fix the mail slot. Jenn's has another cable bill, an envelope with no return address, and a postcard featuring a dancing bear. The bottom of it reads "Circus Capital of America, Peru, Indiana."

I organize the piles, then reorganize them. Biggest pieces on the bottom, then longest, then fattest. Gotta make sure all face the same way—Kimberly says I'm a bit over-the-top, a bit eccentric. When

I pick them up and tap them on the table to even the edges, Jenn's postcard slips out and falls like a pinwheel onto the beige carpet. It lands picture-side down. Handwriting stares up at me.

I don't read it, though. I snatch it from the floor and put it back on top. Then I go straight to the bedroom, flop down on the bed, and watch the ceiling fan. Almost two full minutes go by before I return and read the postcard. It says:

> *Jenn,*
> *Thanks for the weekend. Don't be a stranger.*
> *Paul*

The writing is heavy. The top of the T shoots at a high angle across the card, and Paul is underlined three times. I put the postcard at the bottom of the pile, cover it with the other letters, and walk downstairs to fix the mail slot.

The flap isn't broken, just stuck, which means me going back upstairs for a screwdriver. My eyes are drawn to the mail again. I take the postcard and spin it by its corners, hypnotizing me into circus daydreams. The weight of the screwdriver in my back pocket reminds me of the task at hand. I head for the door.

When I open it, Kimberly's there. It startles me—I didn't hear her come up.

"What are you smiling about?" she teases. She seems happier today.

"Me?" I say.

"No, Harry," she says. That's what we nicknamed Jenn's friend. What an ape.

"Just thinking about something."

In the hallway, with the door open, I grab her tightly around the waist. She squeaks. Her eyes look like river rock.

"What are you doing?" she says, pulling away a little.

"I don't know," I say. "Just playing." I let her go.

"Where are you going?"

"The mailbox." I flash the screwdriver, return it to my pocket.

"Where's the mail?" She says this more seductively, almost in a meow.

I point to it on the table and back out the door. As Kimberly shuts it, I say, "Don't be a stranger."

"Huh?" The door freezes.

"Nothing," I say. "Forget it."

I take the stairs two at a time, palms barely grazing the handrails.

I sleep restlessly and lie awake from five on. When Kimberly finally wakes up, I coax her into a quick session. At first she's a little hesitant. We're on a schedule. We've done it nights for the past year, mostly in clammy backseats and dimmed basements. It got best—I say best, it always was a little guilt-filled—right before the drugstore stick turned purple. It got worse when she lost it in Yellowstone.

I mention that the neighbors can't hear—they're not home. Then she's all right, and relaxes.

I'm late for work. Patrick reams me. When I lie and say I slept late, he calls me on it. The ceiling is paper thin, he says, and doesn't crack a smile.

Thursday, I have Kimberly call in sick for me. She's cool with it, but tries to get me to go out to Hamer. When she asks, I cough violently and pull the covers up to my chin, lying still until she leaves.

I murder the morning around the apartment. Baseball Today, the slop operas—nothing does it for me. All I can think about are dancing bears, acrobats, sharing Cracker Jacks with Jenn. Except, in my mind, everything is bathed in a brilliant sheen of green, the same shade as birthday balloons, avocado skins, kiwi fruit. It's a circus, all right, but the big top looks like a turtle shell, the clowns have pale, grassy faces and cucumbers for noses. I thumb through the mail and reread the postcard.

"Paul," I say out loud in the empty apartment. "Paul."

Kimberly told me that the mail comes around two. I check it at 1:50. Then at 2:10. When it finally comes at 2:31, I'm sitting at the top of the stairs, fists propped under my chin, pigeon-toed, impatient.

After I'm sure the mailman's long gone, I gather up the correspondence and fly upstairs. I sort. More bills, more letters. No postcards. Nothing comes for us. Jenn's pile doubles.

I notice the cable bill's flap has worked slightly open, exposing a corner of bill.

Suddenly, I crave macaroni.

As the water boils, I whistle and glance across the living room toward the apartment door. I would hear Kimberly coming, for sure. Plenty of time. Just in case I open up and look down the flight of stairs.

The steam burns my hand until I put on a tattered oven mitt. The letter pops completely open after a few seconds in the steam. When the bill slides out, I sit back down at the table and read through its contents. My palms sweat from the steam, or something else, I don't know. I'm not hungry anymore. I mean, it's just the cable bill, but it's something more. When I'm done, I examine the other letters for loose flaps and hidden openings.

I have it back in the envelope and glued shut when Kimberly gets home. Before she can ask if I'm feeling better, I'm at her, pushing into the back of her hair, panting.

"What are you, a farm animal?" Kim says. Once she pulls away from me, she asks what came in the mail. I guide her past the letters and to the fridge, encouraging her to eat. No point in getting caught so soon.

While she eats we make small talk.

"Today go okay?" she asks. She seems distant again.

"I missed you. Other than that, fine."

"What's gotten into you?" she says flatly and spoons through her stew.

"Nothing," I say.

"You're just so, I don't know...giddy."

"Really?"

"Yeah, usually you're just kind of quiet."

Her eyes look like pencil lead, bike tire rubber.

"You need to tell me something?" she says. "How come the change?"

"What change?" I say.

"You tell me," she says, and waits until I look at her.

I can't answer for a while. Finally, I say, "Patrick says I might get a raise soon. He came up and told me."

"Really?"

"Yeah," I say.

She's pretty happy about that, and comes around to sit on my lap. We kiss for a while before we go into the bedroom. For the first time in a while, it's easy.

Friday. Ruthless. At work I check my watch every ten minutes. Once it passes two, I'm even more antsy. Time grinds by slower than Christmas Eve.

But there's nothing inside the door when I get home. I trudge up the stairs and take off my clay-covered boots in the hallway. Before knocking, I slide over to Jenn's apartment and quietly try the knob. It's locked. Our place is locked too, and Kimberly doesn't answer. It takes a minute to dig my keys out from the bottom of my lunch pail.

Kimberly is sitting at the table, the two piles of mail in front of her. Two angry pig-tails jutt out near her neck, she's not wearing makeup, and her jaw is squarely set. I tell her thanks for opening the door, that that was really nice. She doesn't say anything back.

When I come out from the kitchen she holds up Jenn's cable bill. The flap is open—my glue job didn't hold. She shakes the envelope and the papers fall out.

"What's this?" she says.

"Looks like Jenn's mail."

"Why is it open?"

I shrug, crack a soda.

She repeats her question, and then zeroes in with a drawn out, "Cal."

"I'm not sure—did you open it?" I head for the TV.

She starts yelling at me. That lasts for a while. She cries some too, sniffling about privacy.

It takes a while, but I bust. "Fine!" I say. "I did it. Happy?"

"Are you?" she asks.

"I'm fine with it."

"Oh really?" she says. She throws it down on the table. "You're happy, opening up someone else's business? What if everyone knew about us? How would that feel?"

"Why would I care?" I shout without thinking.

Kimberly crosses her arms and sticks out her bottom lip.

"You started it," I say, "Asking about her, wondering what she did. It wasn't my fault the envelope ripped."

She doesn't really answer, just grinds her heel into the carpet.

"Yeah, it was open. The papers fell out on the stairs."

She walks around the living room, gathers up the two piles of mail and goes to the bathroom. The door slams hard, and she locks herself inside. I stand there for a while, go over and try the knob, but she yells for me to leave her alone. I pound one sharp, staccato burst on the door with my fist, but leave it after that. It's the second time I've stared blankly at a locked bathroom door during our marriage. Our bed, a hand-me-down from my Aunt's basement, doesn't give when I lie down. It makes for another restless night.

I've made her fume before. There was this girl no one at school knew about, some quiet blonde in Government. Turns out she lived across from me through the neighbor's hay field, and we started meeting up by the headgates. When Kimberly found out, she got drunk for the first time and made out with Jarrett Buckett—dirty style. It took us a while to work things out after that.

So I know it's best to leave her alone.

I don't see her again until I start frying eggs and bacon for breakfast. She pulls on the back of my t-shirt and wraps her arms around my waist.

"Hey you," she says. She's wearing her navy-blue robe. It's covered with white outlines of teddy bears. Her eyes rove around but never meet mine.

"Hey." The grease pops. "You better stand back. It'll burn."

"I'm okay," she says. She squeezes me tighter. It's always this way, even after Yellowstone. Just give her a minute, let her breathe. She's a real trooper.

While we're eating, I say, "Look. About last night..."

"It's okay," she says. "I got a little mad, that's all."

"No big deal, right?" I say.

She smiles and shakes her head no. "Don't be mad," she says. We eat quickly and make love on the couch. She seems A-OK.

After, I go to the bathroom. Surprise—I'm blown away. The letters are scattered everywhere: along the sink's edge, the back of the toilet, in the bottom of the dry tub. I stand in the doorway, confused. Kimberly wraps me from behind again.

"Who do you think Paul is?" she says. I'm stunned.

"You know, Paul from the postcard. You don't have to hide it." She walks in and fishes it out of a pile, points to a cheesy thumbprint covering one corner. I shrug.

"Maybe he's her manager," she says, and starts to tickle me.

I realize something big, and grab the letter with the blocky handwriting, the one with no return address. Side by side, they match nicely.

"Maybe not a manager, but at least something more than a fling," she says.

"What did you think about the cable bill?" I say. It's out of the envelope, under a hairbrush.

"Naughty, naughty," she says.

I hold up the letter and the postcard. "Do you think?" I see her make the connection.

"Maybe." She starts to gather up the mail.

"Did you open anymore?" I ask.

"Not yet. I thought I'd wait for you," she says.

In the living room, I clean the dishes off the table and backhand the crumbs onto the floor. "When's she coming back?" I ask.

"Tomorrow sometime," she says, carrying all the mail in the crook of her arms, like she would a baby. She spreads it out across the table.

I find my stainless-steel trout knife under the bed. Without its sheath, the blade gleams clean, well-honed.

Kimberly is organizing the mail on the table, sorting bills from letters, letters from cards. She sees the knife and scoots two chairs side by side. We cross our legs underneath us and lean over the table.

"Softly," she says. "Carefully."

I bite the tip of my tongue. She grits her teeth.

I slide the blade under one of the letter's flaps, sawing slowly through the glue. We open three letters and read their contents out loud. Halfway through the fourth, the downstairs door slams shut. Light, noisy footsteps ascend the stairwell.

I stare at Kimberly. Her eyes get bigger than I've ever seen them—big gray orbs of panic. My knife stabs clear through the envelope, skewering it.

"It's Saturday, right?" I whisper.

The clacking stops at the top. Kimberly can't answer. We slump down in the chairs and hold our breath. Jenn knocks on our door. "Hello?" she says. "Hons?" She pounds a little harder.

I set the knife and letter on the table. Both of us sit still as China dolls. Kimberly takes my hand and we bow our heads, like children, praying for the knocking to stop.

The knocking reminds me of the steady thump of my mother's borrowed Buick as we pulled onto the shoulder on our way to Yellowstone two weeks before. There, Kimberly's contractions set in. The pee test proved what we knew deep down, so we went to the courthouse and sealed the deal, but kept living with our parents for a while. Finally we decided to tell them, and we let the cat out of the sack separately. They interrogated us about something in the oven, but we denied it, argued that we were just in love. No big deal. "I mean, you guys got married right out of high school," I remember pointing out to my folks. "What's a year early, anyway?"

So the Smithfields called the Bisbees and pooled some money for a honeymoon shack in West Yellowstone. "What's a wedding without a honeymoon?" my dad had said with a grimace. I could tell he was sad beyond belief.

We left, and then Kimberly started cramping. She told me to keep driving, so I slammed the Buick up to eighty and made it to Yellowstone in under an hour. As soon as we got to the room she stripped and showered. I'm not sure what happened, she locked the door. She sobbed and sobbed. Then I took her to this little hippie hospital and they made sure it was all cleaned out. The rest of the weekend we stayed inside watching fuzzy television, wrapped around each other, swearing that no one ever needed to know.

Kimberly says I've lied enough, so I have to take the mail to Jenn. I say I wouldn't have even cared if she hadn't brought up the dancing stuff. She says she's sick of me causing problems. I say she doesn't know what she's talking about.

We glue the flaps back down and lie low in the apartment for a day. Sometimes we hear Jenn leave. Sometimes we don't.

The skewered letter can't be glued, so I cover it as good as I can with transparent tape, hoping it looks like the post office's mistake. On Sunday night, I walk it over to apartment 1B, knock, and hand Jenn the pile of mail without a word. She asks some questions while sifting through the bills. In that brief moment that her mouth moves, nothing registers for me. I notice her dingy tan teeth; her pale, thin lips; the wrinkles forming around her bare shoulders. When she stops and looks up, expecting an answer, I'm long gone.

The next day, Tammy shows up with her Bishop. They sit us both down around the table. Tammy starts in with this stern lecture about growing up. Bishop follows up with the sanctity of marriage. Tammy butts back in about the loss of a loved one. When I look at Kimberly, realizing she's told, she starts crying. Her eyes are duller than ever.

I don't know where Kimberly's mom gets off, bringing in the cavalry, ordering me around. Someone starts knocking. I'm anxious to answer and shoot out of my chair to get it.

I recognize the face—Harry. He's wearing a blue mechanic's jacket with PAUL stenciled above the right pocket. His mouth is one little line, puckered a bit, and before I can say anything he pops me hard with a stiff straight right. From the floor, before my eye swells shut, I see the damaged mail clutched in his left hand. He towers over me and grunts about invasion of privacy. My head aches with a resonant fire alarm echo.

The Bishop lumbers over and shoos him into the hallway and shuts the door. Kimberly scoots my head onto her lap and runs her cool fingers over and over through my hair. She coos and calls me sweet names. Cold sweat forms all across my forehead.

From the kitchen, Tammy brings a bag of frozen broccoli wrapped in a paper towel and plants it on my brow. The two women are speaking in low tones when I black out.

Patrick fires me for lying, and we get booted from apartment 1A. He never did like me. It's okay because we get our deposit back and use the money for a down payment on a 1994 Chevy Corsica that belonged to Kimberly's older sister. It's a solid car. Not what I always wanted, but it'll do for now. Kimberly gets me a job stocking at Triple Js. We carpool three times a week from my parents' place, where we stay. The kiddie table is stashed in the shed.

The swelling and discoloration around my eye are gone in a few weeks. Sometimes, though, when I'm in the canned vegetables aisle making sure the Garden Peas aren't wall-faced, I think about Jenn and my vision of that strange circus, and this flush of curiosity surges through me. It burns around my eye. The Bishop tells me that all of us face temptation, but it's really a matter of action. He says we have to choose. So, sometimes I stay away from aisle nine—but sometimes I can't help but request it and spend all night there.

I climb the ranks faster than usual—the up-and-ups like my organizational skills—and earn a spot as receiving manager within a few months. It's graveyard shift, not bad. Jenn pops in and out of my memory the entire time. I can't wait to see Paul again; I can swing like a champ. I practice with the broom handle in the break room. I'll mess him up good.

Late one night, an eighteen-wheeler brings in a massive shipment. The grizzled old trucker jaws for a bit and says he'll be asleep in the cab. He leaves after opening the trailer. Before Jessie or any of the other stockers come out, I truck down a crate, open it, and extract a can. In the reddish glare of the taillights, even in the haze, I know it's the label for Western Family Emerald Peas. Aisle nine, on the right. I toss it up in the air a few times, judging its weight, and try to picture a perfectly green version of Kimberly.

It doesn't click. I don't know if it's the dark asphalt blanketed by the night, or the cave-like appearance of the closed loading dock door that sets me off, but all I can imagine are Kimberly's shadowy, tear-glistened eyes when she opened the bathroom door in Yellowstone. I cock my arm way back and chuck the can into the desolate parking lot. It soars lopsided, whooshing end over end until it lands with a hollow thunk. Under an empty, starless sky, I listen to the can roll off the curb and disappear. The halogen floodlights flip on; I'm bathed in synthetic yellow light. The others come out with dollies and begin unloading.

I leave before the sun rises, park the Corsica in the barrow pit, and let myself in the back door. In my old bedroom, curled in my old bed, Kimberly is asleep. The sounds of her breathing fill the room. It's timid and soft, comforting beyond belief. I don't undress, just climb in with her, and run my fingers through her long hair until she blinks awake.

ANSELMO PICKS UP ROCKS

2006

The Monday after I graduate high school, on Monday Morning, Pops tells me I'm going to Osgood. "Got a real important job. Need someone with a head on their shoulders."

"What? Osbad?"

"Pay attention. That dirt we put on out there—the lava rock's coming through. Spread out and pick up as many rocks as you can. We don't want to ruin a swather."

"Why not Brandon? He's new."

"Because the Mexicans like you."

We stand in silence. Brandon would quit after a day at Osbad.

"I just need someone with a brain on their shoulders to run this crew."

"Don't we have some plowing to do? Isn't there a tractor job?"

He sighs. "Look, you gonna, or do I need to?"

I shut up. A rotten taste mills in the back of my throat. "What truck am I taking?"

"All we got is the van. Get going—it's supposed to rain."

"Who's coming with me?"

"Sergio and some new guys. They're in the house."

I drive across the gravel yard to the cinder-block shack. The ceiling and wall are stained black from the stove. The guys are lounging on mattresses thrown out on the floor.

"Get your lunches," I say to Sergio, the only one that understands, and look over the new guys—two young kids, and a decrepit, tired man. In the van, Sergio takes front, the old one in the middle bench seat, the kids sit on overturned oil buckets in the back.

I gas it when we leave the shop, and the kids pretend to be riding bulls when I swerve. Sergio, in the front, dramatically shoots his hands down, clamping them onto the seat. He swears in Spanish—I know, he's taught me the words. The old one doesn't budge.

"This is the best I can do, drive you around." I'm not surprised when Sergio doesn't answer. The old one gapes a toothless grin, his cheeks and forehead all long, brown wrinkles. I stare at him in the mirror, and swear in Spanish.

The old man shuts up quick; the grin disappears.

The van handles poorly, floating from one edge of the road to the other. We ride in silence.

"Why he treat like that?" Sergio breaks in. He squints a little, concentrates, and asks again, "Why treat you bad tú papá?"

"Trying to make me a man or something."

"Be man? What mean?"

"Responsibility, I guess. Make me run a crew."

"Run over crew?"

"No. Run crew. Be boss."

"Oh, new boss you?"

"Just today."

He nods. "Make pretty good boss," he says. "Good boss son."

We pass Roberts—twenty bleached singlewides on the south side of the road—and leave the blacktop for good. The van handles worse on the pot-holed gravel; knuckles of half-drowning lava rock jar the old machine and make the doors rattle.

The van revs and rumbles up a rocky incline. "I ought to be running a farm by now, not playing chauffeur."

Sergio just stares straight out the windshield, toward the western horizon. In the rear-view, the two bobble-head boys laugh and push each other off of their buckets. The old man stares at me, smiling. Our eyes connect.

"Ask him what his deal is," I say to Sergio. He turns halfway around and rattles off some tin-can jargon. The old man cracks his knuckles and replies low and deep.

"He say he happy today. Been five years since left Michoacán."

"Michigan?"

"Michoacán, México."

"Tell him he'll be even happier when we get to the fields."

Sergio says nothing to the old man.

I wonder where Michoacán is, and if it's as strange as the high Idaho desert. Cinderblock houses pepper the bare, rolling hills. The only things moving are quarter-mile lines of corrugated steel pivots, crawling across the fields, watering the thin ground. Snaky gravel roads crisscross at lonely intersections.

From above, I've been told it looks flat as Nebraska, but it's different driving through it. Left, right, up, down—Pops says never faster than thirty, especially in the van.

The thought makes me push the accelerator up to thirty-five. That's when the old man starts singing.

Who knows really, really what he was singing? I look over at Sergio. He's glossy eyed; the two in the back, hands resting in their laps, stare at the oil-stained, tool-cluttered floor.

The sound comes out low, guttural, and then smooth and high and floating. He doesn't change the tune, holds the notes like a bear trap. Forceful. Unforgiving. He sings, sings like an old man should, I guess.

As he sings, the morning darkens; the bright clear windows of the van change with the sky around it. The old man stops, and Sergio asks him a question. He answers quickly.

"He say he learn that song as boy. On way to farm in Michoacán, he sing it then too."

Sergio translates more: "Next time, he say I drive and you play guitar."

I look back. He smiles. I don't know how to play the guitar, so I don't smile back. Sergio and the old man talk again. It sounds like a typewriter.

"He say song make him happy be alive. He feel neck muscles move, wind move, sound. Alive."

"Tell him he might not be alive after picking up rocks today," I say.

Sergio tells him. "He sing, he tell me. He sing forever." The old man's wavering voice starts again.

All of us listen for a while before I realize we're lost. Pops gruffly relays the directions over the cell phone. West. Blue Shop. Lone Pine Cellar. Five miles. Two rusty pivots. Dead coyote.

"Dead coyote?"

"Dang dog ran right out in front of me, couldn't stop fast enough," he says. Its carcass is easy to find—green patchy sprouts of hay bending in the breeze.

We empty out of the van. I explain to Sergio the plan, and he explains it to the pack. "We'll stretch out along the bottom here, halfway across the pivot, and we'll all walk to the north." He translates. "Whenever we come across a patch of rocks, come together and pile them up. We're not going to be able to pack them all the way from the middle, so Pops can bring a pickup out if he wants them moved."

I ask Sergio to tell me their names. He does. Pedro, something else. We space out across the field, the old man follows me. He tugs at my sleeve. He points to himself.

"On-sail-moe," he says, and thumps his chest with a withered finger. "On-sail-moe."

"Huh?"

"On-sail-moe." Thump, thump.

I must look confused because he squats in the dirt, right by the road, and scrawls ANSELMO in shaky letters. He points to himself again.

"Oh, your name?"

His head shakes vigorously. "Sí, sí, sí."

"Anselmo," I say, and point to the field. "Go pick up rocks."

By ten we're at the northern edge of the field. We've made about eight waist-high piles of the chalky black rock. My back hurts, but I only rub it when I'm away from the guys. They don't need to see me hurting, I'm the new boss.

Anselmo ends up close to me and smiles as he carries a small boulder, hunched over. It hangs down between his legs like a prison-ball shackle.

I tell Sergio that we can be back to the van by noon if we hurry. We move quickly to the other side and start back towards the gravel road.

When we get close, the scrawniest boy runs to the corner and pulls the van up closer to us. We make it back by noon—the second side not half as bad with the rocks, only three piles. We carry out a load of beer cans and candy wrappers from the hay.

We pile into the van for lunch. I only have a soda. The rest pull out tightly rolled packages of tin foil from plastic grocery bags.

"They want heat them up," says Sergio.

"Tell them to go to town," I say. My stomach growls.

"I show you," he says. He reaches over and turns the key, then walks around and pops the hood. He sticks the food on the van's manifold. "They heat up now."

We nap for twenty-minutes while lunch warms up. I turn the cell phone off just in case Pops calls—he doesn't need to know.

It's one by the time we unload, stretch, and start off on our third swipe. As we walk out into the hay, Anselmo tugs at my sleeve.

He holds an open tinfoil package out to me, looking like a priest. The tinfoil's still warm. I nod to Anselmo and then bite down into the taco. The beans are cold, chewy, but I smile. He looks at the ground and puts his hands together, nods and walks backwards, mumbling to himself as if he's saved a soul.

The weather is worse. To the west, black clouds form, so I tell them to pick up the pace. Given the circumstances, there's a Rio Grande joke in there somewhere, which I almost tell Sergio. We're all gonna get wet. For some reason I don't. It's not funny. I bend down and pick up a rock, moving through the field, parallel with the rest.

I end up next to Anselmo on our second pass to the north. This pivot is covered with hills. My legs feel like anchors. The young ones take advantage, and, once I'm out of sight, lie down in the bottom of the swells to rest.

The wind picks up. The nearest tree—the lone pine by the cellar— is five miles off, so it hits us like a snowplow. That's all I hear, the wind, like I'm swimming in it. I tell Sergio to stay back and move a pile that's close to the edge. The rest of us bend into the wind, forming a line across the thin hay.

We make it halfway down the field. I walk on the backbone of a long-running ridge that meets the gravel road where the van is parked. The ridge's crest forms an upside-down u in the road. The kids trudge along in the bottom of a swell, and Anselmo in another. From the ridge, I can see everyone clearly for the first time.

Anselmo ties his yellow windbreaker around his neck with the sleeves, like I used to do with my pajamas after Saturday morning cartoons. He is tired. I saw that at lunch, while he napped. His chest had moved slowly then, shallowly up and down, barely moving the thin jacket.

Now the jacket flies out behind him, flapping and snapping. He extends his arms, like he's going to pull up in the headwind and take off, and his coal-colored hair stands on end. His mouth—open, open wide and gaping, singing, yelling, screaming, singing, praising—is silent. The wind whips his words away. He begins to jog into the wind, arms out, hair blowing, mouth wide open. Nothing comes out. He gazes up the hill at me and smiles.

I smile back. Then I trip.

Lying in the hay, a jagged bunch of lava protrudes behind me. Only fifty feet from the gravel road, I have to dig it out or Pops will see. Scratching at the edges of the biggest piece, digging into the cold earth, the wind moans in my ears and flips my collar. I dig a six-inch deep trench around it before I can rock it loose.

Standing, both arms wrapped around the big rock, I see the van. One of the kids brings it up the hill quickly. The window is rolled down, the other chases after him. He laughs in the driver's seat and swerves from left to right on the gravel road.

Then I see Anselmo, on the other side. He's walking up the road on the hill's backside towards the van. He can't see it.

I drop the rock and run—run with my mouth open—yelling, screaming, waving, screaming. The wind sweeps my words away. Ten feet from the crest, the boy sees me and turns his head. Anselmo does the same.

The kid locks up the brakes—at least he tries. The four tires leave dark, deep trails on the down side of the hill, before the van hits the old man. It stops hard.

Anselmo is folded underneath.

I fumble with the cell phone as I run, turn it on. I fall to my knees and skid into the van, stopping myself with my elbows, denting the door. The three boys stand in the hay, staring.

I dial 911. Then I crane my neck, see Anselmo, and vomit.

"Emergency Services, how may I help you?" a lady says.

"I'm in the desert—in Osgood. Anselmo just got run over."

"Okay. Remain calm. Stay on the phone. What happened?"

"Anselmo was walking and a kid brought the van. He couldn't stop, ran right over him. He's under the van."

"Is he alive?"

The thought makes me sick.

"Is he alive? Can you hear him breathing?"

I can't hear anything because of the three, crying, wailing, screeching.

"I don't know," I say.

"You have to check his pulse."

My stomach knots, my mouth dries.

"Sir, you have to check his pulse. You can save his life."

"I can't."

"You have to."

I lie flat on my stomach and look back under the van. Anselmo is there. One arm points at me, the hand contracts, relaxes, contracts, relaxes, picking up rocks and scratching five furrows in the gravel. I crawl under the van, away from the arm, towards his neck.

"His hand is moving," I whisper into the phone.

"You have to check his pulse," the voice says.

His hand works at an unpredictable rate—fast, slow, slow, slow, faster, fast.

I drop the phone and crawl deeper. Her voice, incomprehensible, crackles steadily.

It's difficult to free my arm enough to reach. Wedging into position, extending an arm, touching his neck—it's warm. I feel his pulse.

It beats to the song he had sung—his song—guttural, soft, floating, shameless.

The phone crackles again.

I reach for it to answer but when I open my mouth, the song begins to fade, fade. The wind stops—the song stops—and it's silent for a moment under the van until the sky splits open and the heavy drops fall straight down.

SECOND DAY
OF SUN

2005

It happens this time every year.

On the second day of sun, with the ice pulling back from its winter-long stay on the pavement; the mounds of the red and brown stuff, piled up along the roads, shrinks away; the air warms enough that, even though it's coat weather, I wear a jacket; and I walk everywhere—everywhere; and the green grass on the fringes of the sidewalks and around the mailboxes looks coffee-brown from the sneakers that carry the junk into it; but it's showing now, at least the grass is showing, and I know from the sun that it's coming quickly.

It's not the spring that I wait for, or worries me. And it's not the break from academic endeavors—far from it. It's the jab of metal to belly as I lean over the grill of the pickup, standing on the front bumper, spraying ether into the carburetor and yelling at Poncho or Jaime or Cesar—or whoever the hell is at the wheel—to stomp on the pedal and turn it over one more time. The truck fires, blue-black smoke billows everywhere, and it rattles like marbles in a tin can. We head back to the shop for more pipe to lay out, and maybe even some lunch. That's what it's bringing, this second day of sun, and I'm torn and pissed off and elated.

I will be the first member of my family to graduate with a bachelor's degree. The first—ever. My great-grandfather worked the rail-lines, lost four and a half fingers repairing the elephant-sized steel wheels of the cars. My grandfather died at forty-two of kidney failure. When he died, he left my father, then fourteen, and my uncle, twenty-one, a few hundred acres of grain ground and eight thousand dollars of debt. They were chained to that farm—chained to the Ririe bench, and to the west desert of Osgood.

Their binding chain was one of those thirty-foot, rusty snakes with inch-thick links and used to jerk a tractor buried frame-deep out of the sludge. But the brothers took the chain, wound it up, looped it, and roped cows until they had enough for their own herd. The brothers took the loop out, swung it wide, and caught land above the Snake River on the Antelope Bench, some of the prettiest in the county. They took that chain and drug it behind them and turned the thin dusty ground until it was night-black. They put a bucket on one end, lowered it deep down until they struck water. When they reeled it up, they turned it over and watered their spuds.

Now, the chain hangs loosely around both their tanned, thick necks. The brothers—my father, my uncle—have earned the right to do what they please. From that dusty sage-brushed land they have raised cash crops of potatoes and barley, herds of Black Angus, homes, and dozens of girls. They raised me, too—the only son, the only namesake—and that's why the second day of sun scalds my back even though it's cold enough to see my breath.

They'll preach that there are two types of smarts: street and school, and that one of those don't add up to squat. I always questioned why street smarts mattered at all since there were hardly roads in our world—just service trails of wash-boarded gravel. And they question in turn schooling, smarts not worth a fart in a bottle. Instead, they talk of how to rope the sky. I'll nod as the sun bears down, incinerating me completely, wholly.

This is how it goes—how it has gone—my entire life, on this second day of sun. The chain is light, hardly noticeable, and I agree to farmhand one more summer.

Anyways, I think, the fields are close and I've done it forever and I like the guys and the Mexicans with those homemade burritos and dirty jokes. And where else can I get so many hours? Pops and I learned something last year—he'll let me take a few nights off for dinner-and-a-movie, or a dip in the lake, right? We're both a little more mature. Maybe we can even make some deals together, look at some type of future together . . .

The second day of sun cinches it up and seals the deal. My decision is made.

But the seventeenth day of sun is a scorcher, and I'm pushing fourteen hours in the tractor with no AC or a radio; then on the thirty-second I'm shoveling barley in a steel grain bin July oven; then on the sixtieth I'm painting garage doors and telephone poles and fences with a three-year-old brush; then on the one-hundredth-and-eighth I'm underneath the silage truck—that rank, manure-caked jalopy—cutting off runners with the torch, and I don't even own a pair of safety glasses or gloves; and on what seems like the seven-hundredth-ninety-first day I face my father—the man I call Pops on Christmas and when we watch football games together—and I yell and tell him he can take his whole rancid farm and cram it; that I'm never coming back, ever. I leave in my car—tricky bastard won't even lend me a farm truck—windows down, elbow out, swearing, chipping through gears and dreaming about any city in the wide world with an office close to a sushi bar and an indoor pool.

I box up my work clothes and bury them in the closet and quit, this time for good.

Until a day like today—the second day of sun—and I'm walking to class, two months from being a god-danged college graduate, and I watch my breaths wisping in the cold air and the shrinking snow piles and the flattened grass at the bottom of the mailbox posts.

Without thinking, I get my phone and call my dad and say, "Hey, Pops, I'm gonna have some free weekends here. If you got work, maybe I ought to start coming down."

My father pauses to mull this about, then says, "Well, we do got that old red horse trailer that needs welded on, painted up…"

All through class, I fidget, thinking about my work clothes, how they'll smell like stale diesel and sweat and will take a day or two to break in. On my walk back to my apartment, the sun scorches my neck. I pop up my jacket's thin collar, shove hands into pockets, and quicken my step for home.

APPENDIX

THE CLEAN PACKAGE: A PIONEER ASSEMBLAGE – is an archive of the author's Mormon voice in its various forms, genres, and dramas over fifteen years of creative writing, and also a short hybrid cleaned crown essay assembled from twenty-seven lines, one taken from each of the following pieces:

SECOND DAY OF SUN – nonfiction – published in *Idaho Magazine* and later included in BYU-Idaho's textbook *I-Think*

ANSELMO PICKS UP ROCKS – fiction – published in *Black Rock & Sage* and later a finalist in *Idaho Magazine*'s annual fiction contest

THE NEWLYWEDS – fiction – awarded the Eugene England Young Writers Award from *Dialogue: A Journal of Mormon Thought* and published online and in print

CHEDDAR – fiction - earned Honorable Mention from *Irreantum*'s annual fiction contest and published in print

GOD DAMNED THE LAND BUT LIFTED THE PEOPLE – nonfiction – published in print by *South Loop Review*, and later republished in the anthology *Best of Mormonism*

LONG IN THE TOOTH – nonfiction – awarded Second Place from *Irreantum*'s annual nonfiction contest and published in print

INSIDE OUT – fiction – selected for *Fugue*'s special Regional Issue, published in print, and nominated for a Pushcart Prize

THE GOSPEL OF WILD DOGS, HUNTERS, PLIERS – nonfiction – published on the literary website *Shady Side Review* with "The Gospel of Wild Dogs" nominated for Best of the Net

PARTIAL MEMORIES – nonfiction – a true-crime endeavor processing the murder of a cousin, published here for the first time

CLOSE CALL: A FEVER DREAM – fiction – excerpted from dream journal

THE FOURTH ELEMENT – nonfiction – published in print by *Hawk & Handsaw*

FOUR SEASONS OF MAKING HAY – fiction – the only included example of third-person narrative, published here for the first time

MY TIME IN THE DIRT – nonfiction – published online at *Terrain.org: A Journal of the Built + Natural Environments*

BIRTHPLACE OF TV – fiction – excerpted from an abandoned novel by the same name

BRING ON THE SPINS – nonfiction – published by *Tin House* and listed as a Notable Essay in the anthology *Best American Essays*

CLEAN UP, 1997 – fiction – published online at *Menagerie*

NATE BOZUNG: MORE SPIN – nonfiction – published online at the lifestyle blog *The Salty Beatnik*

TELL ME HOW YOU REALLY FEEL: A ROMANCE – fiction – excerpted from dream journal

MY FATHER KEEPS TOUCHING HIS HEART – fiction – an unpublished, unfinished short story

HERE COMES THE HOTSTEPPER – nonfiction – composed for the online music essay tournament *March Fadness: The Tournament of One-Hit Wonders* and published online, the piece knocked out of competition first round by Torn

THE DRIVER – fiction – designed as the narrator establishing the structure of the Nate Bozung novel *Jokers Wild*

DOGMAN: A NIGHTMARE – fiction – published online by *DIAGRAM*

WHAT HAPPENED ON 6.21.18 - nonfiction – produced for *Essay Daily*'s online literary writing event "What Happened on 6.21.18" and published online

WHAT HAPPENED ON 12.21.19 - nonfiction – produced for *Essay Daily*'s online literary writing event "What Happened on 12.21.19" and published online

SAILING: A DUET – nonfiction – co-written with Georgia Pearle for the online music essay tournament *March Badness: The Tournament of Worst Songs*, the essay reaching the Final Four and eliminated by Muskrat Love

ACKNOWLEDGMENTS

SPECIAL THANKS & MUCH GRATITUDE

Sarah Jane Abate
Hosam Aboul-Ela
Brandon & Sarah Alva
Jack Amerson
Brett Applegate
University of Arizona
U. of Arizona Poetry Center
Miah Arnold & Raj Mankad
Matt Babcock
Renae Barzee
The Barzee Family
Robert Stephens Beck
Skyler Bell
Mark Bennion
James & Valerie Best
The B.H.C.
Reed Bills
Judy Blunt
Eavan Boland
Graig Briggs
Brigham Young University-Idaho
Taylor Brorby
Robert Boswell
Nathan Hale Bozung
Severin Bozung
The Bozung Family
Jason Brown
Craig Buchner
Simmons Buntin
Patrick Burns
William Burns
Glade Byington
Corey Campbell
Kai Carlson-Wee
Dave & Michelle Chapple
Mario Chard
Dan Chu
Sally Connolly

Cameron Powers Cox
Ben & Erica Dansie
Alison Hawthorne Deming
Del Denney
Peter Derby
DIAGRAM
Dialogue: A Journal of Mormon Thought
Anthony Doerr
Chitra Divakaruni
Jennifer duBois
Isaac Eldridge
Emily & Jed Erickson
Ford Erickson
Spencer Erickson
Essay Daily
Nick Flynn
Boyd & Laurie Foster
Brad & Sharol Foster
Georgia Pearle Foster
Jenkins B Foster & Aurielle Oyen &
Phyrex Hasten Pearle
Katie Foster
Kara Foster
Greg Fox
Fugue
Andrew Gallup
Mike & Nicole Gooch
Grackle & Grackle
Kendall Grant
Joe Griffin
Lou & Louis & Judy Griffin
PR Griffis
JP Gritton
Gulf Coast: A Journal of Literature & Fine Arts
Don Hammar
Jack Harrell
Abby & Jordan Hamilton
Braden Hepner

NIKI HERD
JON HICKEY
ALLEGRA HYDE
LAWRENCE HOGUE
HELEN HOOPER
ROBBIE HOWELL
UNIVERSITY OF HOUSTON
MURRAY HUNT
IDAHO COMMISSION ON THE ARTS
IDAHO MAGAZINE
INPRINT HOUSTON
INPRINT C. GLENN CAMBOR/MICHAEL &
NINA ZILKHA FELLOWSHIP
IRREANTUM
MARILYN JENSEN
MARSHALL & MALLORY JENSEN
ADAM JOHNSON
FENTON JOHNSON
MAT JOHNSON
J. KASTELY
DANA KLETTER
DAVID HOON KIM
ERROL & DEBRA KING
CHESTON KNAPP
SUZETTE GEE KUNZ
MALLORIE NOEL LAMB
THE LAMB FAMILY
NATHANIEL LANDRY
CHRIS LEIK
RICH LEVY
JEREMY & MELISSA LIVINGSTON
PATRICK MADDEN
JOSEPH MAINS
MICHAEL MARTONE
ANTHONY MARRA
VICTOR & MELANIE MARTINEZ
THE MARTINEZ FAMILY
ISLE MCELROY
RYAN MCILVAIN
NISHTA J. MEHRA
NATHAN MEIKLE
KATHRYN MILES
SHARON MORGAN
ANDER MONSON
MALORIE & TREVOR MONSON
LUISA MURADYAN
CHRISTOPHER MURRAY

MICHELE NEREIM
JODY NELSON
BRENDEN & SARAH & ELIZABETH OLIVA
DANIEL PACKARD
ALEXANDER PARSONS
JONATHAN PENNER
ADRIENNE G. PERRY
CHASE N. PERRY
JUSTIN ROBERT PERRY
DAVID JAMES POISSANT
K. TOM PORTER
JAMIE PORTWOOD
GREG & TASHA PRICE
THE SALTY BEATNIK
SHANNON PUFAHL
KIRSTIN VALDEZ QUADE
PRESIDENT & SISTER QUIST
BEN QUICK
CHARLES M. & ESTELLE H. QUIST
SYDNEE & AUSTIN RASMUSSEN
JIM RICHARDS
TIGH RICKMAN
KENDALL & RACHEL ROLFE
JACOB & LAUREN RUTHERFORD
MATTHEW SALESSES
FEBRONIO & ANTONIA SALINAS
CORY & TARYN SANFORD
DELAINA SCHOLES
LEXIS SCHONTZ
AURELIE SHEEHAN
DEREK SHEFFIELD
GARRETT & BRITTANY SHERWOOD
MAGGIE SHIPSTEAD
AISHA SABATINI SLOAN
MICHAEL SNEDIKER
SOUTH LOOP REVIEW
JUSTIN ST. GERMAIN
BRENDAN STEPHENS
JEFF STEVENSON
STANFORD UNIVERSITY
WALLACE STEGNER/KAREN OSNEY
BROWNSTEIN FELLOWSHIP
YERRA SUGARMAN
DRUE SUMMERS
SUNSTONE
ELIZABETH TALLENT
KAJ TANAKA

Nina Schloesser
Giuseppe Taurino
Mika Taylor
Ryan Teitman
Nan Thorton
Terrain.org: A Journal of the Built +
Natural Environments
Tin House
Justin Torres
Peter Turchi
Armando & Erika Vazquez
Braulio & Damiana Vazquez
La Familia Vazquez
Meredith Wallis
The Wallis Family
E. Jaren Watson
Juliana Xuan Wang
Joe Wilkins
Denry Wilson
Richard Wise
Steve Woodward
Greg Wrenn
Writespace Houston
Tobias Wolff
Rachel Yoder
Jarred & Valerie Young

    — and the multitudinous
    Foster & Manwaring

www.ingramcontent.com/pod-product-compliance
Lightning Source LLC
Chambersburg PA
CBHW032031310726
48972CB00002B/634